THE BALD EAGLE

THE BALD EAGLE

Mark V. Stalmaster

Artwork by Michelle LaGory

UNIVERSE BOOKS
New York

Published in the United States of America in 1987
by Universe Books
381 Park Avenue South, New York, NY 10016

87 88 89 90 / 10 9 8 7 6 5 4 3 2 1

Printed in Hong Kong

Library of Congress Cataloging-in-Publication Data

Stalmaster, Mark V.
    The bald eagle.

    Bibliography: p.
    Includes index.
    1. Bald eagle. I. Title.
QL696.F32S79 1987   598'.916   86-30832
ISBN 0-87663-491-9

To Adam and Helen . . .

Contents

Preface

I can still remember the first time I ever saw a bald eagle. I was fishing near the headwaters of the Mississippi River in Minnesota, where it is hardly more than a creek, when a black bird of astounding proportions flew by. As a lad of only twelve, I was unfamiliar with this bird. I was told that it was a bald eagle, one that had just left its nest, and one that had not yet developed the white head and tail. It was the start of a long association with this species, and sometimes an obsession, though at the time I had no idea I would ever embark on the studies and writings that have brought me to the understanding and appreciation I now have for the bald eagle. But the image of that first bird is as vivid today as it was then.

Since that time, I have watched many eagles. Whether hiking along the seacoast in my home state of Washington, canoeing along the shores of wilderness lakes in Canada, or serving as a backcountry ranger in Yellowstone National Park, I have often had bald eagles as my close companions. I have counted tens of thousands of them, have raised several in captivity, and have observed their most intimate moments from the secrecy of a blind. But it was not until 1974 that I began to study their habits in detail. I have conducted numerous research projects on wintering bald eagles in northwest Washington and other areas. My work continues today as I am often asked to find out where bald eagles are, what they do, why they do it, and how eagle populations can be managed to keep them safe from human interference.

Throughout the years, I amassed a small library of scientific and popular articles concerning the bald eagle. But as my stock of references and data grew, so did my confusion in interpreting it. Here was the eagle's life story hidden away in a myriad of technical details. Apparently, I was not alone in this predicament; many eagle biologists voiced concern for the lack of a standard reference for this species. And because research was expanding at a phenomenal rate, some sort of information pool was sorely needed. Surprisingly, the bald eagle, after two hundred years as the national bird of the United States and an endangered species of intense interest to many, has never had its complete life history told in the form of a book.

It was with this appreciation, background work, and the need to tell their story that I decided to write a book on the bald eagle. This is my attempt to put together a synopsis of the eagle's natural history, to com-

pile and condense the immense collection of literature, and to syn-
thesize it into a form that can be understood by the seasoned bald eagle
biologist and layperson as well. It has been an enormous task, one that
took more than five years to complete, and one that I sometimes regret
having undertaken, but I hope that I have come close to accomplishing
my objective.

Although this book draws on many of my experiences and interpretations, it is a compilation of information from bald eagle biologists
throughout North America. I am indebted to all of them for allowing me
to draw on their data to develop the true picture of the bald eagle. I hope
that in the process I have not misinterpreted their information or altered
the overall intent of their work, for one of the purposes of this book is to
translate and pool all of the available scientific information and present
it in a comprehensive and understandable form.

As can be seen by the extensive bibliography, I have done an exhaus-
tive review of the literature. But a note of caution is necessary. When I
had to decide whether to use a particular reference, pool it with other
data, or ignore it, I relied on my instincts and used the studies that I
thought best represented the actual situation and, more importantly,
were conducted in the most scientifically rigorous manner. This is, of
course, not to belittle any references not used, as I may have simply over-
looked them. But it does point to a possible bias in the presentation,
since I often made value judgments in terms of data credibility. Perhaps
readers' comments on this book will clear up any inconsistencies; I am
sure that numerous passages will spark controversy. But this is the
scientific method: to work toward finding the truth, no matter how difficult or inefficient the process may be.

To date, three major books have been written on the bald eagle. A
literary classic, one that I have used extensively in this book, was written
by Francis Herrick in 1934. His book, *The American Eagle,* has many
observations of nesting behavior that are still valid today. But this text is
well out of date, because most research on bald eagles has been conducted since 1960. Another book, written in 1952 by Myrtle Broley,
describes some of the life history of the bald eagle in Florida, but most
of *Eagle Man* is devoted to the life and research of Charles Broley, a well-
known eagle biologist of earlier years. More recently, George Laycock
published his *Autumn of the Eagle,* which describes the dismal plight
of eagles during the 1960s and 1970s as a result of human activities.

The evolution of science and thought is a continuous process. I have
"built" this book on the solid foundation of these earlier books and on
the plethora of literature available about eagles. And I have "remodeled"
it after conversations with other bald eagle biologists and after my own
personal experiences. Certainly, other writers will come along and
"reconstruct" my thoughts on the bald eagle using this book as a step-
ping stone.

Several people assisted me in the development of this book, but one associate deserves special thanks. Richard Knight critically reviewed this book and acted as a source of inspiration, guidance, and friendship. Brian Millsap, whom I do not know personally, also provided insight when he reviewed the manuscript.

Another special friend, Gail Gladstone, was the first to read this book, although she had to wade through a rough first draft. Her interest in this project and her encouragement made my five years of work seem like much less.

I am grateful to the many eagle biologists who have allowed me to use their information from published and unpublished sources. I have taken particular pains to give credit to studies done by others despite the need to scatter references liberally throughout the text (numbers in parentheses indicate a reference). There are some five hundred references in this book.

Lastly, I want to thank Mildred, Harriet, Gertrude, Ralph, and all of the other bald eagles that put up with my harassment in the name of science.

1

Introducing the Bald Eagle

The bald eagle perhaps evokes more emotionalism, controversy, and mis-understanding than any other North American bird. Some condemn it for its destructive powers; others consider it an unworthy symbol of the United States because of its "decadent" life-style; many regard it with special pride because it symbolizes freedom and independence. Still others, especially those fortunate enough to have seen a wild eagle, appreciate it as an important component of a natural ecosystem. A few regard the bald eagle as a spiritual being, an object of worship. Although I suspect that most Americans have never seen an eagle in its natural habitat, most of us undoubtedly have an opinion of this bird, whether we revere the eagle or loathe it.

Humans have long been fascinated by birds of prey, especially eagles. Ancient man undoubtedly admired and respected the eagle, and this admiration persists today. But what is it about the bald eagle that stirs such appreciation? Although we all differ in our perceptions of the natural world, the eagle seems to have a number of attributes that people regard as inspirational or aesthetically pleasing.

Because the bald eagle is the *national symbol* of the United States, it evokes strong feelings of patriotic pride. The *large size* of the eagle is one of its most impressive qualities. Because eagles are so large, they build huge nests, perch in the tallest trees, and feed on large prey. The *predatory life-style* of the eagle is another source of fascination. For centuries, the eagle has symbolized power, might, dominance, and conquest because of its strength and its lofty position in the animal world. Recently, the *endangered status* of this species has brought it renewed attention and concern. Even though each individual eagle is powerful, the species as a whole is delicate; special care and attention are needed to prevent its extinction. Furthermore, the eagle represents the *wild and free spirit*, perhaps because a wild eagle lives a free life in the wilderness. The *coloration* of the bald eagle is also striking, particularly that of the adults, which sport the familiar black, white, and yellow pattern. Their *facial expression* suggests several attributes that many people admire. The pronounced brow, penetrating eyes, and poised alertness suggest courage, determination, and fortitude. For such a large bird, the eagle is amazingly *graceful and elegant in flight.* Humans have always respected and envied the flight of birds. For some, the eagle represents a *spiritual being* to be honored and worshiped. Some civilizations, even today, believe the eagle is the link between heaven and earth, the spirit that carries the soul to the world of the gods. (1) Whatever the reason, the eagle's symbolic status is shared by few other animals.

Symbols are expressions of desire, purpose, and ideals. On 20 June 1782, an Act of Congress officially adopted the bald eagle as the symbol of the United States. The original seal or symbol depicted the eagle with spread wings, an olive branch in one talon and arrows in the other, and in its bill a scroll emblazoned with the words *E Pluribus Unum.* This emblem, only slightly changed in two hundred years, still appears on the seal of the United States and on currency, coins, and other items (Fig. 1.1). Today, the bald eagle is used on countless symbols for governmental, commercial, and private uses. Though its image pervades many aspects of life in America, little was known of the eagle's natural history during most of its tenure as the country's emblem. Today, after celebrating the eagle's bicentennial birthday in 1982, we have a better understanding of eagle ecology and have finally come to realize that the eagle has not fared well in the United States.

The bald eagle has dwindled from a widely ranging species once spanning all of North America to a few remaining populations. The situation is serious; the eagle is classified by the United States government as being threatened or endangered with extinction in all forty-eight contiguous states. Although still plentiful in Alaska and Canada, many local populations have been severely reduced or completely extirpated.

Some would argue that the preservation of an endangered species is a futile task, because the evolution of a species inevitably concludes with extinction. But man's influences have greatly accelerated this process; in the future, a plethora of animal and plant species will continue to give way to human activities. But in 1973, the Congress of the United States sought to reverse this tide by passing the Endangered Species Act. In this act, Congress recognized that endangered species "are of aesthetic, ecological, educational, historical, recreational, and scientific value to the Nation and

Fig. 1.1 The seal of the United States in 1782 (above) and at present (below).

its people." As Congress put it, "the bald eagle is no longer a mere bird of biological interest, but a symbol of the American ideals of freedom." It is surely this, but the bald eagle is much more.

The eagle is a lingering reminder of the pristine and vast wilderness area that once encompassed the whole of North America. It is a symbol of a distant past, when the natural world of America was untarnished. The eagle is a dying breed, a monarch pitifully subordinated to human progress. But the eagle also is living evidence of perfection in the evolutionary struggle for existence, a tribute to survival despite the influences of man. It is an integral part of its environment, one that is perfectly structured by past evolutionary events and adapted as no other animal is. But it also represents a challenge to the ideals and values of a people. If the bald eagle returns, it will be more than a wildlife management achievement; it will symbolize the growing concern and appreciation for life on earth. It is a gallant bird of many images, of many personae. It is a bird whose history and life are still untold. This, then, is the natural history of the white-headed sea eagle in North America, the so-called bald eagle.

2

Evolution, Classification, and Relatives

ANCESTRY

Tens of millions of years ago, somewhere along the coast of the tropical seas near what is now southeast Asia, a transformation was taking place. A group of birds, known as kites, was providing the genetic framework for the evolution of a new branch on their family tree. From these ancestral kites emerged one of evolution's finest works, a sea eagle. This ancient sea eagle would eventually become the progenitor of at least eight other sea or fish eagles, one of which we now call the bald eagle.

Though few details are known about the evolution of predatory birds, fossil remains of this ancient sea eagle date back some 25 million years, long before the evolution of man. We do not know when the bald eagle, as a species, evolved. Fossil remains indicate, however, that they inhabited North America as far back as one million years, but it is likely that bald eagles were present before that. Fossil eagle bones are well represented in ancient tar deposits in California, and eagle remains from Indian middens are abundant. Though ancient, the bald eagle probably reached the New World fairly recently, at least in terms of evolutionary time. (6, 5, 9)

The bald eagle, a member of the genus *Haliaeetus* in the Accipitridae family tree, probably evolved from the scavenging Asian and Australasian kites of the genus *Haliastur* (Fig. 2.1). Today, the Indian Brahminy kite is perhaps the closest living link of the sea eagles to their past ancestors. Sea eagles and kites share many common characteristics, including their fishing, scavenging, and piratical foraging habits, their courtship displays,

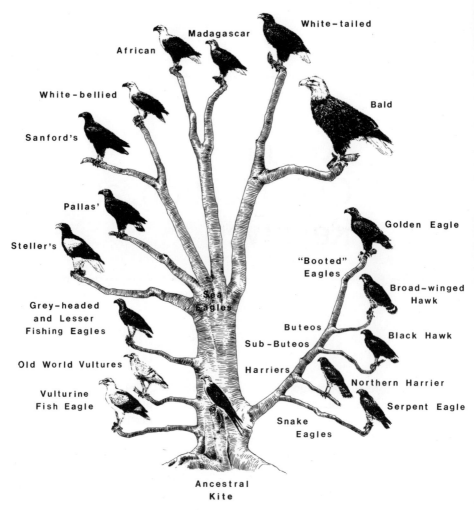

Fig. 2.1 Accipitridae family tree showing the relatives of the bald eagle.

and their breeding habits. The sea and fish eagles are closely related to the lesser and grey-headed fishing eagles of the genus *Ichthyophaga* found in tropical Asia. They are not too distantly related to the vulturine fish eagle (*Gypohierax*), perhaps through the Old World vultures. (2, 4)

The other major lineage in the Accipitridae family is a much more diverse group, but has one ancestor in common with the sea eagle lineage, this again being the fish-eating kite. This family branch includes the snake eagles, harriers, sub-buteos, buteos, "booted" eagles, and others. It is along this branch of the family tree that the golden eagle, one of the "booted" eagles, has evolved. Bald and golden eagles may have many similar characteristics, but they are not closely related; they share a distant relative in the kite group. The osprey, another raptor similar in habits to the bald eagle, is even more distantly related. The seven other sea and fish eagles are close cousins to the bald eagle.

CLASSIFICATION

The bald eagle is a member of the class Aves, which includes all birds, and the order Falconiformes, which encompasses most diurnal birds of prey except owls. Within this order, there are five families. The bald eagle is in the family Accipitridae, which includes 205 species of eagles, hawks, kites, Old World vultures, and harriers. It is within the genus *Haliaeetus*, which includes all eight sea and fish eagles.

The common and scientific name of the bald eagle has been a subject of debate for over two hundred years. The bird has been variously called the black and brown eagle, the fish eagle, the Washington eagle, the grey eagle, the sea eagle, the mottled eagle, the bald-headed eagle, the white-tailed eagle, the white-tailed sea eagle, the American eagle, and the American bald eagle. It has been assigned a myriad of scientific names including *Aquila capite* in 1731, *Falco leucocephalus* in 1776, *Aquila leucocephalus* in 1807, *Falco ossifragus* in 1809, *Falco washingtonii* in 1827, *Falco washingtonianus* in 1832, *Haliaeetus washingtonii* in 1840, *Pandion washingtonii* in 1856, *Falco pygargus* in 1880, and finally *Haliaeetus leucocephalus* in 1898. These name changes reflected the confusion in the bald eagle's taxonomic position in the bird world. (8)

Two subspecies or races of the bald eagle are recognized today. These are the southern race, *Haliaeetus leucocephalus leucocephalus*, and the northern race, *Haliaeetus leucocephalus alascanus*. The bald eagle subspecies differ only in size; the southern race is smaller than the northern. An arbitrary geographic line divides the two races; there is a gradual change in size from low to high latitudes, and where the two races meet, the racial distinction is uncertain. A further complication is the fact that northern birds migrate south in the winter and some southern birds migrate north in the summer, which invariably causes an intermixing of the races. Though the dividing line between the races is debatable, most biologists recognize that the southern race occurs in southern California, Arizona, Oklahoma, Texas, Louisiana, the southern Atlantic states particularly including Florida, and Mexico. The northern subspecies, which is much more common, occurs in all other parts of the eagle's range.

The eight sea and fish eagles are thought to be divided into three unnamed superspecies or "closest cousins." This is a subclassification between the genus and species levels, which indicates the closest relationship without interbreeding. As the branching in the family tree in Figure 2.1 suggests, three pairs of sea eagles are more closely related to one another than they are to the others. The African and Madagascar fish eagles are thought to be either superspecies or variations within the same species. The white-bellied and Sanford's sea eagles presumably are super-species, as are the white-tailed sea eagle and the bald eagle. This makes the white-tailed sea eagle the closest living relative of the bald eagle. The Pallas' and Steller's sea eagles seem to be taxonomically distinct in this respect. (4, 1)

MODERN RELATIVES

The sea and fish eagles are large to very large eagles with unfeathered lower legs and large, powerful talons. Adults of most species have a bold, striking color pattern of black and white, and have yellow legs and beaks. The young are more dull and drab in color and have a mottled plumage with black, brown, and gray hues. The sexes are similar in color, but the females are larger, often much so. As their names suggest, the sea and fish eagles inhabit seacoasts and feed primarily on fish and other aquatic prey. They nest along shorelines and spend perhaps half of the year breeding and raising young. In many respects, all eight eagles are morphologically, physiologically, and behaviorally similar in nature. (2, 4)

The sea and fish eagle group enjoys nearly a worldwide distribution; South America is the only large land mass where they are not found (Fig. 2.2). It is a mystery why they have not occupied suitable habitats of tropical America, but perhaps this is because South America is one of the most distant areas from the sea eagles' evolutionary birthplace, in tropical Asia. Except for a small population of white-tailed sea eagles in Greenland and a few Steller's sea eagles in Alaska, the bald eagle is the only resident sea eagle in the New World.

The modern relatives of the bald eagle are the seven species of the genus *Haliaeetus,* the sea eagles, though two species are referred to as fish eagles. The bald eagle is by far the most studied species, but the white-tailed sea eagle and the African fish eagle also are well known. We know relatively little about the remaining five eagles—the white-bellied, Sanford's, Pallas', and Steller's sea eagles and the Madagascar fish eagle.

As mentioned, the white-tailed sea eagles are the bald eagles' closest cousins. Similar to the bald, they have a distinct white tail, but they lack a white head. They inhabit the temperate regions of Asia and Europe and are often found along the frigid seacoasts of Norway and Russia. They have the widest distribution of all sea eagles. These birds were once common to the British Isles, but persecution has caused local extinctions there and dramatic declines in several other European countries. Thousands of breeding pairs still exist in wilderness areas of Siberia, Norway, and in the Volga delta of Russia. (10)

The white-bellied sea eagle is a coastal inhabitant of southern Asia and Australia. The adult bird has a brilliant white head, neck, and underbelly with a mix of gray-brown on the back and wings. It is nonmigratory, though wintering birds band together and follow local food sources.

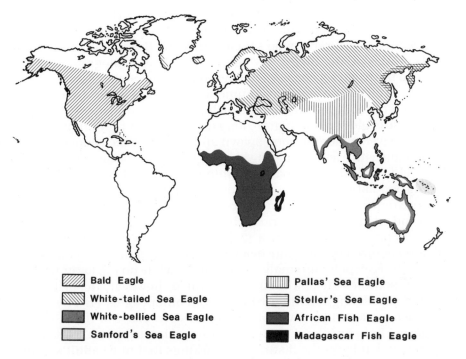

Bald Eagle

White-tailed Sea Eagle

White-bellied Sea Eagle

Sanford's Sea Eagle

Pallas' Sea Eagle

Steller's Sea Eagle

African Fish Eagle

Madagascar Fish Eagle

Fig. 2.2 Worldwide distribution of the genus *Haliaeetus,* the sea eagles. (4)

Although it is a fish eater, its tendency to kill sea snakes is well known. It will often plunge into water to take its prey, whether hunting for fish or snakes. (4)

A close relative of the white-bellied sea eagle, the Sanford's sea eagle is found only in the Solomon Islands in the South Pacific. Its appearance is similar to that of the subadult white-bellied eagle. Black, brown, and gold coloration is mixed throughout the Sanford's plumage, and it is similar in size to the Pallas' eagle; in fact, these two species are the smallest sea eagles. Conspicuously absent are any white patches on the plumage, which all other sea and fish eagles possess. Little is known of the Sanford's eagle, and its status is uncertain. These birds live along seacoasts, but are also found far inland amid montane tropical forests. Here they feed on birds and mammals rather than on fish.

A bird of central Asia, the Pallas' sea eagle avoids seacoastal areas and inhabits the shores of large inland lakes and rivers. This is the only sea eagle that is virtually landlocked. The dull white coloration on the head, neck, upper breast, and central portion of the tail is distinct on the adult. It feeds much as the bald eagle does, preferring fish, especially dead ones, and it frequently steals food. Perhaps the most gregarious member of the genus, Pallas' sea eagles gather in favored feeding areas in large groups, particularly in winter.

Probably the most magnificent sea eagle, and perhaps even more impressive than the bald eagle, is the giant Steller's sea eagle. Named after Georg Steller, a naturalist who sailed with Vitus Bering to the Aleutian Islands of Alaska, the Steller's weighs as much as 9 kilograms! (7) Restricted to the frigid seacoasts of northeast Asia, the Steller's is a striking feature in an otherwise bleak environment. The white forehead, shoulders, thighs, and tail contrast with a brownish black body and massive yellow beak. These eagles do not migrate long distances, but they often congregate along rivers where salmon spawn and die. They occasionally share their domain with a few wandering bald eagles, and an occasional Steller's will travel to the Alaskan coast and mingle with bald eagles. The total breeding population consists of less than one thousand nesting pairs. (10)

The two remaining eagles, usually referrred to as fish eagles, inhabit the coastal and inland waters of Africa. The African fish eagle, a much studied species, occurs in southern Africa. (3) Its numbers appear to be stable. The adult is recognized by the white head, neck, and tail and contrasting dark brown body. Except for its smaller size and the white on the lower neck, it closely resembles the bald eagle. Its voice, however, described as "melodious yodeling," distinguishes it from other eagles. (1) The Madagascar fish eagle, which lives along the western coast of the island of Madagascar or in its inland mangrove swamps, has a grayish white head and white tail. It lacks the distinctive markings that most adult sea and fish eagles possess. Unlike the African fish eagle, its numbers have been severely reduced, and it may be close to extinction. As their names suggest, both eagles prey on fish; they seem to prefer live fish to carrion. Interestingly, both species are somewhat tolerant of humans and can be approached closely, unlike the other eagle species.

The *Haliaeetus* eagles are an exciting evolutionary achievement. Unfortunately, all eight species have suffered persecution and habitat loss as a result of human activities. Many populations have been reduced or locally exterminated, and several species are threatened with total extinction, even more so than the bald eagle. Given their fragile status, research and management are desperately needed to ensure that this impressive and unique group is not destined for extinction.

3

Identification, Description, and Adaptations

IDENTIFICATION

The bald eagle is a large and strikingly colored raptor whose appearance is quite unmistakable. It is immense in size, one of the largest birds in North America. The adult bird displays a distinct white head and tail, which serve as its trademarks. Young bald eagles lack the white on the head and tail and undergo a series of plumage changes until adulthood. They can appear slate black to whitish gray, but are most often seen with a brown plumage interspersed with white, giving them a mottled look. The two sexes are monomorphic in color—that is, their plumages are similar.

The name "bald eagle" is a misnomer. In historic times, "bald" often meant "white" rather than "hairless." Historically, this species was often called the bald-headed eagle, among other names. In the late 1700s, the name was shortened providing us with the common name "bald eagle." This once meant "white eagle," but today it implies that the eagle is hairless, or more appropriately, featherless on its head. Both names are now meaningless; the eagle has a feathered head and is mostly brown, not white. The names "American bald eagle" and "American eagle" have often been used, but they imply geographic and/or political limitations that have not been widely accepted. However, the name "bald eagle" is so deeply ingrained in common usage and scientific literature that it is not likely to be changed. The scientific name for this species, *Haliaeetus leucocephalus*, literally means white-headed sea eagle. This, then, is the appropriate common name for what we call the bald eagle. Perhaps "white-headed eagle" would

Fig. 3.1 Comparison of the bald eagle with other similar species, perched and flying. Above, from top to bottom: osprey, red-tailed hawk, and turkey vulture; facing, from top to bottom: adult bald eagle, subadult bald eagle, adult golden eagle, subadult golden eagle.

also be appropriate as this would complement the name of its closest cousin, the white-tailed eagle. (19, 1)

Several other bird species can be confused with the bald eagle, especially golden eagles and ospreys, but hawks and vultures might also be misidentified as eagles. An identification chart that works well is provided in Figure 3.1. Proper identification is best made by noting as many distinguishing characteristics as possible. Size, color, form, and wing beats are the most helpful clues for field identification.

Young bald eagles and golden eagles of any age are easily confused. Both species are approximately the same size and have very similar plumage colorations. Sometimes only a trained observer can discern the difference, but there are several ways of distinguishing the two. First, any white color on subadult goldens is located in discrete patches on the wings and at the base of the tail. The adult golden eagle has no white coloration. On young balds, white mottling occurs, often extensively, and is scattered about on the wing undersides, breast, back, head, and tail. A white patch where the wing meets the body (the wing pit) is a definitive characteristic of the young bald.

Second, the golden color on the back of the head and the lack of white on the tail of the adult golden eagle will distinguish it from the bald eagle. Third, the head of the bald projects forward of the wings *more* than half the extent of the tail; the golden's head projects *less* than half the length of the tail. (9) Fourth, the lower legs on the bald are naked on the bottom half, but they are feathered down to the toes on goldens. This feature is seen only at close range. And, of course, the white head and tail of the adult bald is shared by no other bird in North America.

Ospreys, some hawks, and vultures might also be confused with the bald eagle. The osprey is much smaller, but occupies similar habitats. Its head and breast are white, and a black line crosses through the eye. A crook or bend in the wing is quite apparent in flight, and in this crook is a conspicuous black patch of feathers. Hawks are best distinguished from the eagle by their rapid wing beats, short wings, and small size. Vultures are smaller than the eagle, hold their wings in a V profile, and tend to teeter while doing so. The underwings of the turkey vulture appear black in front and gray in back; the black vulture has white patches near the tips of its underwings.

DESCRIPTION

Size and Weight   No other feature of the bald eagle is more impressive than its size; it is an enormous bird. Body weights over 7 kilograms are not uncommon. Five eagles captured in Alaska weighed an average of 7.3 kilograms; the largest was 7.5 kilograms. In contrast, though, some eagles can weigh as little as 3 kilograms, less than half the weight of a large bird. Measurements of body weight, however, are not nearly as impressive as those of body size. A northern eagle's wing span ranges from 200 to 235 centimeters. One of the largest eagles on record had a wing spread of 243 centimeters. (John James Audubon recorded a wing span of 310 centimeters on one bald eagle, but he was mistaken.) Body lengths vary from 84 to 95 centimeters for northern birds. Apart from individual variation, three major factors influence the size and weight of eagles: *sex, age,* and *geographic location.* (31, 21, 25)

As with most birds of prey, the female eagle is larger than the male. Among other types of birds, females are usually smaller than males; therefore, this phenomenon with raptors has come to be known as *reversed sexual size dimorphism.* The reasons for this apparent inconsistency in the bird world is still open to speculation. (27, 36) Whatever the cause, female bald eagles have larger wings, tails, bodies, beaks, and other features, but they also are heavier (Table 3.1, Fig. 3.2). The wing chords (distance between bend of wing and tip) of females range from 6 to 7 percent longer than males, and weights are 22 to 31 percent greater, depending on age.

This disparity in size between the sexes can be used with reasonable accuracy to determine the sex of a captive eagle. With paired measurements of the bill depth and length of the hallux talon, the sex of 98 percent of all eagles can be determined (Fig. 3.3). (4) Other techniques, which use measurements of wing chord, wing span, tarsal (lower leg) width, and beak depth and length, also provide accurate means of sex determination. (11, 17) In the field, determining sex can be difficult. A mated pair observed together usually can be sexed by comparing sizes, but differences in parental behavior may also provide clues to their gender.

Age also influences the size and weight of eagles. Young eagles are larger than adults, but they weigh less (Table 3.1, Fig. 3.2). The largeness of young eagles is attributable to longer feathers, especially wing and tail feathers. The lightness of their bodies occurs perhaps because the calcification of the

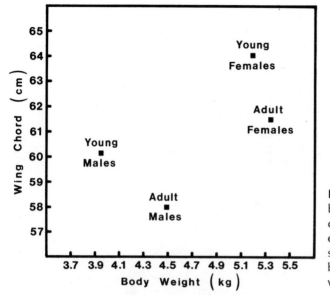

Fig. 3.2 Comparison of body weights and wing chords of 176 northern bald eagles of different age and sex. The wing chord lies between the bend of the wing and the tip. (2, 17, 21)

bones and development of muscles are not yet complete. As the young grow older, their plumages gradually shrink and they gain weight.

No one fully understands why there is such a marked size difference between young and old eagles, but the smaller adults may be more agile in flight, allowing them to kill prey with greater ease, and youngsters may benefit by being larger. (17) They may soar more effortlessly, being larger

Table 3.1. Weights (in kilograms) and measurements (in centimeters) of bald eagles of the northern subspecies.*

	Male		Female		
Feature	Adult	Juvenile/ Subadult	Adult	Juvenile/ Subadult	Reference
Body weight	4.325 (52)	3.917 (38)	5.268 (54)	5.129 (32)	17,21
Wing chord	58.2 (102)	60.1 (94)	62.8 (110)	63.7 (74)	4,10,17,21
Wing span	207.3 (52)	207.8 (38)	221.1 (54)	225.8 (32)	17,21
Tail length	29.1 (101)	30.8 (90)	31.7 (110)	32.7 (71)	4,10,17,21
Body length	84.3 (35)	87.2 (18)	91.1 (37)	94.9 (18)	21
Bill length	5.14 (67)	5.04 (75)	5.50 (73)	5.46 (55)	4,10,17
Bill depth	3.22 (18)	3.22 (45)	3.69 (12)	3.56 (33)	4
Tarsal width	14.6 (38)	14.5 (76)	16.8 (31)	16.5 (57)	4,17
Hallux length	3.98 (20)	3.96 (57)	4.57 (13)	4.43 (42)	4

*Figures in parentheses are the number of birds measured.

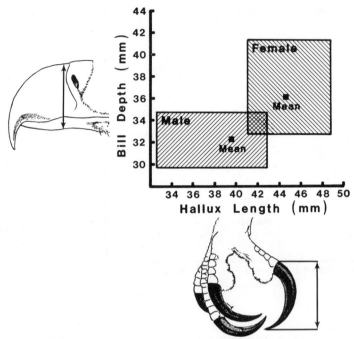

Fig. 3.3 Technique for determining the sex of captive bald eagles by using the bill depth and hallux (rear talon) length. In the following equation, if sex is positive the eagle is a female; if negative, it is a male: Sex = (Bill Depth x 0.392) + (Hallux Length x 0.340) − 27.694, in centimeters. (4)

and lighter, and this could aid in finding prey and reduce the energy costs of flight. Their large size could also increase their success at stealing food from smaller eagles or defending food from others.

Besides sex and age variations, a considerable size difference exists between the northern subspecies *(Haliaeetus leucocephalus alascanus)* and the southern subspecies *(Haliaeetus leucocephalus leucocephalus).* Southern eagles are much smaller than their northern counterparts (Table 3.2, Fig. 3.4). The southern race also is lighter, but few data are available on weights of southern birds. The subspecific size difference is so large that males of the northern race are larger than females of the southern race. Assuming that egg weight is consistently proportional to the weight of the mother eagle, egg size can be used to assess this latitudinal change (Fig. 3.5). The relationship of egg size to latitude demonstrates a distinct and continuous increase in egg dimensions as one goes farther north. As will be discussed in Chapter 9, this trend is related to the eagle's ability to cope with cold stress; large bodies lose heat at a slower rate and therefore are advantageous in colder climates.

Three factors, size, weight, and geographic location, distinguish the two subspecies. But deciding where to draw the line between the two races has

Table 3.2. Ranges of weights (in kilograms) and measurements (in centimeters) of the two subspecies of bald eagles and their eggs.

Feature	Northern subspecies		Southern subspecies		Reference
	Smallest	Largest	Smallest	Largest	
Body weight	3.100	7.484	?	?	20,31
Wing chord	54.1	69.2	50.8	58.8	2,4,10,21
Tail length	23.6	39.4	23.2	28.6	2,4,10
Bill length	4.17	6.06	3.00	5.20	4,10
Egg size					
Length	6.96	8.43	5.81	7.88	3,18
Breadth	5.30	6.34	4.70	5.76	3,18

not been easy (see Chapter 2). With a gradual change in size and weight from north to south, any dividing line is arbitrary. Because of this, some taxonomists believe that two different subspecies should not be recognized. (1)

Plumage Coloration Apart from their large size, the contrasting color pattern of the adult bald eagle is particularly impressive. The white head and tail stand seemingly apart from the dark brown, almost black, body. And at close range, the yellow beak, eyes, and legs blend with the white and black to form a pattern that is pleasing to the human eye.

In comparison to the adults, young eagles have drab plumages. Beginning with the recently fledged bird, five juvenile and subadult plumage types usually can be recognized, though there can be considerable varia-

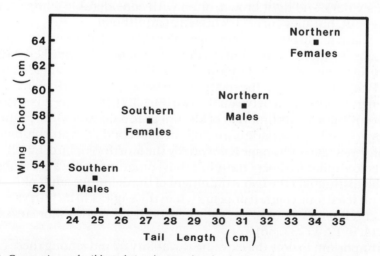

Fig. 3.4 Comparison of tail lengths and wing chords of ninety-eight adult bald eagles of both subspecies and sexes. (10)

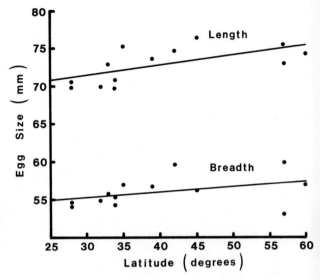

Fig. 3.5 Relationship between egg sizes and the latitude at the nest location. The size of the eggs is predicted by the following equations: Length = 67.38 + 0.14 x Latitude; Breadth = 53.09 + 0.07 x Latitude. (3, 5, 8, 32)

tion. (The plumages of nestling eagles are discussed in Chapter 6.) These five plumage classes show a gradual attainment of the adult color, with each successive class gaining more adult characteristics, especially on the head (Table 3.3, Fig. 3.6). The iris of the eye is transformed from dark brown to yellow or cream in the adult. Similarly, the beak and cere (fleshy area at the base of the beak) change from black to yellow. The blackish head and tail of the juvenile eagle gradually lighten with each successive molt. The lower breast undergoes interesting changes, normally from dark brown to light brown to whitish gray to dark brown again. The undersides of the wings are variously dark and light brown, often with considerable white scattered throughout, but they turn dark brown at adulthood.

The relationship between plumage coloration and age has been a subject of debate for many years, but recent studies of color-marked eagles of known age have addressed this question. Many inconsistencies and individual variations exist in the relationship between age and color, but there is a general correlation between the two (Fig. 3.7). Plumage A is sported by the juvenile during its first year of life, but gradually fades into plumage B. Plumage C is characteristic of an eagle in its second year, and plumage D is the third-year garb. Plumage E is worn by the fourth-year bird, but this color class is so similar to that of the adult that sometimes only a close observation can distinguish the two. Attainment of the definitive adult plumage requires at least four years; it appears when the eagle is in its fifth year of life. Further refinements to this scheme may be discovered as more research is done. (4, 9, 12, 17, 37, 38)

It is important to note the extreme variability in and among these classes of plumage coloration. Some eagles will skip a plumage class or retain one for long periods; individual variation can be so great that many features just

Table 3.3. Descriptions of juvenile, subadult, and adult plumages of the bald eagle.*

| Feature | Juvenile plumages | | Subadult plumages | | | Adult plumage |
	A	B	C	D	E	
Eye	Dark brown	Brown	Light brown	Cream	Dull yellow	Yellowish white
Beak and cere	Black and gray	Black and gray	Black, gray, and some yellow	Gray and yellow	Dull yellow	Yellow
Head	Dark brown to black	Brown	Brown to light brown	Gray and light brown	Dirty white	White
Lower breast	Dark brown	Brown	Usually mottled gray	Usually brown with some gray	Dark brown	Dark brown
Under-sides of wings	Dark brown, black, and gray	Dark brown, gray mottling especially at wing pit	Brown, much gray mottling especially at wing pit	Brown, some gray mottling especially at wing pit	Dark brown with some gray mottling	Dark brown
Tail	Black with gray near vane	Black with gray near vane	Black with gray intermixed	Gray with black	Dirty white	White

*The relation of plumage types to age is shown in Figure 3.6.

do not fit any pattern. Possibly the least variation is seen in the head characteristics. In many respects, the plumage classes are not distinct but should be thought of as a gradual transition to the adult appearance.

Besides individual variation, there can be extreme aberrations in color. "Blond" bald eagles have been seen; they are very light, almost cream in color. Albinism also occurs; it is a consistent, though uncommon, genetic trait. (9) Albino birds are completely white because they lack any pigmentation. Most variants are, upon closer examination, strange-looking juveniles or subadults.

Attainment of the adult plumage may not be concurrent with sexual maturation. Breeding eagles have been seen while still in subadult plumage, although rarely, and birds that have recently attained the adult plumage tend to be less adept at breeding. It has also been suggested that northern birds mature earlier than southern ones and that wild birds mature earlier than captives, but this needs verification. Healthy eagles may mature sooner than those in ill or marginal health. (3, 16, 4)

Biologists who study bald eagles do not agree on the terminology used to denote young eagles. They are called either juveniles, subadults, or immatures, and there is complete confusion over distinctions among the three types. I have used *juvenile* to identify the first-year bird, prior to its first

Fig. 3.6 Juvenile plumages A and B (lower left and middle left); subadult plumages C, D, and E (upper left, upper right, and middle right); and adult plumage (lower right).

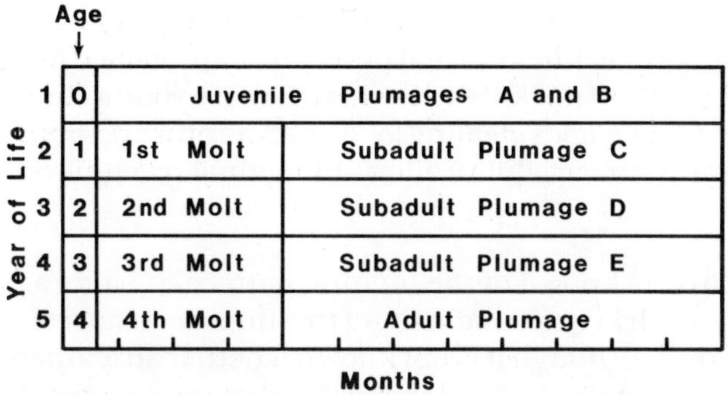

Age

Year of Life			
1	0		Juvenile Plumages A and B
2	1	1st Molt	Subadult Plumage C
3	2	2nd Molt	Subadult Plumage D
4	3	3rd Molt	Subadult Plumage E
5	4	4th Molt	Adult Plumage

Months

Fig. 3.7 Best approximation of the relationships between juvenile, subadult, and adult plumages with age, year of life, and molt sequence. (12, 17)

birthday; this includes plumages A and B. Juvenile might also refer to the nestling that has attained the juvenile plumage and is close to leaving the nest. *Subadult* and *immature* both refer to the young eagle after its first birthday and prior to reaching adulthood. This includes plumages C, D, and E. The *adult* may also be called a *mature* bird.

Reasons for Coloration   Most animals are colored so as to influence the behavior of other animals; these visual signals are an important means of communication. We do not know why bald eagles look the way they do, but their plumage coloration undoubtedly conveys important messages or serves vital functions. Deciphering these vital signals is difficult, and we are only beginning to understand the reasons for animal coloration. (29)

A number of hypotheses have been suggested to explain the color of bald eagles. Some seem quite plausible, others are farfetched, and all of them need scientific verification. Listed below are some thoughts on why plumages appear as they do. There probably is no single reason; colors may serve several purposes.

Adult Coloration
   1. Signals sexual maturation and breeding readiness, and aids in attracting potential mates.
   2. Signals the occupation of a breeding territory.
   3. Warns and threatens other animals to keep their distance or avoid entering a territory.
   4. Indicates a condition of social status such as dominance or subordination.
   5. Serves to attract other eagles to resources such as food and roosts.

Juvenile and Subadult Coloration
   1. Signals a lack of sexual maturity and inability to breed.
   2. Indicates a condition of social status such as dominance or subordination.

3. Signals a non-threat status to territorial adult eagles.

4. Provides concealment so that prey can be ambushed more effectively, so that predators will not kill them when they are young, and to reduce the likelihood of other eagles stealing food or some other resource from them.

5. Extreme color variability allows individual recognition among relatives and associates.

Molting Little is known of the molting pattern in bald eagles; perhaps future studies will help us understand this important aspect. A molt takes place every year, although it is not known whether all feathers change annually. Juveniles and subadults change in appearance after every molt, but adults maintain their basic coloration for life. Molt is a gradual process occurring mostly in the summer, but extending into spring and autumn. Because the flight feathers are not lost all at once, as is the case with some birds, eagles are never flightless during the molting period. (22, 34)

Longevity Bald eagles are physiologically capable of living a long life. Often, however, eagles in the wild die well before reaching physiologic old age (also see Chapter 11). Wild birds surely do not live as long as those kept in captivity, because captive birds are pampered, fed regularly, given nutritional supplements, and protected from calamities. The life span may be as much as fifty years, but the actual life of a free-living eagle is much less. Two captive eagles lived to be at least forty-seven years old. Other records of exceptionally long lives of captive birds are fifteen, twenty, twenty-one, twenty-five, thirty-one, and thirty-four years. Bald eagles are thought to have a reproductive life of twenty to thirty years. (16, 39, 23)

Voice The calls of the bald eagle are simple and limited in variety, but quite distinct. Their voice has been described as "ridiculously weak and insignificant, quite unbecoming [for] a bird of its size and strength," "metallic with the quality of an unoiled caster," "a loud harsh scream," "an ear-splitting scream," "more of a squeal than a scream," "shrill, querulous squealing," "weak in volume and trivial in expression," and "a snickering laugh expressive of imbecile derision." (3, 28, 19, 5) Unlike its other qualities, the eagle's voice is not especially admired by naturalists. The voice is best described as a loud, high-pitched scream, most similar to the sound of a sea gull, but broken into a series of notes in rapid succession. It can carry for long distances, and within a confined space, the boisterous calls can be uncomfortably loud.

Eagles communicate primarily by visual means, but vocalizations can, at times, be an important medium for the exchange of information. We know virtually nothing of the purposes of most vocalizations, and past researchers have often anthropomorphized in describing the functions of eagle talk. A "greeting" call is used during the breeding season when a mate arrives at the nest or territory, but this same call is used by both birds during courtship. A "solicitation" call occurs during courtship, just prior to copulation, and is a single, soft, high-pitched note used by the female. Vocal displays denoting "annoyance" and "threat" are common and seem to intensify when intruders enter the territory or approach the nest. The eaglets have "begging" calls, which are described as "remarkably persistent peeping" by the very young chicks or "peculiar whining cries" by the older nestlings. Juveniles and subadults occasionally make clucking sounds similar to those of domestic fowl. (30, 13, 19)

Eagles also vocalize in winter, especially when they gather in large groups. Vocalization is most intense during communal feeding and when eagles arrive at perching and roosting areas. When perching or loafing throughout the day, roosting at night, or flying around, eagles are usually quiet. An eagle possessing food will call frequently, perhaps as a warning threat to others, but these calls may attract or induce others to gather and feed. Vocalizations are especially common after an eagle has successfully stolen food, arrived at a communal roost for the evening, or engaged in other social activities.

Other aspects of vocalization have been little studied. Some characteristics of voice development have been measured using sonagrams and other researchers have attempted to measure "voice prints" by which to identify individual birds. (14, 40) There is a dire need for research on vocal communication particularly during winter when eagles are most gregarious.

PHYSICAL ADAPTATIONS

Senses Without question, vision is the most important sense of the bald eagle. Its eyes are exceptionally powerful. Few, if any, animals can match the eagle's ability to see distant objects. Its visual acuity, the degree of resolving power, is three to four times greater than that of humans. Generally, then, eagles can see objects three to four times farther away than can a human. Anyone who has watched an eagle through a telescope from afar and found the eagle staring back will attest to this bird's remarkable visual ability. One study suggests that one eagle can detect another eagle soaring from a distance of 23 to 65 kilometers! (7, 35, 24)

The eagle has eyes so large that they occupy most of the space of its head. Although they have only a slight ability to move their eyes in the sockets, eagles can rotate their heads to possibly three-quarters of a circle. An eagle will frequently turn its head to obtain a better view. The position of the eyes allows both monocular vision, where both eyes operate somewhat independently to see objects to the side, and binocular vision, where, like those of humans, both eyes focus on an object directly in front of the head. The eagle's eye is functionally similar to that of a human, but it is more refined and adapted for superior performance.

Several anatomical features provide the eagle with its superb eyesight (Fig. 3.8). Because the eye is large, the retina has a large surface area on

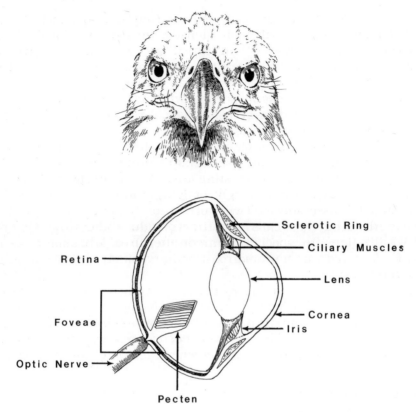

Fig. 3.8 Anatomy of the eagle's eye.

which the visual image is registered. The retinal surface is densely packed with sensory cells called *cones* and *rods.* The cones are more numerous because they allow for visual acuity and color perception. Rods allow sight in low illumination, but eagles do not have particularly good night vision. Nerve fibers connecting the sensory cells to the brain and forming the optic nerve are exceptionally dense, again promoting superb resolving power. On the retinal surface, two foveae exist in each eye, one for monocular or sideways vision, and the other for binocular or forward vision. The foveae are deep depressions in the retina where sensory cells are especially concentrated; it is here that the eye attains its maximum optical resolution. Extruding from the retinal surface is a peculiar structure, replete with blood vessels, called the pecten. Perhaps it provides nutrition and oxygen to the retina. Toward the front of the eye is the lens, with ciliary muscles that alter its shape to provide exact focusing ability. The iris, the pigmented portion of the eye, regulates the amount of light entering by changing shape, thereby either enlarging or constricting the pupil, through which light passes. The cornea is the outer surface of the eye. A ring of bones, the sclerotic eye ring, surrounds the cornea for protection. The nictitating membrane, the so-called second eyelid, sweeps across the cornea to cleanse the surface and also to protect it. A parent eagle will often draw it across the eye while feeding its young so that the eaglet does not inadvertently strike the parent's eye while trying to grab food dangling from the adult's beak. (7, 35)

Hearing is another sense that is known to be important to the eagle. Its hearing may be comparable to that of a human. Covered by a layer of feathers designed not to impede the passage of sound, the outer ear opening is situated just behind the eagle's eye. Not unlike the human ear, the opening leads to the eardrum or tympanic membrane, which is vibrated by sound waves. These vibrations are transmitted to the oval window by several small bones. The inner ear, known as the labyrinth, is where the auditory signals are relayed to the sensory cells and eventually transmitted to the brain. Semicircular canals in the labyrinth assist in equilibrium.

The eagle appears to have a rudimentary sense of taste, developed enough to allow it to distinguish foul-tasting prey. But bald eagles do not seem to mind the taste of many food items that are repulsive to humans. The sense of smell is poorly developed. If foul-smelling food is covered by snow, for example, an eagle will be unable to find it. The sense of touch seems to be well developed throughout the skin, but is especially acute on the beak and feet; this aids in the capturing and killing of prey.

Predation The bald eagle is well equipped as a predator. Its keen eyesight allows it to see prey at great distances, and its stealth in flight can be an effective weapon. With its large appetite, the eagle has evolved several important adaptations for efficient capturing and killing of prey.

The feet and talons are the eagle's main predatory equipment for capturing, grasping, and killing prey (Fig. 3.9). The feet and talons are surprisingly large even for such a huge bird. When spread on a flat surface, the eagle's foot extends 15 centimeters or more. (26) The talons alone seem disproportionate to the toes because they are so long. The hallux, or hind claw, being the largest, ranges from 3.5 to 5.0 centimeters long. (4) If measured along its curvature, the hallux can be 7 to 8 centimeters in length. The other three talons are successively smaller than the hallux. It is easy to imagine the grasping ability of these claws, but the muscular force behind them also is tremendous. When the muscles of the legs contract, the tendons in the lower legs tighten, and the talons close together. This locking system also allows the bird to secure its toes around a perch and keep its body steady during rest and sleep. The talons can easily penetrate to the bone and even crush some bones in the prey animal; those unfortunate enough to have been grabbed by an eagle are not likely to forget the experience.

On the undersides of the fleshy toes are small, rough projections, called spicules, which help the eagle to grasp and hold slippery prey such as fish. Why the lower legs are unfeathered is open to speculation, but perhaps the feathers are kept drier when the bird wades in shallow water. The eagle is ungainly and awkward in its stride; its feet are obviously adapted for predation and perching, not for walking.

The beak is massive, especially on the females. Like the talons, it may be used for capturing prey, particularly if the victims are small. But its main purpose seems to be for tearing and killing, if the job was not accomplished with the talons. The beak is a formidable weapon. The end has an elongated and sharp tip which, when closed, can impart severe injury (Fig. 3.9). The powerful muscles supporting the beak and the beak's destructive shape can be appreciated only by the eagle's victims, but compared to the feet, the beak plays a secondary role in predatory conquests.

The mouth has a large gape that permits the eagle to swallow sizable objects. Eagles do not chew their food; they tear it into manageable portions and swallow it with a biting motion. If the item is too large, they will pull it out and rip at it again. After ingestion, the food is temporarily stored in a huge sack, called the crop, in the esophagus. An eagle that has recently eaten will have an obviously distended bulge in the throat area. The crop can accommodate up to about one kilogram of food; it allows the eagle to gorge itself when food is abundant.

Fig. 3.9 The feet, talons, and beak are the bald eagle's predatory equipment.

Fig. 3.10 Comparison of wing shapes between a juvenile (below) and adult (above), showing that young eagles have larger wings.

Flight At times, eagles can soar and glide in a seemingly effortless fashion, much to the delight of many earthbound observers. At other times, however, their flight is awkward, laborious, and apparently exhausting. Because of their bulky size, eagles need optimal flying conditions to display their true elegance in flight.

As a modern airplane needs ample room in which to take off, so does an eagle. Obstructions, such as trees and branches, can play havoc with flight. Flight often appears strenuous when the eagle takes off from the ground, and even after it attains cruising speed, it must use a deliberate and steady beat of its wings to maintain altitude. Eagles reach their epitome of grace and form while flying during optimal atmospheric conditions. When the sun heats the earth, large masses of warm air rise in thermals. These thermals attract eagles and other soaring birds because the rising air lifts the birds to great heights. When winds pass over hills and mountains, an updraft of air is created along the windward sides. Eagles also recognize these vertical wind profiles and will glide in them for long distances, especially during migration.

One reason flying is difficult is that eagles have a greater amount of "wing loading" than do most other birds. Wing loading is the weight carried by the surface area of the wings. It averages 0.8 grams per square centimeter, and some interesting differences occur with age. Adult wing loads are about 15 percent greater than those of young eagles, because adults weigh more and because their wings are narrower (Fig. 3.10). The wings of adults are adapted for speed and attacking, whereas young eagles' wings are adapted for soaring and lift. This disparity may make adults more effective at killing live prey and allows young eagles to soar and glide more easily so that they can search for carrion. (17)

All eagles possess wing slots on the ends of their wings. These are the fingerlike gaps between the large primary feathers. These wing slots are constantly adjusted to maintain a steady flight pattern and to permit precise maneuvering. Slots also increase lift, especially during soaring, so that less energy is needed to stay airborne. Eagles frequently adjust their tail feathers by spreading them as well as by tilting them to aid in quick turns and stability.

Other flight adaptations of eagles are shared by most other birds. A lightweight yet strong skeleton is one feature. In fact, the skeleton of an eagle weighs less than half as much as the feathers. Feathers, of course, are the principal adaptation for flight, even though they are thought to have originally evolved for the purpose of maintaining body warmth. One plucked eagle contained 7,182 feathers. (6)

4

Populations, Distribution, and Movements

Historical documents reveal that bald eagles were once widespread throughout North America. There are many past accounts of eagles that nested where they no longer exist today. In New York State, for example, some sixty-three breeding pairs were known to exist a century ago. In 1982, however, only two nesting pairs inhabited the entire state. But there are large gaps in our knowledge of historic numbers; it was only a few decades ago that the first concerted effort to count eagles was launched. One researcher estimated that a quarter of a million bald eagles inhabited North America a century ago, but this and other estimates are only rough guesses of past numbers. It can be assumed that eagles were never especially abundant because predators rarely are, but there is no question that the population has declined in the past two centuries. (33, 11, 42, 6)

Although the bald eagle has been exterminated or greatly reduced in many parts of its range, this species is not in any immediate danger of becoming extinct. But many local populations are now gone, and though many bald eagles still live today, there are few pristine populations left in the contiguous United States. Populations have suffered a slow decline mainly due to a gradual, piecemeal destruction of their habitat and food sources; humans and eagles are rarely compatible. Because of these severe reductions, the bald eagle is now classified as either threatened or endangered with extinction in all forty-eight contiguous states.

NUMBERS

A complete and accurate count of all eagles is difficult to achieve, but there have been many censuses of nesting pairs and wintering birds. Most nests are counted from small airplanes, but wintering eagles are often surveyed on foot or from a boat. Whatever the method or time of year, most censuses are conservative estimates of actual numbers.

A survey of nests in 1982, during the eagle's two hundredth anniversary as the national symbol, showed that only 1,482 pairs occupied nesting territories in the forty-eight contiguous states (Table 4.1). Of these 1,482 pairs, only 954 successfully raised young. The number of breeding pairs in southeast Alaska ranges from approximately 7,000 to 8,000; thus, the breeding population in the United States is less than 10,000 pairs. (11, 20, 24)

Counts of overwintering birds are better estimates of the actual eagle population because they include juveniles, subadults, and nonbreeding adults, which are not included in counts of breeding pairs. The numbers of wintering eagles counted during five years of surveys conducted throughout the forty-eight contiguous states were 9,815 in 1979; 13,046 in 1980; 13,710 in 1981; 13,804 in 1982; and 12,098 in 1983. (32) In Alaska, numbers are much higher, with 35,000 to 45,000 being the best current estimate. In 1982, the "Year of the Eagle," more wintering eagles were counted in the United States than ever before, though this probably was due to more comprehensive surveys (Table 4.2).

Table 4.1. Number of breeding pairs of bald eagles in the United States, 1982. (11)

State	Number	State	Number
1. Alaska	7,500*	26. Illinois	2
2. Florida	340	27. Oklahoma	2
3. Wisconsin	207	28. Iowa	1
4. Minnesota	207	29. New Jersey	1
5. Washington	135	30. Arkansas	1
6. Michigan	96	31. New Mexico	1
7. Oregon	93	32. West Virginia	1
8. Maine	72	33. Alabama	0
9. Maryland	58	34. Connecticut	0
10. California	52	35. Indiana	0
11. Virginia	48	36. Kansas	0
12. Montana	37	37. Kentucky	0
13. Wyoming	22	38. Massachusetts	0
14. South Carolina	21	39. Mississippi	0
15. Louisiana	18	40. Nebraska	0
16. Idaho	15	41. Nevada	0
17. Texas	14	42. New Hampshire	0
18. Arizona	10	43. North Dakota	0
19. Ohio	7	44. Rhode Island	0
20. Colorado	6	45. South Dakota	0
21. Pennsylvania	4	46. Tennessee	0
22. Delaware	4	47. Utah	0
23. Georgia	3	48. Vermont	0
24. New York	2	49. North Carolina	0
25. Missouri	2	50. Hawaii	—

*Estimate. (20, 24)

Table 4.2. Number of overwintering bald eagles in the United States, 1982. (32)

State	Number	State	Number
1. Alaska	40,000*	26. Maryland	109
2. Washington	1,378	27. Wisconsin	83
3. Missouri	1,234	28. Nevada	74
4. Utah	1,001	29. Minnesota	61
5. Florida	920	30. South Carolina	55
6. California	872	31. Alabama	41
7. Illinois	810	32. North Dakota	40
8. Oklahoma	706	33. New York	40
9. Idaho	668	34. Michigan	39
10. Colorado	628	35. Louisiana	38
11. Arkansas	569	36. Connecticut	31
12. Oregon	480	37. Mississippi	26
13. Montana	470	38. Georgia	20
14. Kansas	453	39. Massachusetts	13
15. Wyoming	362	40. Pennsylvania	13
16. Texas	359	41. Indiana	12
17. New Mexico	357	42. New Jersey	12
18. South Dakota	356	43. Ohio	7
19. Nebraska	348	44. Delaware	6
20. Tennessee	285	45. West Virginia	3
21. Arizona	208	46. New Hampshire	2
22. Kentucky	199	47. North Carolina	1
23. Iowa	167	48. Rhode Island	1
24. Virginia	159	49. Vermont	0
25. Maine	110	50. Hawaii	—

*Estimate.

The breeding and wintering populations in Canada have not been surveyed as extensively as have those in the United States. It is believed, however, that Canada has tens of thousands of nesting pairs and about 30,000 wintering birds (Table 4.3). Only a handful nest and winter in Mexico.

A 1975 estimate of the total number of bald eagles in the world was between 35,000 and 60,000. (2) A more reliable estimate made in 1980 revealed a figure of 70,000. (8) Because these counts are likely to underestimate the population, perhaps 80,000 would be a more reasonable statistic. Unfortunately, the accuracy of censuses is poorest where eagles are most abundant. Eagle numbers are well documented and closely monitored in the continental United States, but surveys are sorely needed in the wilderness areas of Canada and Alaska where the largest populations exist.

DISTRIBUTION

Bald eagles are indigenous to the North American continent. They do, however, occasionally stray to coastal areas in Siberia and Greenland, and there have been unconfirmed sightings in Sweden and Bermuda. Their

Table 4.3 Estimated number of breeding pairs and overwintering eagles in Canada.

Province	Breeding Pairs (8, 19, 27)	Wintering Birds (8)
Alberta	?	569
British Columbia	4,500	28,507
Manitoba	?	0
New Brunswick	12	65
Newfoundland	?	461
Nova Scotia	106	235
Ontario	?	108
Prince Edward Island	?	0
Quebec	?	112
Saskatchewan	3,900	112

principal breeding range includes most of southern Alaska and southern Canada, the northern contiguous states, and parts of the eastern and western seaboard (Fig. 4.1). Their wintering range encompasses areas mostly south of this, but especially includes the northwestern and central states and the Alaskan and British Columbian seacoasts where large concentrations breed and overwinter. Bald eagles are absent from the far arctic areas and are generally rare north of the arctic timberline. Their most southerly distribution is in Baja California.

The major strongholds of breeding populations in the United States are Alaska, the Great Lakes states, Florida, the Pacific Northwest, the Chesapeake Bay area, and several other coastal states (Fig. 4.2). Excluding Alaska, Florida has the greatest number of breeding eagles; 340 pairs occupied nesting terrritories in that state in 1982. Other large concentrations occur in Wisconsin and Minnesota, each with about 200 pairs; Wahington, Michigan, and Oregon have approximately 100 breeding pairs apiece; and Maine, Maryland, California, and Virginia each host 50 to 75 pairs. Scattered populations persist throughout many other states, but eighteen states have no breeding pairs left. As mentioned, Alaska maintains a substantial population of at least 7,000 to 8,000 pairs, and breeding eagles occur in all of the provinces of Canada. British Columbia has at least 4,500 pairs. (11, 19)

For every breeding pair in the forty-eight contiguous states, there are nearly ten wintering eagles (Fig. 4.3). The winter population is higher because many birds migrate south from Canada to join resident birds in the lower states. Except for seacoastal populations, the bulk of the Canadian nestling population winters in the United States. Alaska has a wintering population of 35,000 to 45,000, more than any other state. Washington has the largest winter population in the lower forty-eight states with nearly 1,400 birds counted in 1982. Many eagles gather along the Mississippi River, particularly in Missouri and Illinois; each state has about 1,000 birds. Utah, Florida, California, Oklahoma, Idaho, Colorado,

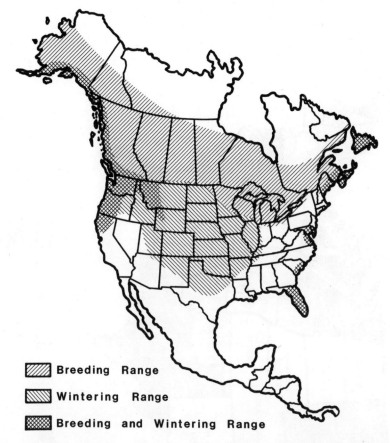

Fig. 4.1 Primary distribution of breeding and wintering bald eagles in North America.

and Arkansas also are major wintering areas; from 500 to 1,000 eagles are found in each of these states. The bulk of the winter population resides in the western states. The size of the Canadian winter population is little known, but for the most part, few birds spend the winter in the central provinces; they prefer the milder climate of the States. Coastal winter concentrations are large, however. More than 28,000 eagles overwinter in British Columbia. (32, 8)

SPECIAL AREAS OF ABUNDANCE

Although their range encompasses most of the North American continent, bald eagles are found only in areas where suitable habitat is available. An abundant food supply is the prime reason for a gathering of eagles, but the birds also need old-growth forests and freedom from human disturbance. Eagles usually select wilderness settings for their nesting activities.

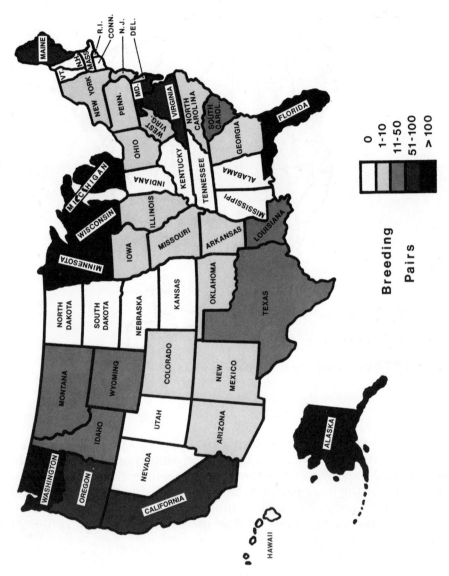

Fig. 4.2 State-by-state number of breeding pairs occupying territories in 1982. (11)

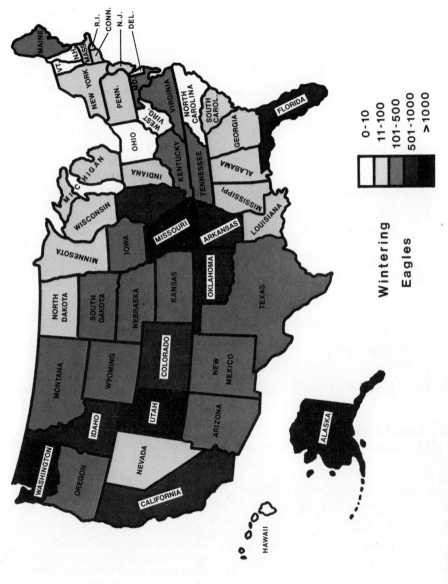

Wintering
Eagles

0-10
11-100
101-500
501-1000
>1000

Fig. 4.3 State-by-state number of wintering eagles in 1982. (32)

Table 4.4 Twenty-five areas in the United States where bald eagles are common.

Name	State	Specific attraction
Sanctuaries		
1. *Chilkat River Bald Eagle Preserve	Alaska	Largest concentration of bald eagles in the world. In autumn, over 3,000 can be seen.
2. Seymour Eagle Management Area	Alaska	Islands set aside where a particularly dense concentration of nesting eagles can be observed.
3. Skagit River Bald Eagle Natural Area	Washington	Established by the Nature Conservancy, this sanctuary hosts several hundred eagles that dine on salmon.
4. Three Sisters, Caldwell, Cougar Roosts	California	Three large communal roosts near the Oregon border. Eagles feed at Klamath and Tule Lakes (see 16).
5. Ferry Bluff Eagle Sanctuary	Wisconsin	Small winter roost protected by Eagle Valley Environmentalists and the National Wildlife Federation.
6. Eagle Valley	Wisconsin	Winter communal roost protected by Eagle Valley Environmentalists, a bald eagle conservation group.
7. Oak Valley Eagle Refuge	Illinois	Bald eagle wintering area established by the National Wildlife Federation.
8. Prairie State Eagle Refuge	Illinois	Large overwintering concentration on the Mississippi River.
9. Cedar Glen Eagle Roost	Illinois	Large winter roost in the forested floodplains of the Mississippi River.
10. Pere Marquette Eagle Roost	Illinois	Protected winter communal roosts at Pere Marquette State Park.
National Parks		
11. Olympic	Washington	One of the last wilderness beaches in the 48 states where bald eagles are common year-round.
12. Glacier	Montana	Densest winter concentration in the 48 states along McDonald Creek. Photography blinds available.
13. Yellowstone	Wyoming	Small nesting population particularly on Yellowstone Lake, but some birds winter here, too.
14. Grand Teton	Wyoming	Small nesting population, but wintering eagles too. Most are found on the Snake River.
15. Everglades	Florida	Large concentration of nesting pairs that remain on their territories throughout the year.

Table 4.4 (cont.)

Name	State	Specific attraction
National Wildlife Refuges		
16. Bear Valley, Klamath Lake, Tule Lake	Oregon and California	Three refuges where eagles feed, nest, or roost. Used in conjunction with three other roosts (see 4).
17. Bear River	Utah	Feeding grounds with a large communal roost in Willard Canyon. Status now uncertain due to flooding.
18. Karl Mundt	South Dakota	One of the first bald eagle sanctuaries protects wintering birds along the Missouri River.
19. Swan Lake	Missouri	Large overwintering aggregation that feeds primarily on migrant waterfowl.
20. Reelfoot	Tennessee	Many wintering eagles on Reelfoot Lake make this a popular attraction. Photography blinds available.
Other Areas		
21. San Juan Islands	Washington	One of the densest nesting populations in the 48 states, but also many wintering birds.
22. Cedar and Rush Valleys	Utah	Unique communal roosts and wintering areas associated with a desert environment.
23. San Luis Valley	Colorado	Several hundred eagles wintering on the Rio Grande and Conejos River and other areas.
24. Chippewa National Forest	Minnesota	A large nesting population that is well studied. A special bald eagle nesting area has been set aside.
25. Chesapeake Bay	Maryland, Virginia, Delaware	Excluding Florida, this is the largest nesting population on the eastern seaboard; over 100 nests.

*Numbers correspond to map locations in Figure 4.4.

Wintering groups, on the other hand, tend to be transient in nature, depending on the food supply. They traditionally winter in the same areas year after year. A listing of many of these "eagle haunts" is found in Table 4.4, and Figure 4.4 shows their location.

By far the most spectacular eagle gathering in the world is on the Chilkat River near Haines in southeast Alaska. No other eagle concentration is as large, as dense, and as impressive as this. Within a 60-kilometer run of river, as many as 4,000 birds have been counted! These eagles feed on salmon that spawn and die in the river in fall and winter. Upsurges of warm

Fig. 4.4 Selected areas in the United States where bald eagles are common. Numbers correspond to those in Table 4.4

water keep part of the river free of ice so that carcasses are accessible throughout the long winter months. November is the time of peak concentration, but many eagles are present throughout the year, and some nest in the valley. Timber harvesting, mineral development, and other human activities threaten this population, but parts of the Chilkat Valley have now been set aside as an eagle preserve. (6, 5, 16)

The most abundant breeding population is found along the seacoastal islands of Alaska and British Columbia. Many shorelines have such large populations that an active nest can be found every kilometer or two. It is the last remaining eagle stronghold still virtually untouched by man. Nearly all of the major islands in southern Alaska harbor some eagles, but Admiralty Island is noteworthy (also see Fig. 10.1). On the eastern portion of this island, the Seymour Eagle Refuge has been established to protect vital habitat. In British Columbia, the Queen Charlotte and Vancouver Island archipelagos are home to thousands of birds. Similar numbers winter along the Fraser River system and many other rivers along the coast, including the Squamish. Eagles thrive in these locations even though human encroachment reaches farther into these wilderness areas every year. (20, 24, 15)

The largest inland breeding population exists in the glacier-carved lakes and the streams in south central Canada, particularly in Saskatchewan, Manitoba, and Ontario, but scattered nesting populations persist in all Canadian provinces. These provinces support thousands of eagles. Breeding populations in Quebec and Labrador are relatively small, as are those in other provinces, but in British Columbia, eagles abound. (12, 49, 48)

In northwest Washington State, hundreds of eagles congregate on the Skagit and other rivers every winter. They gather to feed on spawned salmon as do many in the coastal Pacific Northwest. The Skagit River Bald Eagle Natural Area has been set aside to protect many of these wintering birds. The nearby San Juan Islands have both breeding and wintering birds. Also in Washington is one of the last remaining wilderness seacoasts in the contiguous United States. Here, along the ocean shores of Olympic National Park, a vast diversity of wildlife species can be found; these provide an abundant prey source for the many breeding and wintering eagles. (37, 26, 36)

One of the largest winter communal roosting areas is located in the Klamath Basin of south central Oregon and north central California. Here, up to 500 birds congregate at five different communal roosts. The Bear Valley roost, located in Oregon near the California state line, was set aside as a special eagle refuge in 1979. Three California eagle roosts—Three Sisters, Caldwell, and Cougar—also are protected. Many nesting eagles also inhabit the Klamath Basin and surrounding areas. South of Klamath Falls in the Shasta and Trinity national forests of northern California, both breeding and wintering eagles can be found; this is the largest population in the state. (23)

Most of Idaho's eagles are migrants, but a few birds nest throughout the state. Wintering birds are particularly common on the Snake River in the south. A small number of transient eagles pass through the Snake River Birds of Prey Natural Area, famous for its dense raptor breeding population. In northern Idaho, Lake Coeur d'Alene hosts the largest winter concentration in the state. (21, 28)

Perhaps the best-known and densest collection of wintering birds in the lower states is at McDonald Creek in Glacier National Park, Montana. Many hundreds of bald eagles gather along a 4-kilometer stretch of river in autumn to feed on landlocked kokanee salmon. A peak count of 618 birds was made in November of 1978. The National Park Service strictly regulates access to this area to prevent unwarranted disturbances, but viewing and photographic sites are available. These birds leave the park early in winter and continue south, perhaps to Utah, Idaho, or Oregon. (30, 39, 31)

Many winter concentrations form in Utah; about a thousand eagles were counted there in 1982. The Bear River Migratory Bird Refuge just north of the Great Salt Lake is an important stopover and feeding area, but in the early 1980s it was flooded by rising lake waters. This is a treeless, arid region, and eagles must perch on the ground during the day. At night, they roost in a dense stand of coniferous trees some 29 kilometers from the refuge in Willard Canyon. Daily arrivals and departures from this communal roost, where up to 300 birds have been counted in late winter, can be observed from the town of Willard. West of Utah Lake near Provo is another large winter aggregation; these birds inhabit the Cedar and Rush valleys. Eagles here are unique in their habits; they live in a desert environment far from any water and prey on black-tailed jackrabbits. In 1983, an active nest was discovered on the Colorado River. It is the only bald eagle nest in the state of Utah. (34, 41)

Yellowstone and Grand Teton national parks in Wyoming have small breeding and wintering populations. Most nests are on the shores of Yellowstone Lake or along the Snake River. A few overwintering birds gather to feed on the large mammals that die during harsh winters in both parks. Only a handful of eagles nest in nearby Colorado, but in the San Luis Valley in the south central part of the state, several hundred birds gather each winter. The White River has numerous wintering eagles as do many other river systems in Colorado. (25, 45, 17)

The Karl Mundt National Wildlife Refuge in southeastern South Dakota was established in 1974. It is one of the first such refuges founded for the sole purpose of protecting bald eagles. This refuge includes a stretch of the Missouri River just below the Fort Randall Dam. Here many types of fish fall prey to the hundreds of eagles that hunt below the dam. Many other rivers, reservoirs, and refuges provide sanctuary in the central states. A large population at the Swan Lake National Wildlife Refuge in Missouri is noteworthy because waterfowl are sought. Eagles follow these migrant waterfowl from Canada and feed on the many that are crippled by sport hunters. In Oklahoma, wintering birds are found on almost every large reservoir, but they are also common along rivers and on wildlife refuges. (10, 44, 13, 29)

Many of the present-day eagle management practices were developed and first implemented in the Chippewa National Forest in north central Minnesota. No other breeding population has been studied to the extent that this one has. The countless lakes and rivers provide superb nesting habitat, as is true throughout much of the remote Great Lakes region. Wisconsin and Michigan also contain dense breeding populations, but most birds leave these states in winter. Northern Wisconsin and the upper peninsula of Michigan are havens for hundreds of nesting pairs. (7, 35)

The northern Mississippi River is a migration corridor for thousands of wintering birds. From Wisconsin to Missouri, the banks of the Mississippi are often dotted with the familiar white heads of bald eagles. The first comprehensive research ever conducted on wintering bald eagles was done here near the Savannah Army Depot. A number of sanctuaries have been established to protect eagles in this region. These include the Ferry Bluff Eagle Roost in southern Wisconsin; Eagle Valley, also in Wisconsin; and a string of refuges along the Mississippi River including Oak Valley Eagle Refuge, Prairie State Eagle Refuge, Pere Marquette Eagle Roost, and the Cedar Glen Eagle Roost. In Tennessee, Reelfoot Lake is a popular eagle viewing area in winter. (40, 41)

Overwintering eagles are less common east of the Mississippi River, but sizable breeding populations still exist in both inland and coastal Maine, in the Chesapeake Bay area in Maryland and Virginia, and in Florida. Breeding pairs can be found throughout Florida, but Everglades National Park has a particularly dense population. A combination of jagged coastal shorelines and inland swamps provides optimal living space for the southern subspecies. (46, 1, 3, 4, 41)

MOVEMENTS AND MIGRATION

Bald eagles are not usually thought to be a migratory species. But, in fact, some populations migrate while other eagles stay on or near their breeding territories year-round. The decision to migrate or not is linked to the food supply. When food dwindles or when access to it is lost, eagles will move elsewhere, but if food supplies are stable throughout the year, eagles may opt to stay where they are.

Most populations travel south in autumn and north in late winter or early spring. This is especially true of those birds that nest in central Canada. When the lakes and rivers of the north freeze, fishing is impossible and waterfowl migrate south, leaving eagles with a scant food base. Such ecological conditions seem to cause fall migration, but in spring, changes in day-length are thought to bring about spring migration. Some sedentary populations, whose movements are minimal, are found along the coast of southern Alaska—on Amchitka Island, for example—and in many states in the southern latitudes. Some of those in Florida, Arizona, and Louisiana are not migratory.

Some bald eagles migrate between the same nesting and wintering areas each year, but others travel about in a wandering, nomadic fashion. This is certainly true of subadult eagles, especially first-year birds or juveniles. They may find and stay near a large food supply throughout much of the winter, or they may move in a leapfrog fashion in their endless search for prey. Juvenile eagles tend to migrate longer distances, travel farther south, and move in a more random pattern than older birds. The wanderlust of young birds may be an adaptive behavior that promotes expansion of the population and reduces competition for limited resources with breeding adults. (47) With the many hazards of long migration, especially for those birds attempting it for the first time, it is no surprise that many young eagles do not survive their first winter.

The timing of migratory flights depends on the age of the eagle. In many western states, adults arrive on wintering grounds earlier than subadults, although considerable overlap occurs. (37, 43) In the Midwest and the Rocky Mountain region, however, the reverse is true: young birds move south earlier than older ones do. (31, 44) A particularly interesting phenomenon takes place in Florida. Many nesting pairs remain there year-round, but first-year birds migrate north shortly after fledging in late winter and spring. Normally, young eagles migrate south after fledging. Northern birds travel south in winter, and eagles from southern latitudes migrate north in summer; this creates considerable intermixing of populations. (3, 4)

Few people actually witness the migration of bald eagles. Eagles migrate during the day; nocturnal migration has never been documented. Migration speeds average about 50 kilometers per hour. Most birds travel alone rather than in large flocks, though some mated pairs may take wing together. During spring migration, males may begin their northward journey before females. The altitudes of migration flights vary, but have been measured to be between 1.5 and 3.0 kilometers on the average. Eagles seldom fly all day long, preferring to forage in the morning and migrate in the afternoon. Daily flights of up to 435 kilometers have been recorded, but flights between 150 and 200 kilometers a day are more typical. Weather patterns have a particular influence on migration. More eagles migrate when sunshine creates updrafts of air and when wind provides lift, but strong winds can throw an eagle off its flight course. Favorable air patterns enable them to soar and glide over long distances with ease. Rain, snow, and low clouds hinder and sometimes completely stop migration; eagles will wait out inclement weather. (17, 37, 40, 50)

MIGRATION ROUTES

Migration patterns have been determined by three methods: (1) compiling information from returned bands that were attached to the eagles' legs at an earlier time, (2) resighting eagles that were fitted with color markers, usually on the wings or legs, and (3) following birds equipped with radio transmitters. A summary of eight major migration studies is provided in Figure 4.5.

Charles Broley was the first to study the migratory habits of the bald eagle. In the 1930s and 1940s, he banded 1,168 eagles in Florida; 108 bands were later recovered. Some of them were found over 2,000 kilometers north of Florida in eastern Canada. Broley discovered that fledglings migrated north, but that most adults remained on or near their nesting territories in Florida. (3, 4)

In the Great Lakes region, bands placed on eagles by researchers in

Fig. 4.5 Migration of bald eagles. The smaller numbers represent the movement of an eagle from its origin at the larger number. The larger numbers mark these locations: (1) west central Florida, (2) Swan Lake National Wildlife Refuge, Missouri, (3) Great Lakes states, (4) Besnard Lake, Saskatchewan, (5) San Luis valley, Colorado, (6) Glacier National Park, Montana, (7) Skagit and Nooksack rivers, Washington, and (8) Chilkat River, Alaska. (3, 4, 13, 14, 7, 18, 9, 17, 50, 22, 38, 16)

Minnesota, Wisconsin, Michigan, and Ontario have been recovered southward over a wide area in the Midwest. (18) Eagles wintering in Missouri, for example, are from breeding sites along the Great Lakes and in central Canada. (14)

An extensive migration study in Saskatchewan, where 300 eaglets were banded and/or color-marked from 1967 to 1975, showed a fall movement to wintering grounds across a broad square extending from Montana to Missouri and from Texas to southern California. Interestingly, subadult eagles reared in the study area usually returned during subsequent summers, and after reaching adulthood, some even established nesting territories in the vicinity of their parents' nest. (9)

In the western states and Alaska, migration has been studied by following winter migrants rather than nestlings. Birds spending the autumn in Glacier National Park come from nesting grounds in Alberta and Northwest Territories and then travel south in winter to the Great Basin states. (50) Wintering eagles in the San Luis Valley of southern Colorado returned to breeding and summering grounds in central Canada, particularly Saskatchewan. (17) In the Puget Sound region of Washington, wintering eagles migrate back north along the northwest seacoast and also into the interior of British Columbia. (22, 38) Eagles in the Pacific Northwest migrate shorter distances than most other birds. Some birds do, however, migrate between southeast Alaska and Washington State. Many juveniles and subadults winter on the Chilkat River in Alaska and summer along the Canadian coast south of Alaska. In contrast, adults travel less and generally stay in southeast Alaska. (16)

Although many eagles seem to wander at random, they use some general routes for southerly and northerly migrations. (50) The *Pacific Coast* flyway encompasses the northwest seacoast primarily west of the Cascade and Sierra Nevada mountain ranges. The *Intermountain* route encompasses the Great Basin of the western states in the south and Alberta and parts of northern Canada in the north. It is bordered by the Cascades and Sierra Nevadas on the west and the Rocky Mountains on the east. The *Central* route includes much of north central Canada and the plains states east of the Rockies. The *Mississippi* flyway is a migration corridor between central Canada and the Great Lakes to southern states along the Mississippi River. The *Atlantic* pathway lies generally east of the Appalachian Mountains between Florida and New England, but a few birds travel to the Great Lakes states. But some birds completely ignore these flyways. Eagles have been known to travel in east-west directions for considerable distances or to follow one pathway south and then another north. For example, fledglings from Michigan have been found in Florida, eaglets in Saskatchewan were later seen in Alaska, and many birds from Yellowstone National Park end up on the West Coast. (9, 3)

5

Breeding and Nesting Biology

The breeding behavior of bald eagles has been well studied by research biologists, and this life history phase rarely fails to intrigue any who have seen it. And because reproduction is vital to the health of an endangered species, this aspect is of paramount importance in assessing the status of the species. Francis Herrick's book, *The American Eagle*, is still the most comprehensive work describing breeding biology, but numerous more recent studies have provided us with deeper insight into this intimate behavior of the bald eagle.

MATING BEHAVIOR

The courtship behavior of bald eagles is both elaborate in detail and predictable. Most events seem to be "programmed," and certain behaviors must precede others before successive events can occur. Nevertheless, experience and individuality can create considerable variation in breeding and nesting.

Pairing The first act is the pairing of the male and female. They establish a "pair bond," which is the equivalent of a marriage. It is generally assumed that eagles mate for life, but only a handful of observations support this contention, because it is difficult to recognize individual birds year after year. Nevertheless, several accounts do indicate that pairs mate for life. In Ohio, for example, a mated pair was seen together for several consecutive years. They were distinguished by their peculiar behavior patterns and their appearance. Even if the pair bond is permanent, if one of the pair dies or disappears, the remaining bird will take a new mate. New pair bonds have been formed in as little as three or four days, but one remating took eleven weeks, and some birds probably remain alone until the next breeding season. (29) One female took a new partner on two separate occasions after her previous mates had died. (4) And eagles sometimes exhibit unusual mating arrangements. Although rare, three eagles have been known to form "trio bonds." The purpose and significance of this ménage à trois have not been determined. Occasionally, a bird in subadult plumage will mate with an adult, but there is no record of both parents lacking the adult plumage. (4, 13, 52)

When and where pair bonding occurs is open to speculation. Perhaps the bonds develop before the breeding season when eagles socialize in wintering areas, during migratory flights from wintering grounds to breeding sites, or on the breeding territories. Displays, which may be courtship rituals, have been seen during these times. If the mated pair is apart during the winter, the pair bond is rekindled at the start of the nesting period.

Courtship   One of the most fascinating events in the life of the bald eagle is the courtship ritual. Few spectacles compare to the majestic, aerobatic maneuvering of a courting pair, but unfortunately, few persons have witnessed it. Those who have seen it say that the bald eagle and the other sea eagles have the most elaborate and beautiful nuptial displays of any raptor. (9)

Vocal displays are very common; one or both birds will call to the other either while perched, flying, or soaring. If perched, a vocalizing bird will sometimes throw its head back to a vertical position and scream loudly. *Chase displays,* featuring numerous aerial antics, are also quite common. The two eagles will pursue each other, sometimes in rapid dives, or they may just follow each other in erratic chase flights. During some chases, one eagle may fly upside down beneath the other and either present its talons to or touch talons with its playmate. Often, both birds will "roll" together, exchanging places in flight. A more elaborate show is the *undulating* or *roller-coaster flight.* In this display, an eagle will fly to great heights, fold its wings, and dive at tremendous speed; before hitting ground, it will swing up again and possibly repeat this sequence. This results in an undulating flight pattern, much like the movement of a roller coaster. This undulating flight often occurs in combination with chase flights. (9)

Without question, the best-known and most spectacular exhibition by the bald eagle is the *cartwheel display* (Fig. 5.1). In this nuptial dance, the courting pair will fly to a great altitude, lock their talons together, and fall to earth spinning and whirling in a series of cartwheels. Just when a crash seems imminent, they disengage and fly off, sometimes to repeat the

Fig. 5.1 The cartwheel display of courting bald eagles.

performance later. These displays either establish or renew the pair bond and are a precursor to sexual activity. (9)

Copulation Sexual union by bald eagles is seldom observed. It was once thought that they copulated while locking talons during the cartwheel display, but they do not; they engage in sex as most other raptors do. Although the following description is based on captive birds, wild eagles are assumed to behave in kind. (16)

Copulation usually takes place after the mated pair have perched together for a while. Either the male or the female makes the first amorous advance, but the female often assumes a "solicitation" posture: she perches on a tree branch or on the nest, crouches low, and holds her body horizontal, head forward and wings slightly apart; she will then call to and

Fig. 5.2 Copulation.

nudge the male, thus soliciting his services. In response, the male calls back to the female, flaps his wings, and moves his tail up and down. Then, he jumps on the back of the female, curls his talons so as not to injure her, flaps his wings and calls again, and begins to engage his mate. The female twists her tail sideways, and the male presses his cloaca to hers; this copulative act is often referred to as the "cloacal kiss" (Fig.5.2). After union, the pair may perch together again, preen their feathers, and they may fly to the nest and arrange nest materials.

Copulation takes place in as little as five to fifteen seconds, but can last one to two minutes, and may occur several times a day. (28) Most copulations occur from six days before to three days following the laying of the first egg. (58) Sex is more common in the early morning hours. (16) The sex act, however, has been observed after construction of the nest, and might even happen outside the breeding season. (28, 29, 24) Although not documented, the fertilizing ability of the sperm probably lasts several days or more. The eagle's egg is fertilized internally, before it is laid.

TERRITORY

The earliest mention of territoriality was made by Aristotle about 350 B.C., and, appropriately, he made it in regard to eagles: "Each pair of eagles needs a large territory and on that account allows no other eagle to settle in the neighborhood." (44) His observation is still valid today, but other aspects of living space also need to be mentioned.

Three areas are of concern to the breeding pair: the nest site, the breeding territory, and the home range. Bald eagles will establish a breeding territory and defend it against other eagles, but the nest site is the focal point of activity. Eagles will vigorously protect their nests and their families against most intruders. Surrounding the territory is a much larger land area called the home range. Eagles will wander throughout their home range, often in search of food, but they will not defend it.

Aggressive Behavior   Aggressive interactions in the vicinity of the nest indicate that a territory has been established and is being defended. Several types of defensive behavior have been observed. The most subdued defense is the *threat vocalization*. This is a high-pitched call given by one or both adults when an intruding eagle approaches. (47) Another type of response is the *circling display* in which the defenders will soar over the vagrant eagle until it leaves the area. Interestingly, if the intruding eagle is looking away from the nest, the reactions of the inhabitants are less intense. (37) The most aggressive and commonest display is the *territorial chase*. When an intruder is seen, one or both adults will fly directly at the bird and give chase. They may pursue the interloper until it leaves the territory, or a fight may ensue. Sometimes the defender extends and presents its talons or dives to harass the unwanted visitor. (40) Physical contact is rare, but it can happen. One defender was seen to strike an intruder seven times with outstretched talons; another grabbed an interloper by the wing, causing both birds to fall close to the ground, narrowly escaping injury. (12)

Although eagles will actively defend their nests and territories, aggressive interactions are not common. Once territories are established, other eagles apparently recognize and avoid these areas. When the mated eagles soar above their nest or perch in conspicuous trees, they may be "advertising" that the site is an active territory and warning others to stay out. Perhaps the highly conspicuous white heads of the adults communicate this intent. In this way, eagles can defend their territories with a minimal amount of fighting.

The territorial pair will drive eagles of any age from their breeding area. Defense against juvenile and subadult eagles, however, may not be as vigorous as it is toward adults, but this is not proven. Younger birds seem to be tolerated closer to the nest. Perhaps the territorial pair recognize adult trespassers as a greater threat to their security, and perhaps the younger eagles are, in some instances, the offspring of the pair. If so, the adults may show more tolerance to their presence because they are genetically related. On occasion, fledglings will stay in the nesting territory for several years after leaving the nest. (37, 47, 52)

Eagles may also drive other birds from their territory, but they are not usually as aggressive to them as they are to their own kind. Because all bald eagles have similar living requirements, the greatest threat of competition comes from another eagle. Thus, territories are most forcibly defended against those most likely to interfere. One other bird that is aggressively evicted, however, is the osprey. A territorial pair of eagles can force ospreys to relocate their nests and can reduce the ospreys' nesting success, but after the two species have nested near each other for many seasons, they show some mutual accommodation. In most cases, bald eagles ignore other species, but they sometimes drive other birds of prey from the nest, along with crows, gulls, and other large birds. (45, 29)

Purpose of the Territory The nesting territory gives the breeding pair a monopoly on the resources in the area. Favored perch, roost, and nest trees are exclusively used by the pair. The territory also provides an element of isolation from other eagles, allowing the pair to conduct breeding activities without risk of interference. Nestlings, too, are afforded more protection within the territory because potential predators are kept away.

Many types of birds defend territories in order to monopolize food. But this does not seem to be true of bald eagles, which often gather food outside the territorial boundaries. Little is known of this, but we do know that eagles will forage in many areas throughout their home range. They may share foraging areas, or they may establish a feeding territory separate from their nesting territory and defend the food supply therein. These feeding territories may increase in size as the food requirements of the nestlings increase. (23, 37, 49)

Territory Size and Shape The size of a territory is difficult to determine and can vary greatly. Problems arise in distinguishing a territory from an eagle's home range; studies have attempted to do both, but the division between the two is not always clear. Three general ways of determining territory and home range sizes have been employed.

If perch trees surrounding a nest are plotted and the enclosing area is measured, a conservative size estimate can be made. Territories in Nova Scotia were found to average 0.16 square kilometers in area; in Alaska, 0.23 square kilometers was the common size. (18, 26)

A more reliable technique is based on plotting locations where interactions and displays occur. Assuming that aggressive encounters are more common on the edges of the territory, this method more accurately represents actual size. In Minnesota and Michigan, territories were determined to be 1.09 and 1.55 square kilometers in area, respectively, using this procedure. (37, 40)

The most common method for measuring territories is to locate all occupied nests in a large region, measure their distances apart, and plot a circle about each nest until all of them abut one another. This is best done in a saturated population, because the smallest values recorded are likely the best indication of territory size; larger values are combinations of territory and home range areas. Using this technique in Florida, territories were found to be 2.06 square kilometers in size, but in Washington, they were as much as 8.14 square kilometers. (7, 20) Four studies in Alaska showed territories to be 2.54, 3.87, 7.55, and 12.69 square kilometers in area. (50, 49, 52, 11)

Using these data, a best guess of normal territory size might be from 1 to 2 square kilometers. One study showed that home ranges were a minimum of 10 to 15 square kilomters. (15) Perhaps future studies using radio transmitters attached to eagles will provide additional information on this important aspect of nesting behavior.

Many circumstances influence the distribution of nests and territories. Figure 5.3 shows the minimum boundaries of territories and the locations of nests on Karluk Lake on Kodiak Island off the coast of Alaska. (10) Clearly, three factors influence the distribution of eagles here and in most other areas: (1) nests must be located near water where food can be acquired; (2) suitable habitat (trees) must be available for placement of the nest; and (3) there must be an unoccupied area in which to establish a territory. Only a limited number of nesting eagles can inhabit a given area.

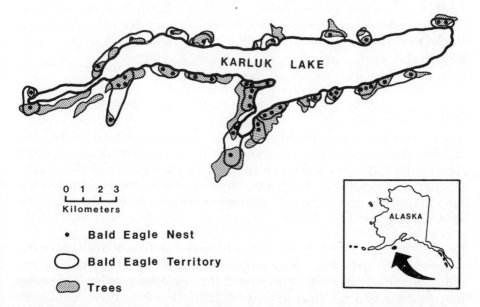

Fig. 5.3 Karluk Lake on Kodiak Island in Alaska, showing the distribution of bald eagle nests and territories. (10)

Once the maximum number is reached, the region is saturated and new territories cannot be formed.

When suitable conditions are available and when the region is filled with eagles, as in some areas of Alaska, the average distance between occupied nests is between 1 and 3 kilometers. (11, 26, 49, 52) Of 3,850 occupied and unoccupied nests in southeast Alaska, the average distance apart was 2 kilometers. (32) There is a natural spacing of nests due to the influence of territoriality. Eagles do not normally build a nest closer than 1 kilometer to another occupied nest. There are exceptions, of course; in Alaska, occupied nests have been seen as close as 640, 365, and 137 meters together. In Florida, three occupied nests were 305 meters from one another, and seven nests were observed in an area encompassing only 6.8 square kilometers. (4, 7) Distances between unoccupied or abandoned nests can be shorter, perhaps half the average distance. Of thousands of nests in Alaska, the average spacing was 0.9 kilometer for unoccupied nests, but 1.8 kilometers between occupied nests. (50)

A territory can be of most any configuration, from near circular to oval to linear. The number of trees and the location of water are particularly influential in determining the shape. (10, 37) Preferred perching trees can delineate the territory boundary, but forested areas also can obstruct the view of adjacent eagle territories. When forest impairs the eagle's view, territories are smaller and nesting pairs are ostensibly more tolerant of each other. An eagle's territory may extend out over open water, unlike that shown in Figure 5.3, and may extend farther over water than over land because the view is less restricted. (37) The configurations of the nearby shoreline also determine the shape of the territory. Some territories are linear, encompassing the shoreline of a lake, a seacoast, or perhaps a section of river.

NESTS

The nest is the home and focal point of domestic activity for mated eagles. It is here that the pair will rendezvous, copulate, lay and incubate eggs, and raise young, but the nest serves other purposes as well. It provides shelter from adverse weather and protection from enemies, and its conspicuousness may act as an "occupied" sign advertising to other eagles that the nest is being used.

Nest Building   Once a territory is established and a suitable nest tree is selected, both birds will gather large branches and sticks and begin the arduous task of constructing the nest. If the nest already exists, the eagles may construct an addition on top of it. (29) The sticks are meticulously arranged, usually by the female, so that they intertwine like the fibers in a basket and provide a rigid support for the many activities of home life.

Construction can take as little as four days, but nest maintenance occurs throughout the breeding season. (28) Sometimes an eagle will acquire nest material by breaking branches from trees. The bird will plummet against the branch with outstretched talons, snap it off, and carry it to the nest. (3) A slight depression for the eggs is formed in the top and center of the structure and lined with a variety of soft vegetation such as grasses, sedges, conifer needles, and feathers. (4) Interestingly, bald eagles will bring fresh leafy sprays to the nest, not for use as part of the structure or lining of the nest, but as a sort of decoration on top. The birds often replace these adornments in an apparent effort to maintain a green or fresh appearance. In Minnesota, nests almost always contained a sprig of white pine even though red pine was the more common tree species in the area. (39) Why eagles chose white pine is not known. Clorox bottles, clothespins, light bulbs, shoes, gunny sacks, golf balls, and lace-trimmed pink panties also have been found in nests. (8) One explanation for the presence of these knicknacks is that they serve as an advertisement that the nest and territory are occupied and tell interloping eagles to stay away. The fact that a piece of green and fresh vegetation is kept at the nest indicates recent activity there.

Nest Size and Shape   If one finds a staggeringly large nest along a shoreline, it may well be that of a bald eagle. Bald eagles build the largest nests of any bird in North America; these nests must be big enough to support the weight of both adults and their young. But some nests are much larger than an eagle family needs because they are rebuilt and added to year after year. In 1925 in Ohio, after thirty-six years of use, a nest crashed to the ground during a violent windstorm. It measured 2.6 meters across, was 3.7 meters tall, and was estimated to weigh about two metric tons—approximately as much as a small car. (29) The largest recorded nest was found in Florida: the top diameter was 2.9 meters, and it was 6.1 meters tall. (7) One other huge nest blew down during a hurricane in Maryland. This nest, which had been occupied for thirty years, weighed 1.3 tons. (53)

Most nests, however, are much smaller. A typical nest will be 1.5 to 1.8 meters in diameter and 0.7 to 1.2 meters tall. The dimensions of the nest cup, where the eggs are incubated, are much smaller. A depression of 10 centimeters with a 25-centimeter diameter is typical. As eagles tend to add new nest materials each year, the largest nests are more likely to be occupied. (2, 10, 20, 25, 26)

Nests are built in a variety of shapes, but the supporting structure largely determines both the shape and the size the nest will assume. A nest may be shaped like a cylinder, a bowl, a disk, or an upside-down cone (Fig. 5.4). *Cylindrical nests* are most commonly built between two upright branches that are parallel to each other. *Bowl nests* are "cradled" on several sides by supporting branches and the tree trunk. *Disk nests* occur

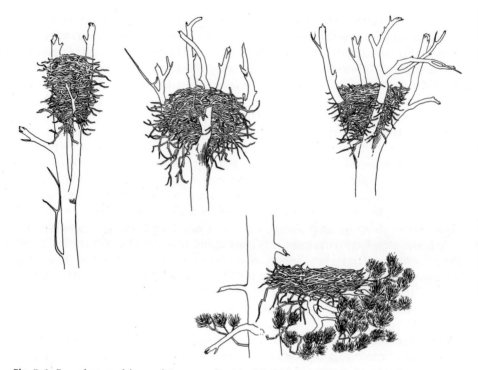

Fig. 5.4 Four shapes of the eagle's nest: cylindrical (left), bowl (middle), inverted cone (right), and disk (lower). (29)

close to the trunk and sit atop several strong branches, mainly in coniferous trees. *Conical nests* occur where the tree branches cause the structure to be small on the bottom and increasingly larger toward the top. These are most common in deciduous trees. (7, 27)

Bald eagle nests can be confused with those of other birds, especially golden eagles and ospreys. Nests of bald eagles tend to be larger, however, and they vary in shape, whereas osprey nests tend to be round. If the nest size and shape do not aid in distinguishing these species, placement of the nest usually does. Bald eagles normally select the tallest live tree for nesting and they place their nests below the top of the tree. Ospreys, which also live close to water, build their nests on the very top of the tree and may prefer dead trees. Golden eagles usually nest in cliffs, but when they use trees, they build their nest at a lower level, usually below the canopy of the forest. In contrast, bald eagle nests are almost always above the canopy. Also, bald eagles may select larger nest sticks than golden eagles. (2)

With careful maintenance, a nest will serve the needs of the breeding pair for many years. A nest first seen during the Lewis and Clark expedition in 1805 lasted more than fifty years. (29) Other nests have lasted forty, thirty-six, and thirty years. (30, 29, 53) The life of most nests, however, is considerably shorter. In Saskatchewan, the average life of an eagle's nest is five years. About 50 percent of these nests are destroyed every six years. (14) In Alaska, 5 percent of all nests are lost every year; the average life expectancy is about twenty years. Fifty percent are destroyed every thirteen years. (31) But severe winter storms in Alaska can destroy up to 20 percent of all nests in a single year. (11) Nests built in sheltered trees are more apt to survive stormy weather than are exposed nests. A nest may also grow so large that the nest tree collapses under its weight.

Alternate Nests   In most but not all instances, bald eagles will have more than one nest in their breeding territory. In 924 territories surveyed, eagles were found to have an average of 1.5 nests in their breeding area. (10, 14, 20, 34, 35, 38, 52, 55) In some regions, such as on Amchitka Island in Alaska, no alternate nests are built, but in other areas, such as Karluk Lake in Alaska, as many as 2.1 nests are found in each territory, on the average. (52, 10) Out of 318 territories studied, 55 percent had one nest, 29 percent had two, 13 percent had three, 3 percent had four, and 1 percent had five nests. (10, 20, 35, 55)

Sometimes it is difficult to determine which breeding pairs possess the many alternate nests that exist, especially when many pairs live close together. Generally, a nest more than 1.6 kilometers from the occupied one is not likely to be an alternate nest in that territory. But this is not always the case; in Florida, for example, there are records of several pairs using alternate nests more than 3 kilometers apart. (33) The average distance of seventy-four alternate nests from the occupied nest in Washington was measured to be 320 meters. (20)

Since only one nest in a territory is occupied at any one time, what is the purpose of an alternate nest? Several hypotheses have been suggested. A proximate function, one that has an immediate explanation, is that eagles are programmed to construct or refurbish their nest as part of the sequence of breeding events. Hence, egg laying may not occur until the urge to build a nest has been satisfied. This may be accomplished either by rebuilding an old nest or by building a new alternate nest. But it is likely that the possession of several nests has an ultimate function that has evolved because of some adaptive advantage. Alternate nests may serve as insurance; if the occupied nest is destroyed or rendered undesirable for some reason, the eagles can quickly occupy the alternate without having to build a new nest. In this way, a disruption to the occupied nest is not likely to cause a nesting failure. Unfortunately, no data are available to support this hypothesis. In fact, the nesting success on Amchitka Island, where no alternate nests exist, is higher than in many other regions. (52)

The use of alternate nests could also be a means of avoiding parasites, many of which remain in the nest, ready to reinfest the birds the following year. By shifting from one nest to another, the birds may be reducing the chance of infestation. A particularly intriguing explanation is that of territorial advertisement, which suggests that the presence of alternate nests further serves to announce that a territorial pair is present in the vicinity and to warn intruders to stay away. (43)

EGGS

The eggs of bald eagles are dull white and unmarked, except for rare specimens with pale brown spots. Sometimes brown stains will be present, but they are not part of the eggshell. Rarely, an egg will have a light bluish appearance, but this seems to be more common on the inside of the shell. It is rounded ovate in shape, not unlike a domestic goose egg. There is no luster or shine to the egg's surface; it is drab, rough, and coarse to the touch. (4)

In comparison to the size of the bird, the eagle's egg is quite small. It averages only about 3 percent of the body weight of the female. The average weight of eight eggs in Alaska soon after laying was 130 grams. (26) This compares to an average body weight of about 5,000 grams. Nine eggs from captive breeding pairs of unknown origin averaged 109 grams. These captive birds laid eggs of decreasing weight; the first of the clutch was the heaviest, and the last was the lightest. (17) Of nearly 300 eggs measured throughout the range of the bald eagle, sizes varied from 8.4 to 5.8 centimeters in length and 6.3 to 4.7 centimeters in breadth. Average eggs are 7.6 to 7.0 centimeters long and 5.8 to 5.3 centimeters wide. The size of the eggs depends on the location in which they are found. (51) As the average body size of the eagle increases the farther north it is found, so does the size of the egg. The largest eggs are found in Alaska and the smallest in Florida; there is a gradual change in size between these two extremes (also see Figure 3.5).

The clutch size—the number of eggs laid in the nest—ranges from one to three (Fig. 5.5). Clutch sizes of four have been recorded, but they are thought to be the result of two females laying eggs in the same nest. (4) The vast majority of clutches have two eggs. The average clutch size, based on hundreds of nests, varies from 1.90 to 1.97, or just under two eggs. (10, 22, 23, 25, 50, 52) The number of eggs laid is predetermined; if eggs are removed, eagles usually will not continue laying to fill the clutch and will incubate only the ones remaining. But if all eggs are removed, they will likely relay an entirely new clutch.

Why do bald eagles lay only about two eggs when they can easily incubate many more? Studies have shown that, over time, birds have evolved an optimal clutch size which produces the maximum number of young that will survive and eventually reproduce. This serves to maximize the rate at which the parents pass along their genetic material. A small clutch produces fewer young than could be raised, whereas a large clutch produces more young than environmental resources can provide for. For bald eagles, food might be the limiting resource; it might be difficult to provide enough food for a large batch of hungry eaglets.

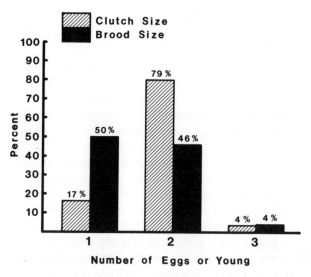

Fig. 5.5 The average number of eggs (clutch size) and young (brood size) produced by nesting bald eagles. (10, 12, 14, 19, 20, 22, 23, 25, 31, 41, 48, 50, 52, 54, 55, 57)

The interval between egg layings is two to four days. (29) Thus, a clutch of three eggs could take a week or more to lay, but the usual clutch of two eggs requires about a half week to produce.

INCUBATION

Eagles must keep the developing embryos inside the eggs warm for a long period. This incubation process takes, on the average, thirty-five days, but it can vary by a few days. (28, 29) For many birds, and perhaps for eagles as well, as the temperature of the egg increases, the incubation period grows slightly shorter. (56) A higher incubation temperature increases the metabolism of the embryo and accelerates tissue development.

Eagles develop an incubation patch which helps keep the eggs warm. This is an area on the lower breast that has lost feathers and is richly supplied with blood vessels, thus facilitating the transfer of heat from the adult to the eggs. It appears only during the nesting season. Because the male and female share the incubation duties, they both develop a patch.

Although both the male and female incubate the eggs, the female does most of the work. In one study, 72 percent of the incubation was done by the female and 28 percent by the male. (16) The eggs are rarely left unattended. There is an adult at the nest over 99 percent of the time and the eggs are incubated 98 percent of the day. But during the 2 percent of the time when the eggs are not incubated, there is little threat to them. In cold and windy weather, the eggs are left exposed for less than a minute out of each hour, but if conditions are mild, the eggs may be left for several minutes during each hour. Sometimes, the incubating bird will cover the eggs with soft nesting material before leaving them unattended. (7, 29)

This could prevent the eggs from chilling as well as camouflage them from potential predators such as crows. Very young chicks may also be covered with materials from the nest. (52)

The diligent care given to the eggs is comparable, but perhaps not equal to the care provided to the eaglets. The male and female take turns incubating the eggs throughout the course of the day. Exchanges are initiated when the incubating bird gives a sharp chitter to the mate, ostensibly indicating a desire to be relieved of duties. Once the shift change is made, the bird will rearrange the nesting materials and poke with its beak in the nest cup, in an apparent effort to arrange the nest in a comfortable fashion. The eagle will then ball its feet, perhaps walk about the nest for a moment, step into the nest cup, grasp a nest branch with its beak, and using it as a pivot, rock its body from side to side and settle on the eggs. Immediately after settling, the adult will reach out with its bill and pull nest material into a mound surrounding its body. The incubating bird sits extremely low in the nest and is difficult to see except from the air. Interestingly, an eagle may assume the incubation posture even when no eggs are present. This pseudoincubation behavior is quite common, especially just prior to egg laying. (16, 29)

Turning the eggs over is necessary for the proper development of the embryos. Eagles will turn the eggs about every hour, usually while they rearrange nesting materials. Rotating the eggs ensures that the warmth of the incubating bird is more evenly distributed to the eggs and lessens the likelihood that the embryonic membranes will adhere to the inner shell, which would be fatal. (56)

Like most birds of prey, bald eagles start the incubation process as soon as the first egg is laid. This causes the eaglets to hatch at different times, depending on the interval between egg layings. This is one reason why eagle siblings are of different sizes.

If the clutch is destroyed early in the egg-laying or incubation process, eagles will sometimes lay a new clutch of eggs. (36) The chance of a new clutch being formed is much less, however, if the original clutch is lost in the late stages of incubation or after hatching has occurred. In one study, nine of eleven pairs renested after their eggs were collected during the first week of incubation. (58) One captive pair consistently laid second clutches after the first clutch was lost. (17) In contrast, a study in Alaska showed that eagles failing to incubate their eggs had no inclination to renest. (26) A new clutch may be started two to three weeks after the first failure, but some birds have laid the new clutch up to two months later.

HATCHING

A day or so prior to hatching, after hearing the cries of the shellbound chick, the adults bring food to the nest in anticipation of a hungry mouth to feed. (29) But the adults are only spectators in the hatching process; if an eaglet has trouble breaking free of its shell, the parents will not assist in any manner.

It is often difficult to know exactly when the eaglets hatch, because the adults constantly cover both the hatchlings and the eggs. Because the eggs hatch at different times, the parents must simultaneously incubate the unhatched eggs and brood the hatchlings. They do this by positioning their bodies closely over the eggs and spreading their wings slightly to accommodate the youngsters. This particular posture indicates that hatching has occurred.

All of the eggs may not hatch. Excessive chilling, heating, or jolting can kill the embryos, or the incubating adult can accidentally break the eggs if frightened from the nest. Predators can abscond with them, windstorms can destroy the nest and clutch, and parents may desert the eggs for no apparent reason. If the eggshells are abnormally thin, as when pesticides are present, they may break. These are just a few calamities that can befall the eggs. Specific hatching rates will be dealt with in Chapter 11.

Because not all of the eggs may hatch, the brood size (the number of young in the nest) is smaller than the clutch size (Fig. 5.5). There is about an equal chance that a nest will have either one or two young present. Rarely will a nest contain three eaglets, but it does happen in a small percentage of nests. On the average, a successful nest contains 1.6 eaglets (also see Chapter 11). No known nest has ever had more than three young, though there are records of nests containing four eggs.

NESTLING CARE

With the arrival of the young, the parental instincts of the adults are put to the test. The parents must provide for the eaglets in a variety of ways and submit to every whim and demand of the young birds. Parental care is instinctive and follows a precise and predictable pattern, but all parents differ somewhat in their routine, depending on individual quirks and past experience.

Brooding   One of many parental duties is brooding, or keeping the young warm. Even though the eaglets hatch with a downy coat, they are unable to maintain proper body temperature for a number of weeks. The parent bird crouches in the nest, and the young scurry underneath, where the temperature remains comfortable (Fig. 5.6). Sometimes the brooding adult will rake nest material all about its body to give the young a warmer bed. Brooding of the young is intense for the first month, but sporadic thereafter. After about two to three weeks, when the eaglets have developed their second coat of down, the parents will sit up and droop or half spread their wings over the young rather than brood them closely. Brooding of the eaglets at night lasts three to four weeks, sometimes longer. During inclement weather, parent birds pay special attention to keeping their

Fig. 5.6 Brooding and feeding the nestlings.

offspring warm. Using their wings, they will shield the young from rain, hail, wind, and, in the more southern latitudes, heat from the sun. The adult will stand with wings held half open, taking the brunt of the nasty weather while the nestlings huddle below, safe from the elements. (29, 28)

Feeding Providing food for the nestlings is an enormous chore. In one study, five or six prey items were brought to the nest each day. (5) Feeding begins when the young are a day old. The adults will bring a prey item to the nest, rip it to small bits, and dangle it from their bills above the eaglets (Fig. 5.6). The hungry chicks will reach for and gobble the tidbits. The parents do this for six or seven weeks, at which time the young begin to feed themselves, but adults will feed their young on occasion even after this period. (29) The eaglets are fed soon after they start begging for food; their persistent squeals cease only after they are satiated. The young also indicate their hunger by pecking at food even though they may be unable to feed themselves. (47) Feeding is intense early in the morning and then again in late afternoon, but the parents do not always adhere to this schedule. In one study, 31 percent of the prey items were brought to the nest early in the morning, 24 percent at midday, and 45 percent late in the day. There usually were two or three feedings a day, averaging fifteen to twenty minutes in length, but feeding was less regular after the young were able to tear prey on their own. Feeding occurs rather fast. In only ten minutes, an adult provided fifty-eight bits of fish to her three nestlings. In another study, ten to fifteen bits of food were offered to the chicks each minute. Feeding bouts end when the young no longer accept food; afterward, the parents quickly take up another chore. (47, 29)

During the first month, the male brings most of the food to the nest because he has more free time to hunt. When the eaglets are more than a month old and the female has finished her brooding duties, both parents bring about the same amount of prey to the nest. Both parents share in the duty of feeding the chicks, but the female probably handles most of this task. Occasionally, one parent will rip prey and pass it to the other, which then feeds it to the nestlings. Interestingly, the parents tend to feed the largest chick most often and seem little concerned when one of the nestmates does not get its fair share. Feeding behavior is purely innate. The youngster that is largest and fusses the most receives the most attention from the parents. Consequently, the largest and most assertive eaglets receive the most food and they grow fastest. (47, 29)

Nest Defense Some parents will leave the area when humans approach; others will defend their young in a variety of ways. In general, eagles are more aggressive in areas where they have not been persecuted by humans, and more timid where they have been persecuted. (19, 52) When eggs are present, one or both members of the pair will circle overhead and scream, but if the human activity is particularly disruptive, the adults may abandon the nest. If nestlings are present, the adults may again soar above and call, or they may temporarily leave the area, returning only after the intruders have left. Rarely will they abandon the nest when they have young. One study describes defensive behavior reaching a peak during egg hatching and gradually waning thereafter, while another study suggests that defense increases as the young grow older. (18, 52)

Parents have been known to defend their family by attacking researchers climbing to or entering their nests. The strike of an angry eagle has been likened to a blow from a "moderately swung baseball bat," resulting in superficial lacerations from the talons. In Alaska, adults will often "stoop" or swoop down at nest intruders. Researchers there have been hit in the back of the head with such force that the blows knocked them to the ground. Some eagles may even attack helicopters that venture close to the nest. In Alaska, a research helicopter was attacked by an eagle at one out of every fifteen nests visited. (21, 31, 42, 52)

Nest Attendance Parental attendance at the nest is closely related to the ability of the young to care for themselves. During the first few weeks, the nestlings are almost constantly cared for, but attendance gradually diminishes thereafter (Fig. 5.7). In the latter weeks of the nestling period, the adults are at the nest only a small portion of the day. When they are away, however, at least one parent will watch the nest from a distance. (47) Keeping the young warm (or cool) requires long periods of special care, but when the young can stay warm on their own, the parents need to visit them only to provide food. Late in the nestling period, the adults will not even roost with the young at night.

BREEDING CHRONOLOGY

Bald eagles follow a prescribed sequence of breeding events from the start of nesting to the eventual dispersal from the breeding area. Some of these events can vary in length, but the durations of others are more or less pre-determined. In general, egg laying takes a few days to a week, incubation lasts five weeks, the hatching period takes as long as the egg-laying period, and the young are in the nest for ten to twelve weeks. From the time the first egg is laid until the last young has fledged, sixteen to eighteen weeks will have passed. If courtship and nest building are included, the adult eagles devote roughly a half of every year to reproductive activities.

The timing of various breeding events is closely related to the latitude at the nesting area. As one travels north, eagles breed at progressively later dates (Fig. 5.8). When eagles in the arctic are completing their nesting efforts and preparing to migrate south for the winter, eagles in Florida are already starting the next breeding season. At any time of the year, some populations in North America are in some stage of the reproductive cycle.

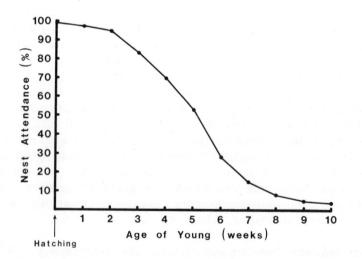

Fig. 5.7 Parental attendance at the nest is high during the first few weeks after the young hatch, but gradually declines as the nestlings begin to feed themselves and require less brooding. (6)

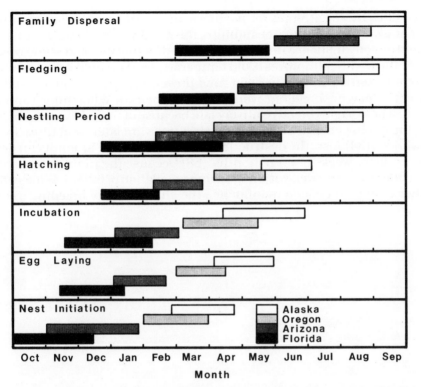

Fig. 5.8 The breeding chronology depends on the latitude of the nesting population. Northern populations also may compress their breeding season into a shorter time span. (4, 7, 34, 46)

There is some evidence that eagles that breed as far north as central Alaska and northern Canada compress their breeding season into a shorter time frame (Fig. 5.8). This seems necessary because the summer season in the arctic is so short. Eagles may begin egg laying almost immediately after arriving in the North, and they may disperse south as soon as the young have left the nest. (59) Egg laying, incubation, and raising the nestlings are activities that cannot be hurried.

Bald eagles in the most southern latitudes, especially Florida, are of particular interest because they begin nesting when days are becoming shorter. It is well known that the stimulus for breeding in birds is the lengthening of daylight hours. The Florida eagles seem to have adapted to a unique situation. It has been suggested that they breed early so that the young will be able to leave the nest before the intense heat of the summer, thereby reducing heat stress. And the fact that these fledglings migrate north just after leaving the nest, and just before summer, supports this contention. Northern migration also could reduce competition between fledglings and adults because only the young migrate; the adults remain on or near their territories year-round.

Besides these extremes for northern and southern populations, other circumstances can affect the timing of the nesting cycle. Cold, wet weather could directly influence the nesting pair by delaying the production of eggs until the weather improves. Cold temperatures also could keep lakes and rivers frozen for longer periods thus preventing access to food and indirectly delaying breeding events. This happens in Yellowstone National Park, where eagles breed relatively late because of the cold weather in the spring. (1) In general, nests at high elevations are later than those in the lowlands. (34) Also, the destruction of the first nesting attempt can delay the cycle for weeks or even months. (58) Because the timing of breeding activities can vary even within the same population of birds, it is likely that other unexplained factors influence the chronology of breeding events.

Eaglet Biology

A new generation begins with the hatching of the baby eagle. The *hatchling,* a newly hatched eaglet in its first days of life, is virtually helpless and is totally dependent on its parents for warmth and food. Once the first critical days of life are past, the *nestling* gradually becomes more self-reliant, though it is still confined to the nest. The nestling grows rapidly, and after months, it will leave the nest and begin to explore the world. This *fledgling,* an eaglet that has left the nest, may continue to depend on its parents for some food, but will eventually learn to fend for itself in the wild.

HATCHLINGS

Birth After the thirty-five-day incubation period, if the embryo has not succumbed to some calamity, the eaglet begins to hatch from the eggshell. The cheeping of the eaglet is a sure sign that hatching is close at hand, as this indicates that breathing with the lungs has started. At this stage, the eaglet derives some air from the air chamber in the egg, but soon must "pip," or puncture, a hole in the eggshell in order to breathe. Hatching usually occurs one day after the eggshell is pipped. The actual hatching process takes four to five hours or more, but it can require up to two days from the moment the shell is pipped until the eaglet breaks free (Fig. 6.1). (15, 11, 14, 17)

The eaglet breaks the eggshell with a special device called the "egg tooth." This is a pointed, chisel-like structure on the tip of the beak specif-

65

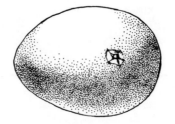

Fig. 6.1 A bald eaglet hatches.

ically used for cracking the shell. Special muscles on the head and neck assist the bird in forcibly piercing through. The eaglet rotates its body during hatching so that it can pip a ring around the entire eggshell. The actual breaking of the egg seems to occur in "violent struggles," which are renewed about every five minutes. (17)

Description   The eaglet hatches with its feathers wet with amniotic fluid and with its eyes closed. But in four hours or so, the eyes open, the feathers become dry and fluffy, and the eaglet is "transformed into a bright, attractive youngster full of vim and enterprise" (Fig. 6.2). It is covered with silky down, which is longest on the head and gray except on the throat, where it is white. The head is extraordinarily large, and its neck is thin and long. The legs are pink at hatching, but soon turn flesh-colored. The skin also is pink, but later becomes bluish. The chick is weak at first and spends most of its

Fig. 6.2 Sequence of development showing the bald eaglet in the natal down stage (upper left), the secondary down stage (upper right), the transition stage when the juvenile feathers are emerging (lower left), and the juvenile stage (lower right).

time lying in the nest and sleeping. But in only a day, it will begin to accept food from its parents. During its first week of life, the chick can crawl about on the shanks of its legs, supported by its wings, and will peck at any nest-mates. Its stage of development at birth is referred to as "semi-altricial"; it is covered with down and can see, rather than being naked and blind, but it is confined to the nest. (3, 17)

At hatching, the eaglet weighs from 70 to 105 grams; two captive hatch-lings weighed 70 grams and 89 grams; six Saskatchewan hatchlings weighed an average of 92 grams; and one Alaskan bird weighed 105 grams. (11, 17, 5, 7) Its weight depends on the size of the egg, the weight of its parents, and the geographic latitude at the nest (northerly chicks are larger). The weight of the hatchling is much less than the initial weight of the egg because the developing embryo has lost water and metabolites through the porous eggshell. One chick weighed only 65 percent of the weight of the freshly laid egg, and six others weighed 80 percent of the weight of the egg prior to hatching. (11, 5)

If more than one egg is present, the chicks hatch at intervals of two to three days, because incubation begins before the entire clutch is laid. This results in a mixture of hatchlings of different sizes, with the firstborn being the largest. This effect may be accentuated if the first egg laid is larger than the rest. (11) A brood of three eaglets can differ in age by a week and can be many different sizes. Size and sex differences of the hatchlings can have ex-treme effects on survival as will be discussed later.

NESTLINGS

Description   The nest-bound eaglet seems always to be in transition. Before it leaves the nest, it will have sported three different plumages and grown from a small toddler to one of the largest birds in North America. Figure 6.2 illustrates the development and plumage changes of the nest-ling. (2, 5, 15, 16, 17)

The primary or natal down plumage, as already described for the hatch-ling, is well developed from the moment of hatch and is retained for several weeks. By the third week or so, a second downy plumage has replaced the natal down. Compared to natal down, the secondary down is long, thick, woolly, and a much darker soot-gray. The legs are now yellow. Within another week or two, the young bird begins to show the first traces of the juvenile plumage. This is the dark brown to black garb so characteristic of the juvenile eagle. It grows most rapidly on the back, shoulders, breast, and especially on the wings. In this transitional stage, when the eaglet is four to six weeks old, parts of all three plumages are evident. By the seventh or eighth week, the juvenile plumage has all but replaced the secondary down, and in the next several weeks, it is fully developed. Unlike the adult, the juvenile has a bluish black beak and dark brown eyes, but the feet are bright yellow and the talons are black, just like those of the parent birds. Although

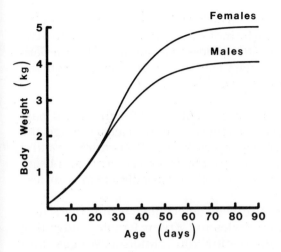

Fig. 6.3 Growth of typical bald eaglets of the northern subspecies showing the characteristic S-shaped curve and divergence of weights of the sexes. (5)

there can be variations, most young eagles bear all or most of these characteristics.

The behavioral patterns of the developing nestlings change rapidly. During their first few weeks of life, antagonism among nestmates is at its peak. The eaglets begin flapping their down-covered wings and, when the new plumages begin to emerge, they preen regularly. When a month has passed, they begin grasping with their talons, pecking at prey, and casting pellets. In another week, they can stand on their feet and scream loudly. After seven weeks, their wings can carry them above the nest, and they are playing games. At two months, they have been described as "bold and masterful"—they steal and monopolize food, their play behavior becomes intense and sometimes violent, and they exercise frequently. At nine weeks, they may, for the first time, perch on branches near the nest and, in several more weeks, they will leave the nest for good. (15, 16, 17)

Growth The rate of growth of the eaglet is staggering. In only three months or so, the nestling's weight will increase from about 100 grams to between 4,000 and 5,000 grams, depending on the sex of the bird. It may gain up to 180 grams in a single day; no other North American bird grows this fast. (5) The bald eagle's growth curve appears S-shaped (Fig. 6.3). Development is rapid during the first month, it slows during the second, and it levels off in the third. After twenty to thirty days, the weights of the two sexes diverge; females gain weight faster than the males, resulting in lifelong differences in size. Males, however, develop their plumage faster than the females. (3) Characteristically, most of the growth in the early stages of development occurs in the body tissues; later gains in weight occur when the plumage grows. Three major circumstances influence the relative sizes of the nestmates: (1) early hatchers are larger than late ones; (2) females outweigh males when more than a month old; and (3) eaglets may be larger in smaller broods.

Two features of the eaglet grow at such predictable rates that it is possible to determine the age of the nestling by measuring them. The length of the bill is used to judge age when the nestling is less than about twenty-five days old, and the length of the eighth primary feather (the third feather from the tip of the wing) is used to age birds that are older (Fig. 6.4).

Sex Determining the sex of nestlings is possible only after they are at least two months old. When eaglets of the northern race are at least this age, the female's bill, from top to bottom, measures more than 3.2 centimeters, and the foot length, measured between outstretched toes, is more than 14 centimeters. Because males are smaller, their bill and foot dimensions are less than these values. (4)

Sex ratios of nestlings have, to date, been determined in only one study. Of 103 nestlings examined, 53 were males and 50 were females, indicating that the sex ratio is about equal. Interestingly, in a clutch of two eggs and a brood of two young, the first egg laid and the first hatchling to appear is more likely to be a female. This happened 63 percent of the time in 37 nests studied in Saskatchewan. (3) Why have bald eagles evolved this pattern of females hatching first? To answer this question, we must examine a phenomenon known as fratricide.

Fratricide Fratricide is defined as the act of killing one's brother, but eagle biologists use this term to describe an eaglet killing its nestmate. (It might best be called "siblicide" or killing of one's sibling.) It can occur as a

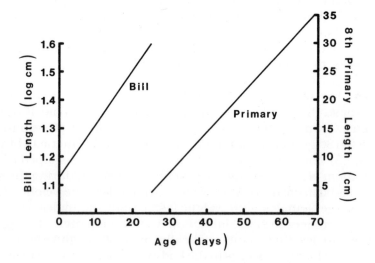

Fig. 6.4 Technique for determining the age of a bald eaglet. Bill length is used for eaglets less than twenty-five days old, and the eighth primary feather length is used for older nestlings. Age predictions: Age (1 to 25 days) = −57.7 + 52.0 x Bill Length (log cm); and Age (26 to 70 days) = 19.9 + 1.4 x Eighth Primary Feather Length (cm). (4)

result of fights, or because a bird starves when the other monopolizes the food supply. (6)

Fratricide occurs when nestlings are of different sizes; the larger one always dominates the smaller one. Size differences occur, as we have noted, because the eggs hatch at different times; the larger, early hatcher may kill the smaller, late hatcher. Fratricide is most common during the first week or two when the size disparity is greatest. Fratricide also is more common when the first to hatch is a male and the second is a female. In this instance, the male is initially larger and grows more rapidly than the female. (3) Through evolutionary time, male-then-female broods may have resulted in fewer surviving eaglets because of these killings. Although this hypothesis is still speculative, bald eagles seem to have adapted, in a way, to minimize fratricide by producing clutches in which female nestlings hatch first. In female-then-male broods, fratricide is less common.

Vicious fighting between nestlings begins soon after hatching, and quarreling can be intense. Combatants will peck at each other's heads with such vigor that they may topple over if they miss their target. The aggressor may peck the smaller eaglet about the head, grab at its beak, or seize its miniature wing and drag it around the nest. The unfortunate nestling may suffer physical injury and may lose its share of food as well. In one observation, the older eaglet gobbled seventy-six tidbits of food during feeding by the adults; the younger bird received only two bits and was constantly tormented by the other while eating. The beleaguered infant may be so intimidated by the larger nestling that it may not beg for food and may not eat even if food is offered to it. If the smaller bird lives for a month or so, it has survived the most critical stage of nestling rivalry. (17, 19)

Though fighting between nestmates is known to be very common, we do not know how often fratricide occurs among bald eagles. Of seven nests in Ohio, only one young of sixteen died due to sibling rivalry. Many nests have only one survivor of several hatchlings and this may suggest that some fratricidal behavior is occurring. Sometimes nestling mortality is higher in nests where several young are present and lower in nests where only one bird hatches, but this does not prove that fratricide is happening. Fratricide probably occurs in a small percentage of bald eagle nests. (17, 24)

Apparently, fratricide is nature's way of reducing the number of mouths to feed when food is scarce. It is thought that fratricide is less likely to occur if the parents bring an abundance of food to the nest. In this way, the availability of food can limit the number of offspring that survive. As noted earlier, the parent birds do not interfere in behalf of the weaker nestling. They appear "unconcerned" when fighting occurs and feed the youngster that is largest, most aggressive, and most demanding.

Thermoregulation The age at which the nestling can thermoregulate (produce enough heat on its own to stay warm) is at least two weeks, if the weather is not especially severe. (3) During rain, hail, and wind storms, nestlings need protection and are brooded by the adults. Several nestlings may huddle together for warmth; this appears to be one advantage of having a nestmate, despite the fighting that frequently takes place. The development of the juvenile plumage is the eaglet's best defense against inclement weather; within two months, this feathering provides an effective barrier against the chilling effects of wind, rain, and cold.

For birds in southern latitudes, coping with intense heat may be more of a problem than cold. Nestlings cause water to evaporate from their bodies by panting; this keeps them from overheating. They might also spread their wings and stand in a cool breeze, or crouch in a shady corner of the nest. If these methods fail to prevent heat stress, the parents must provide sunshade for the eaglets; they spread their wings above the eaglets, much like a parasol.

Routine Behavior The behavior of the growing nestlings changes according to a prescribed pattern, but each eaglet develops its own personality. The daily activities of the young are more or less "linked in serial fashion, with constant repetitions, but with endless variations in detail." (17) The most common activities include feeding, preening, playing, sleeping, and exercising.

Feeding is the highlight of the eaglets' day. If the nestlings are not hungry, they show little excitement when the parents bring food. (17) But more often than not, the eaglets take the food from the parents and feed voraciously. When very young, the birds may beg incessantly for food, but when they are older, they will whine, squeal, cry, or even scream at the adults for a meal. If several young are present, these screams may act as threat calls to one another during competition for food. When nestlings are old enough to feed themselves, struggles for food are common. The eaglets will steal food back and forth until one finally monopolizes the prey item or the other loses interest or waits for an opportunity to steal the food back (Fig. 6.5 A). This predilection to steal food will last throughout the life of the eagle and will provide a means of obtaining a meal when prey cannot be found or caught. An observation of the feeding behavior of young at a nest in Ohio provides a picture of the struggling life of the eaglets:

> After a chicken was brought to the nest, both eaglets crouched with their feathers on end and clamored lustily, but only one of them seized the fowl. The other began at once to romp about and flap its wings. It clutched at sticks, stabbed them with its bill as if they were living prey, and more than once assailed its fellow and tried to secure the appropriated chicken. After a while, the first eaglet gave way to the aggressor, who laid hold of the prey with one talon, dragged it aside, and set to work. The first bird, however, not being quite satisfied, went after the fowl again but was immediately warned off by the squeals and spreading attitude of the other. Then they stood up, and for two minutes, with wings raised, they faced each other like fighting cockerels waiting for an opening, until the bird who had secured the first chance, snatched the chicken with one talon and, dragging it to the op-

Fig. 6.5 Some routine activities of the nestlings: (a) feeding, (b) preening, (c) playing, (d) sleeping, and (e) exercising.

(Continued on following page)

Fig. 6.5 (Continued.)

posite side of the nest, began treading it with both feet and after each hasty mouthful it would glance around and warily watch its nest mate. The robbed bird stood still, as if dazed, but after some moments, lowered its head and moved slowly and stealthily towards the feeding bird following its every movement intently. Interestingly, the eaglet that stood over the prey tore out pieces of the flesh and intestines and held them up, as if by way of peace offerings, to the other bird, who received but did not eat them. It was not to be so easily beguiled, but, watching its chance, it seized the whole chicken and went to feeding with a will on its own account. (17)

Preening the feathers occupies a large part of the growing nestling's day, especially when a new plumage is emerging (Fig. 6.5B). The young eagle meticulously cares for its feathers by stroking itself with its bill, removing the older feathers. When a feather sticks on its tongue, the eaglet will open its beak wide, extend its tongue, and shake its head vigorously to remove the feather. (25) The uropygial gland, near the base of the tail, provides a fluid which the bird spreads on its plumage for waterproofing and grooming.

In between feedings, long periods of rest, and the casual business of preening, the eaglets will *play* a variety of games. If only one eaglet is in the nest, however, very little play occurs. One can only guess at what effect this lack of a playmate may have on the social life of the lone eaglet. But when two or three nestlings are together, they engage in a number of antics. Broad-jumping across the nest has been observed, but romping about is more common. The eaglets may jump up and down, flap their wings, and seize sticks with bill or talons and drag them about or use them as a toy hammer. Playthings include old feathers, leaves, sticks, leftover prey, or any other item that is available, not excluding a nestmate. Birds will often stroke each other with their beaks. Sometimes play sessions become so lively that one bird comes close to being pushed out of the nest. Eaglets will sometimes grab the same stick and battle for it in a tug-of-war (Fig. 6.5C). There are frequent bouts of fighting, but in the latter half of the nesting period, most of it is play behavior. One bird may engage in a mock attack on its nest companion; this behavior is occasionally directed at a parent bird, especially if no nestmates are available to play with. When an adult landed at one nest, the nestling would spring at the bird in a sham attempt to overpower it. The nestling would flap its wings, leap up, and land on the back of the adult or take a fighting stance and peck at the adult. The parents totally ignored these antics. Sometimes it is difficult to tell whether the eaglets are playing or are actually serious in their frolicking. But these instinctive capers will play an important role in the business of surviving later in life, since play behavior readies the individual for other, more important activities. (17, 25)

The eaglets and the adults *sleep* throughout the night. The nestlings will doze intermittently during the day as well, between other activities and especially after eating (Fig. 6.5D). When they are not asleep, they may lie or stand side-by-side, face into the wind, and watch whatever is of interest.

When several young are present, behavior becomes synchronous; eaglets are lulled to rest or stirred to action by the activity of the other.

Exercise gradually becomes more intense with each succeeding week in the nest. The eaglet will exercise its legs by treading, trampling, and prancing around the nest. This behavior will later aid in subduing prey. Flight exercises are even more common. The eaglet will stretch a wing or both wings as a warm-up exercise, then flap them vigorously. If the wings are developed to a point where the eaglet can lift itself off the nest, the bird may hold on to a stick or branch so it will not fall from the tree. As it gains more confidence, it will rise above the nest, at first a short distance, then several meters high, and may hover there for a few seconds (Fig. 6.5E). (17, 23)

Defensive Behavior   Some of the defensive behavior of the young in response to humans or predators at the nest is interesting to note. During the first month of life, eaglets either ignore the intruder or respond to it as they would to the parent birds. They might, for example, beg for food from a researcher who has climbed to the nest. But as the nestlings grow, they have a variety of ways of protecting themselves. Nestlings five to six weeks of age raise themselves up, throw their heads back, and scream threats at the trespasser. Eaglets from six to nine weeks of age react most violently. They may face the intruder, spread their wings, ruffle their feathers, open their mouths and hiss, and display or strike with their talons (Fig. 6.6A). Any researcher who has confronted a combative eaglet will attest to the unnerving effect this display has. Nestlings ten weeks or older might retreat to the opposite side of the nest or, as a last resort, jump from the tree or attempt to fly away. This can have severe consequences for the flightless nestling, which may injure itself. A well-grown eaglet might also feign death by lying prostrate in the nest, apparently in an attempt to divert the attention of the intruder. They may also assume a stoop-shouldered posture with the head bowed and wings held limp; the significance of this display is unknown (Fig. 6.6B). (12, 24)

FLEDGLINGS

Three general periods describe the life-style of eaglets at and following fledging (their first flight from the nest). These include the early, intermediate, and late stages.

Early Stage   Once most of their wing and tail feathers are developed, the eaglets can finally leave the nest. This occurs anywhere from eight to fourteen weeks after hatching, but is most common when the birds are ten to twelve weeks old. In one study, 75 percent of the eaglets fledged within this two-week period. (9, 10)

The timing of fledging can be affected by several circumstances. If the nestlings are disturbed by humans or predators, for example, they will leave

Fig. 6.6 Two defensive displays by older bald eaglets: (a) fighting-stance display, and (b) stoop-shoulder, head-down display. (12, 24)

the nest early to avoid a confrontation. When a male and a female are in the same nest, the male is likely to fledge at an earlier age. Older birds of the same sex are quicker to leave than the younger ones. And finally, a single nestling will fledge more rapidly than one that has nestmates. (3)

In most cases, the first flight from the nest can be an unheralded event in which the eaglet will simply begin flapping its wings and venture forth. At other nests, though, the young may be reluctant to leave, and the parents may coerce them to fly. Adult eagles have been seen taunting their nestlings into flying by luring them with food.

The female eagle appeared with a fish in her talons and was circling just above the nest, and the eaglet was jumping with legs rigid and flapping frantically. Suddenly it rose in the air and for a second seemed to be poised over the eyrie; at that moment the circling eagle began to scream, and swooping down at the hovering and now screaming youngster, she passed within a few feet of him. A moment later the excited eaglet, still holding to the air, drifted fifteen feet or more beyond the margin of the nest; and with vigorous wing beats it began moving eastward, following the mother eagle with the fish, and eventually made a mile in this its maiden flight. It finally landed in the branches of an elm on the border of the woods and without doubt was rewarded with a goodly portion of that tantalizing fish. (17)

Fledging can be a critical moment for the eaglet. The inexperienced birds are awkward in flight, lack coordination, and can have traumatic crash landings. They have extreme difficulty landing on tree limbs, as they are often unable to slow their flight speed in time to arrive safely. (23) Many fledglings fall to the ground after leaving the nest, often because they leave the nest before their flight feathers are fully developed; the reason why they do this is unknown. (5) Birds that fledge early are more likely to fail in their first flight and land on the ground. The proportion of fledglings that are grounded after their first flight ranges from 33, to 52, to 80 percent; on the average, perhaps half do. (9, 18, 8) Life on the ground can be dangerous. The eaglet is exposed to a variety of predators, and it may be unable to find food, but the parents usually will feed it. And because ground vegetation can be dense, the fledgling may not be able to fly again. Eagles are so large that they require large open areas in which to flap their wings and become airborne. One way in which the parents can alleviate this problem is to choose a nesting area that has forest openings nearby so the young eagles can eventually take off from the ground. (9)

Intermediate Stage   Following departure from the nest, the fledglings begin to master their skills at flying, but they still depend on their parents for most food. At this time, they learn to refine their landing technique, soar to great heights, and even perform some limited aerobatics. This is a time for scouting the surroundings, learning how to find and kill prey, and discovering the many nuances of life.

The adults will bring food to where the young are perched, but fledglings also will meet the parents at feeding perches where food is transferred. The young are bold, aggressive, and will take food away from the adults. This dependency gradually diminishes as the young learn to forage. Because the eaglets are poor hunters, they are more likely to scavenge on dead prey than are their parents. Proficiency at killing prey takes one to two months after leaving the nest, but some successful hunts can occur soon after fledging. (13, 18, 20, 21, 1)

The eaglets stay close to the nest and nest tree during the first few weeks after fledging, but they eventually explore areas farther away. In Saskatchewan, they will often return to the nest even up to six weeks after their first flight. A month after fledging, about a quarter of all fledglings are present at the nest or nest tree, another quarter roam within 200 meters of the nest, and the remaining half have ventured some distance away. Through their twentieth week, seven weeks after fledging, most young are still within 1.5 kilometers of the nest. (10)

Within a month after fledging, eaglets will have mastered the art of soaring and may drift about the general area in a wandering fashion. Their movements seem to be influenced by the presence of shorelines and associated food sources, and by the direction of the prevailing wind. Eagles tend to disperse downwind from the nest, but they remain close to water. Soon they may begin to socialize, gathering in areas where food can be easily acquired. (18, 21, 1, 10)

Late Stage   Approximately six to ten weeks after fledging, when they are seventeen to twenty-three weeks old, the young eagles begin to break family ties and leave the nesting area. (10, 18) By this time they are more or less self-sufficient; they are able to fly with ease and acquire prey on their own. It is a time to migrate south if their natal area is in the North, or time to go north is they are raised in the southern latitudes. In some populations that are not migratory, the young may remain in the vicinity of the nest for several years. (24) And even the migratory juveniles may return to the general area of their birth, perhaps to establish a territory of their own and continue the cycle of breeding.

7

Winter Ecology

The annual cycle of the bald eagle can be divided into two periods. In spring and summer, the adults are engaged in breeding activities, the nestlings and juveniles are growing and learning, and the subadults and nonbreeding adults are wandering about trying to make a living. But as the last colors of autumn fade into the icy grip of winter, the life of the eagle changes dramatically and the second half of the annual cycle begins. A sudden scarcity of food, caused by icing of northern lakes and migration of waterfowl, forces eagles to wander southward and band together in large aggregations. In many areas, winter conventions, of sorts, are formed as birds of all ages gather where food is most easily acquired. By joining an assemblage, eagles may be able to find food more easily; this increases their chances of surviving the long ordeal of winter.

These winter concentrations are fascinating to observe and study. Groups of eagles squabble over food, vie for favored perches, soar together in entertaining aerial displays, and even bathe together. Many areas have become traditional sites for public viewing, photographing, and enjoying eagle antics. It is a perfect time to catch a glimpse of the national bird without upsetting its delicate reproductive life.

WINTER CONCENTRATIONS

In mid-January, when winter concentrations are at their peak and are thought to be sedentary, hordes of eagle counters make their way to the favored haunts of the national symbol. This nationwide eagle census, hosted by the National Wildlife Federation and state, federal, and local agencies, was started in 1979 and is now becoming an American institution. These counts have been invaluable in monitoring eagle numbers and distribution so that biologists can deal with the problems of population management, but many other studies have answered questions concerning the winter ecology of the eagle. (28, 35)

Timing Winter populations follow some general rules. Fall migration begins in October; it is at this time that concentrations begin building. By the end of March, most birds have started to migrate back north. High population counts can be as early as November or as late as February, but most aggregations reach their peak in January. The number of birds and the arrival and departure characteristics of each group principally depend on the amount and seasonal availability of food. Aggregations can consist of only a handful of birds, which is the most common situation, to thousands such as those seen on the Chilkat River in Alaska. There are dozens of concentrations in the lower states where several hundred eagles are present throughout much of the winter. Figure 7.1 shows the population trends of six typical concentrations in the United States. These are but a few of the many that exist (also see Chapter 4).

Age Ratios There can be considerable variability in winter age ratios (usually expressed as percentage of young eagles seen). The foremost factor influencing the age ratio is, of course, the demographic structure of the eagle population. A population that is growing will have more young birds than one that is declining. In the early 1960s, young eagles constituted between 22 and 26 percent of the population during three nationwide censuses. (29) In the early 1980s, however, proportions ranged from 30 to 36 percent during the National Wildlife Federation's nationwide surveys. (19, 20) The lowest percentage, 5.6 percent, was recorded in 1962 on the Mississippi River. (26, 27) In contrast, 53 percent was the age ratio for a population on the Skagit River in Washington in 1975 and 1976. (23) This suggests, but does not establish, that the eagle population is healthier now than it was two decades ago. This reasoning assumes that mortality rates remain unchanged and that other factors affecting age ratios are inconsequential. But it is best to use age ratios only as a rough guess as to the population structure and to look only at long-term trends.

Young eagles and older ones migrate at different times, and this can have a profound effect on the age ratio at various times of the year. Several studies indicate that juveniles migrate earlier in autumn and travel farther south than do subadults and adults. (27, 30) Glacier National Park, Montana, where censuses have been conducted for more than fifteen years, is a good example of how differences in migration times can affect age ratios. (18) Early in the wintering season, 45 percent of the birds in this park are

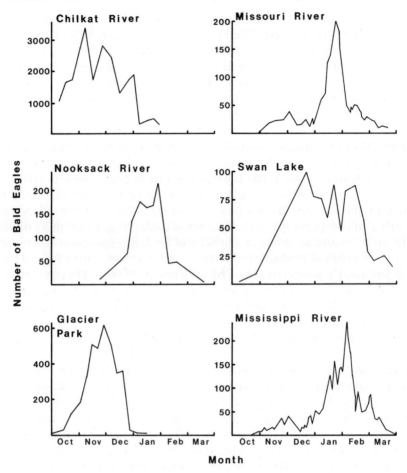

Fig. 7.1 Population characteristics of six selected winter concentrations in the United States: (a) Chilkat River, Alaska, 1981–82; (b) Nooksack River, Washington, 1980–81; (c) Glacier National Park, Montana, 1978–79; (d) Missouri River, South Dakota, 1974–75; (e) Swan Lake National Wildlife Refuge, Missouri, 1977–78; and (f) Mississippi River, Illinois, 1962–63. (2, 15, 18, 34, 6, 27)

young, but late in the season, the age ratio drops to 30 percent. The opposite is true in many other wintering areas, especially out west where adults are more numerous early in winter and the buildup of young birds takes place later. In the San Luis Valley of Colorado, the age ratio is 47 percent; adults are more numerous in early winter, but the number of younger birds gradually increases. (10) The same is true on the Chilkat River in Alaska though the overall age ratio, 22.5 percent, is much lower. (2) In central Utah, 34 to 37 percent were young eagles in the late 1960s and early 1970s, and these percentages gradually increased during each winter. (3, 12, 21)

Another study found that the proportion of young eagles was higher where food was particularly easy to find and exceptionally abundant. On the Nooksack River in Washington, for example, the age ratio in the mid-1970s was about 34 percent. But in the early 1980s, after salmon runs on the river increased several fold, over 50 percent of all birds were young. (30, 15) It remains to be shown whether this phenomenon is commonplace with other wintering concentrations.

Another important consideration is the ability of the observer to see all eagles. Because young eagles are more drab in appearance, they are easily missed by the census taker, and this may result in a lower ratio of young birds. Younger eagles also tend to perch on lower branches, at least in some areas, and this could reduce their visibility. (8, 30)

Census takers have plotted age ratios of other eagle populations that range from 29 percent on the Columbia River, Washington, 30 percent in west central Illinois, 34 percent on the Mississippi River in the early 1980s, 35 percent in southeastern South Dakota, 36 percent in the Klamath Basin of Oregon, and 39 percent in the Gulf Islands of British Columbia. Thus, roughly a third of all eagles in any concentration are juveniles and sub-adults. (14, 4, 11, 34, 13, 8)

Influence of Food   Available food is the key to attracting eagles to a particular wintering area; all other resources are of secondary importance. Eagles seek out a variety of prey sources (also see Chapter 8). Fish is the favored delicacy in winter even though the supply may not be as plentiful as it is during summer. Eagles like to congregate below dams to feed on fish that are killed while passing through the turbines, and to hunt in the open waters immediately below the spillway. (28, 35, 26) On the Pacific Coast, hundreds, sometimes thousands, of eagles are attracted to spawning areas where dead salmon can be scavenged. (2, 23, 30) Other major fish kills can be a temporary smorgasbord for transient birds. Waterfowl is another frequently used prey, especially birds that have been crippled by sport hunters and those that gather in open water below dams and on wildlife refuges. A third food source, carrion, can supplement the eagle's diet when other prey is scarce. Carrion may include winter kills of deer, elk, and large domestic animals.

The number of eagles present and the timing of the aggregation is so closely dependent on the food supply that sometimes eagle numbers can be predicted if the quantity of available food is known. Where eagles congregate to feed on salmon on the Nooksack River in Washington, computer simulation models have predicted population densities within a 10 to 20 percent level of accuracy (Fig. 7.2). (32) Other studies, where both eagle and prey numbers were counted, also show this intimate relationship. (6, 18, 23) Everywhere throughout its range, where prey are vulnerable or carrion is accessible, one can almost expect to see the opportunistic wintering eagle taking what it needs.

DAILY ACTIVITY

The daily life of the overwintering eagle can be filled with a repetitious sequence of activities. Winter is spent making the best of an uncomfortable and sometimes life-threatening situation. On closer examination, however, eagles are not just passing away the days until spring, but are cleverly taking advantage of all situations that will enhance their health and survival.

Nothing about the wintering eagle is more striking than its laziness. Studies indicate that most birds spend the great majority of their time in a quiescent state. This sedentary life allows the eagle to conserve its precious energy stores. Eagles spend about 68 percent of their twenty-four-hour day roosting during the long winter nights, and they devote another 30 percent to loafing on perches during the day. This leaves only about 1 percent of each day for flying and 1 percent for foraging and feeding. The bald eagle is an efficient machine, remarkably well adapted to meet the rigors of winter. It conserves energy by remaining inactive throughout much of the day, by seeking shelter from adverse weather, and by living in groups so that others help find food. (33)

The daily life of all wintering eagles is much the same (Fig. 7.3). Leaving the roost at dawn, they will fly to and loaf near their foraging grounds. In midmorning, feeding is brisk, especially by those who have not fed in several days, but a midday lull in feeding seems to follow. Soaring is most common in early afternoon when eagles can glide effortlessly in the warm, rising air. A less extensive feeding period may occur in late afternoon after which the eagles fly back to their roosts. (7) There can be many variations in this routine—during migration, for example—but this typical chain of events usually ensures a minimal expenditure of effort and energy and an adequate daily meal. (31)

The weather can affect eagles' winter activity. During particularly severe winters, when temperatures are low and winds are chilling, eagles are less

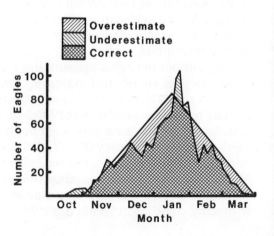

Fig. 7.2 Comparison of a population simulation model (triangular plot) predicted by food availability and the actual numbers of eagles (irregular plot) on the Nooksack River, Washington, 1975–76. (32)

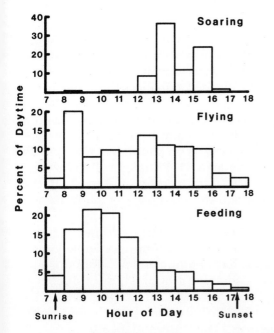

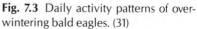

Fig. 7.3 Daily activity patterns of over-wintering bald eagles. (31)

active; they will fly less, are not as likely to feed, and might even remain in a protected roost throughout the day. When wind speeds are greater than 20 kilometers per hour and when temperatures are considerably below freezing, feeding is uncommon. Brisk winds and sunny skies are conducive to flight. When the sun heats the earth and produces rising columns of warm air, eagles will often soar to great heights. Soaring is especially common when wind velocities are between 10 and 20 kilometers per hour. During overcast, rainy, or snowy weather, eagles will perch, loaf, and feed instead of flying or soaring. (10, 23, 36, 26)

The time of arrival at and departure from roosts has been studied. Departures usually average a half-hour before sunrise, but can be as late as a half-hour following sunrise. Arrival at roosts occurs in a broader time frame from several hours before sunset to a half-hour afterward, but averages about a half-hour before sunset. Birds may return to the roost early in the afternoon if they were able to gorge themselves during the day. A few individuals might travel back and forth between the roost and foraging areas throughout the day. Eagles leave their roosts only during daylight. On cloudy days, they will vacate their roosts later in the morning and return earlier in the afternoon. (24, 34, 15, 17, 3)

SOCIAL ACTIVITY

Group Feeding Why eagles have evolved into gregarious animals in winter may well be explained by how they find food. Overwintering populations locate food in two special ways. First, many eagles wander over a large area, enabling more birds to search for prey. Second, once they find food, eagles attract others to it. Like vultures, eagles will congregate near abundant prey not just because there is plenty of food for all, but also because the presence of other eagles signals that food is available. This phenomenon, whereby birds use each other to find food, enhances the ability of the entire population to exploit their prey. (33)

Soaring increases the eagle's visual field and thus aids in detecting prey, but it also serves as a signal to others that food may be waiting. With their remarkable vision, eagles from as far away as 65 kilometers might see a soaring group and be attracted to the area. (18) Eagles will follow one another to feeding areas while departing from communal roosts in the morning, and birds perched in prominent sites purposely or inadvertently act as a signal that prey is nearby. (16, 31)

Above all, the act of eating is the stimulus that attracts other eagles to feed. This socially facilitated behavior, whereby a hungry eagle joins a flock of foraging birds, is known as "local enhancement" (foraging efficiency is enhanced in local areas by a foraging group). These birds convey to others the message that the food is edible, and soon a large group begins a feeding frenzy (Fig. 7.4). Eagles will also find dinner by watching crows, gulls, coyotes, and other scavengers at a food carcass. (16, 33)

It is interesting to speculate on how this social foraging system evolved. Are eagles behaving altruistically when they signal to others that food is available? Why should an eagle share its food with others? If food is scarce in winter, each bird could increase its own chances for survival by being secretive and selfish when it discovers food. When food is abundant, however, the advantages of living in a group may outweigh the disadvantages of competing for food. With plenty to eat, it may not matter if there are fights and squabbles over food, as long as everyone gets an adequate meal. And there may be other advantages of living in groups; for example, eagles may be evaluating and selecting their mates for the upcoming nesting season. A trade-off exists: being in a group helps an individual find its next meal and may have other benefits, but it must fight to get access to the food and vie for other resources. But what if some eagles are closely related? If so, cooperative hunting and feeding may well enhance the survival of the family group. Nevertheless, most winter concentrations should not be thought of as cooperative family groups, but as aggregations of hungry thieves, each determined to get its fair share of food.

Antagonistic interaction during feeding is a most impressive sight. Though physical contact and injury are rare, a number of ritual displays are used to convey messages of dominance, submission, threat, displeasure, hunger, and a host of other behavioral states. These types of behavior have been named and described (also see Chapter 8). (5, 15, 31) Wing displays are most common; sometimes one or many eagles will outstretch their wings to vie for the right to feed on a carcass. Occasionally, two eagles will lock their talons together and jostle with each other until a winner is pro-

Fig. 7.4 During winter, eagles often feed in large groups with much squabbling over feeding rights.

claimed. Given the power behind these mighty birds, it is surprising that more injuries do not result from such encounters. In an attempt to evade would-be thieves, an eagle may grab a food item and fly away with it. An aerial chase is likely to follow; the pursuing birds will relentlessly harass the food holder until it drops the prize or finds a protected place to hide from its tormentors.

Communal Roosting Communal roosting is the eagle's social nightlife. A communal roost is an area where a group of eagles spend the night in close proximity. It can consist of two birds together in one tree, or more than five hundred in a large stand of trees. Two important features distinguish communal roosts: they are traditionally used year after year, and they contain special habitat characteristics that eagles especially desire (also see Chapter 10).

Interactions and fights are common at communal roosts. Eagles chase one another off favored perches until some semblance of order is achieved, until a new arrival upsets the balance, or until darkness prevents any further haggling over perches (Fig. 7.5). If one eagle lands or moves closer than a half-meter to another, the second eagle will assume a threat posture: it will raise the feathers on the back of its neck, lower its head, and strike at the intruder. Sometimes one displacement will trigger a chain reaction in which most, perhaps all, birds are displaced from their perches and renewed jostling begins. In one study, 21 percent of new arrivals to the roost displaced others, and the entire roosting group relocated 3 percent of the time when a new bird entered the scene. Although few data are available, it may be that adult birds are dominant in these disputes and they thus acquire the most desirable perches. Vocalizations are common when a new bird joins the flock, whether or not it supplants others. In the morning, interactions and vocalizations are less frequent, but the younger birds will often chase one another through the roost; for some reason, most adults refrain from these playful antics. (12, 17, 21)

We are unsure why bald eagles roost in groups, but several hypotheses seem plausible. First, roosting together may provide the means by which eagles obtain information on food location from one another. (9, 16, 23) Soaring above the roost just before dusk may entice other eagles to join the roosting group. In the morning, those who do not know where to find food may follow others to feeding sites, thereby gathering valuable information. (16) Sometimes the eagles leave the roost one after the other, forming a procession as they follow the leader to a food source. The cues used for communicating foraging information may be vocalizations (we still do not understand "eagle language"), the presence of a bulging crop indicating a well-fed eagle that knows where to eat, or a particular flight pattern out of the roost in the morning. Thus, communal roosts may serve as information centers. (37, 1) Communal roosts may also have a sexual function. Although mating is not likely to occur at a roost, a pair bond may be

Fig. 7.5 Jostling for preferred perches at a winter communal roost.

formed or renewed there, especially late in the winter just prior to the breeding season. (38) A third hypothesis suggests that eagles roost communally to discourage attacks by predators. Any experienced predator knows that it is more difficult to sneak up on a group of prey animals that are alert to potential danger than on a single one. Whether eagles benefit in this respect is questionable, however, since they have few nocturnal enemies capable of killing them. Fourth, perhaps eagles band together at

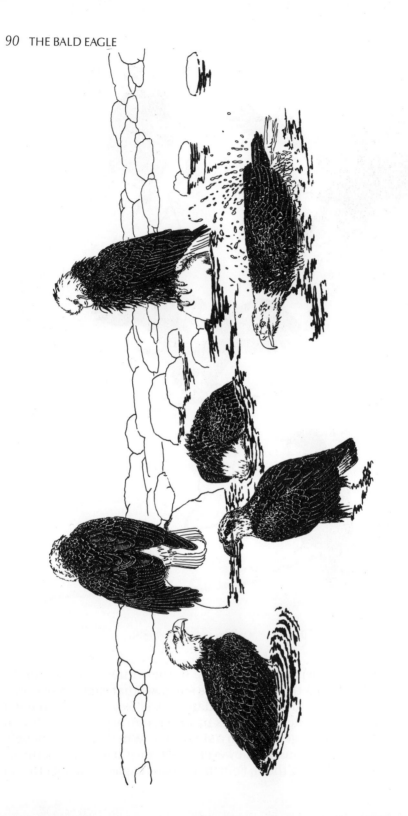

Fig. 7.6 Communal bathing is a lively, though uncommon winter activity.

night to take advantage of a particular kind of shelter. But unless this type of shelter is very scarce, this hypothesis seems unlikely. (33) It is doubtful that eagles stay warmer at night when together; they occupy large personal spaces and rarely huddle together even during extremely cold weather. Lastly, communal roosts may serve as gathering points prior to long-distance movements. (1) These hypotheses are not mutually exclusive; some or all could be acting at the same time.

Other Winter Events Eagles perform other winter activities in groups. Flying and soaring bouts are, of course, highly contagious; a soaring bird will likely attract many others to do the same, until a large flock is formed. Interactions during flight are prevalent, but the significance of these aerial encounters remains unknown. Even in winter, eagles can be seen locking talons and cartwheeling in a manner similar to the courtship displays of a mated pair (see Chapter 5). Interestingly, these displays usually involve juveniles and subadults; rarely will adult birds display in winter. (22, 17)

Although eagles rarely bathe, when they do so, it often is a social soak. When a bird first wades into the water and starts flipping its wings to spray water on its back, the idea spreads fast, and before long, an entourage of eagles is wildly splashing about (Fig. 7.6). Bathing is most common during sunny weather and just after feeding. Afterward, they may loaf nearby and preen their freshly rinsed plumages. (24, 25)

Little information is available on winter migration, but this seems to be one event that is performed alone. Groups of eagles may travel together in local areas, but rarely do so during long-range movements. This is not always the case, however, as mated pairs have been seen together along their migratory routes and small, close-knit bands may journey as one.

Diets and Foraging Behavior

A naturalist attempting to categorize the culinary habits and foraging methods of the bald eagle may, at first, falter in hopeless desperation. The observer will see some eagles flash through the sky and pounce on prey with amazing stealth and agility. But others will scavenge on decomposing, rancid flesh rather than hunt on their own. In another place or time, the naturalist will witness an act of thievery; rather than fend for itself, the eagle steals a meal from others, even from its own relatives. Some eagles will chase after vultures and feast on their vomit, others will eat fecal matter, and some, accustomed to human enterprises, will rummage through garbage dumps.

Had it not been for the eagle's diverse diet and varied foraging tactics, the species might have succumbed long ago. But eagles have, in many areas, adapted to human influences and are adept at finding food despite constant changes in their prey base. Few other predatory birds exploit so many different opportunities to take food from the environment as eagles do, and eagles' methods of acquiring prey are as diverse as the composition of their diet. This, then, is what the naturalist discovers: diversity and variety characterize the eagle's prey; it will eat virtually anything that has food value.

DIETS

There are several problems in accurately determining what bald eagles eat. The best approach is to observe and identify the captured prey, but this is often difficult. Most studies use an indirect method for determining dietary habits. The eagle's diet can be reconstructed either by examining food remains at nests and feeding perches or by analyzing regurgitated pellets, which contain the undigested portions of the food item. Pellet analysis is, however, a poor research technique because fish remains are either totally absent from or underrepresented in pellets, since fish are more easily digested than other foods.

That eagles exploit a vast diversity of prey is exemplified by the variety of prey items found at their nests or under their feeding perches. A list of prey species throughout their range would constitute a lengthy monograph. And eagles will feed on prey of any size. Bald eagles are known to eat small rodents, but they also dine on beached whales. Their food habits can change daily or seasonally and from one location to the next, and their varied foraging tactics mean that their diet will also be diverse. When eagles steal prey from other predators, for example, they exploit a whole new range of food sources. Perhaps the only restriction the eagle faces is in the location it seeks prey. Eagles require large, open expanses of water or land for foraging (searching for and acquiring food) and feeding (eating food).

Bald eagles feed primarily on fish, birds, and mammals. Table A, in Appendix 1, summarizes the results of twenty food-habits studies of nesting eagles throughout North America. Based on information in these studies, an overall average diet can be calculated: 56 percent fish, 28 percent birds, 14 percent mammals, and 2 percent miscellaneous sources (Fig. 8.1). Nesting eagles eat twice as many birds as mammals, but twice as many fish as birds.

When a choice is available, bald eagles invariably select fish over other prey. Preference tests, in which fish, bird, and mammal carrion were placed at feeding areas or provided to captive birds, showed that fish were chosen most often, followed by birds, then mammals. (77, 71) Although fish may be the preferred prey, prior experience can greatly influence a bird's choice. An eagle that has been eating a particular item will likely continue foraging for it as long as it remains available.

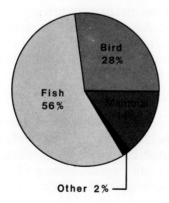

Fig. 8.1 Diet of nesting bald eagles. Values are based on data from Table A, Appendix 1.

Fish A key food supply for thousands of eagles in the Pacific Northwest is salmon, especially in winter. But most salmon are too large to kill; instead, eagles eat them as carrion. The coastal rivers of Alaska, British Columbia, and Washington, where natural runs of salmon still thrive, are often, overrun with hungry eagles. Chum salmon is the main source on the Chilkat River in Alaska, on the Fraser River in British Columbia, and on the Skagit and Nooksack rivers in Washington. (11, 25, 61, 57, 69) On Kodiak Island in Alaska, fish constitute 62 percent of the diet with sockeye salmon and char being the most sought after prey. (22) Nesting eagles in the Pacific Northwest use less salmon than overwintering birds, since the bulk of salmon runs occur in the autumn and winter months. (10) An introduced run of kokanee salmon attracts many eagles to Glacier National Park in autumn. (43, 44) Herring and oolichan runs offer prey for bald eagles in the Pacific, and, in Newfoundland, eagles gather in spring and autumn to fish for herring. (5, 10) Alewife is used in New York. (49) In the Midwest, gizzard shad form an important prey item, especially after they are killed while passing through the turbines of large dams. (62, 63, 64) Gizzard shad are also eaten in Oklahoma, sometimes constituting more than 80 percent of the eagle's diet. (42) They are common prey on the Karl Mundt Refuge in South Dakota, too. (70) Suckers and catfishes are selectively killed in many areas. Brown bullheads seem to be widely used by nesting birds; they are the prime food source in Maine, Florida, and Minnesota (Table A, Appendix 1). In a preference test, eagles selected them over all other fish species. (77) In west central Idaho, nesting eagles consumed an all-fish diet of yellow perch, northern squawfish, largescale suckers, trout, and brown bullheads. (75) Northern pike is another common food type in several areas. (13, 55, 73)

Birds Nearly all bird species eaten are those associated with aquatic habitats. Ducks and sea gulls are taken along the Maine seacoast, and in the Midwest, eagles hunt and kill many species of waterfowl, especially on wildlife refuges. (74) Waterfowl, particularly Canada geese, provide food for wintering eagles in Missouri, South Dakota, and many other areas. (20, 70) Mallards, widgeons, and pintails are favored in southern Oregon and northern California. (18) In central Washington, chukars, partridgelike game birds, are sometimes killed. (16) High use of birds occurs in the Aleutian Islands of Alaska. (48, 60) These islands are heavily populated with a large diversity of seabirds, many of which fall prey to eagles. Fulmars, a large seabird, seem quite vulnerable to the talons of nesting adults as are sea gulls. (29) Seabirds along the coast of British Columbia are an important food source, and Cassin's auklets and various species of petrels succumb in Alaska. (5, 9) Loons are killed, too. (23) Domestic fowl rarely are a part of an eagle's diet, but 13 were counted in 800 nests in 1923. (31) Other seabirds taken include grebes, alcids, cormorants, puffins, pelicans, herons, and others. Perhaps because they are easy prey, coots make up a major portion of the eagle's diet in many areas. (5, 47) Several raptors, such as red-tailed hawks, harriers, and ospreys, have been found as food remains, but it is not known if eagles killed them or scavenged on their carcasses.

A large proportion of prey, especially waterfowl, are crippled, diseased, or sickly individuals. Eagles seem adept at recognizing the unusual behavior of debilitated birds, and they selectively kill these prey. Waterfowl crippled by hunters are especially vulnerable.

Mammals Mammals, the least preferred of the three major vertebrate groups, can be an important source in some areas. In central Utah, wintering bald eagles forage as golden eagles do; they prey almost entirely on black-tailed jackrabbits. (52) Similarly, on the San Juan Islands in northwest Washington, the introduced European rabbit is a common victim. (54) In southern Colorado, white-tailed jackrabbits are the favored prey. (26) Throughout much of their range, and especially in the western states, bald eagles scavenge on large mammalian carcasses. Winter kills of deer, elk, and other mammals are common food sources. In Wood Buffalo National Park in northern Alberta, eagles feed on bison carrion. (78) There is evidence that they kill fawns, especially in Alaska, but this is probably rare.

Among marine mammals, eagles are known to scavenge on the bodies of adult sea otters and to kill the pups. (59) In Alaska, they scavenge on whales, seals, sea lions, and porpoises. Fifty-five bald eagles completely devoured a small beaked whale in less than ten days after it washed up on shore. (60) The largest known food item is reported to be the sperm whale! (59, 37)

Fascinating is the description of wintering food habits in southern Oregon. In the Klamath Basin, flood waters force mice and other small rodents to move to higher and drier ground. Bald eagles patrol the waterline and snatch the emerging mice. (36) Brown rats are taken on Amchitka Island in Alaska. (60) Some other oddities include porcupines, nutria, and muskrats. (3, 12, 61, 73) Eagles eat muskrats that get caught in leg-hold traps; a nest in Ohio contained fourteen such traps. (31) Other mammalian prey include foxes, tree and ground squirrels, prairie dogs, opossums, raccoons, and skunks.

Some domestic animals, including cows, sheep, and pigs, are eaten, but essentially all of these are scavenged, not killed. On rare occasions, eagles will kill newborn lambs and pigs and will sometimes, though rarely, take dogs and cats. (3, 50, 61, 31)

Other Prey Besides fish, birds, and mammals, bald eagles will sample an assortment of other culinary delights. They sometimes eat reptiles, especially turtles; diamondback terrapin and musk turtles provide a favored meal in the Chesapeake Bay region. (3, 8) Snakes are an unusual dietary item, but a black swamp snake was seen in one nest. (45) Eagles seldom eat amphibians. A myriad of invertebrate species find their way to the dinner table of the eagle. Bald eagles will eat squid, octopus, crab, shrimp, starfish, and many species of shellfish including freshwater mussels, abalones, clams, blue mussels, and snails. (74, 33, 21, 28, 13, 22) Eagles along the Washington coast have been seen feeding on large masses of eggs of some unknown sea creature.

Eagles will eat leaves on very rare occasions; epiphytes and persimmon seeds have been found in nests. (31, 4, 33) They will even ingest dung from sea lions; such coprophagic behavior probably is more widespread than is believed. And, as mentioned earlier, eagles will consume the food vomited by other animals, especially vultures. (50) They also seem to relish garbage from human settlements, at least in some areas. On Amchitka Island, hundreds of eagles gather at garbage dumps, especially when natural food supplies are scarce. (34, 60) It is hard to imagine the national symbol rummaging through table scraps and eating bread and pastries, but such flexibility in food habits is obviously advantageous when eagles are stressed by energy shortages. This behavior also suggests that eagles can exploit unusual food sources in times of desperate need.

Much has been written regarding the weight of prey that eagles can carry in flight. The largest prey items taken to nests include geese, cormorants, and sea otter pups in Alaska and brown pelicans, great blue herons, and cormorants in Florida. One goose found at a nest in Oregon weighed 4.1 kilograms. When the weights of the above prey items are compared to the average size of the eagle, just about half of an eagle's weight seems to be the heaviest load that the bird can lift and carry. (60, 4, 18)

Lastly, what about the claims of eagles having attacked humans? There are accounts of unprovoked attacks on infants, but most of these are difficult to verify and are undoubtedly imaginative or at least greatly exaggerated. It is doubtful that a single unprovoked attack on a child or adult has ever occurred, though researchers have been attacked while visiting nests (also see Chapter 5). (31)

FORAGING BEHAVIOR

A predator has two options in acquiring prey. One evolutionary strategy is to specialize in killing one or a very few types of prey. Predators of this type often are keenly efficient at capturing their quarry. The other strategy is to feed on whatever is available or most easily acquired. Bald eagles fit into this latter category; they use a wide variety of foraging techniques.

Bald eagles acquire food by three means: (1) stealing prey from others, (2) scavenging on carrion, and (3) hunting and killing. This may be the order of preference; eagles seem to prefer to steal rather than scavenge and to scavenge rather than kill prey, although this may be simplifying a complex situation. Indeed, one study showed that the decision to steal or scavenge was based on many different circumstances, and other information suggests that eagles may kill even when carrion is available. (25, 58) The reasons for these preferences may lie in the evolution of the species. It is suspected that throughout the evolution and adaptive "development" of the bald eagle, food shortages caused, at times, high mortality rates. Those individuals who were able to steal food when prey could not be acquired were the ones that survived and eventually reproduced, thus carrying on the genetic tradition of thievery. (68) And birds that conserved energy by scavenging on carrion instead of burning precious energy stores by hunting and killing also had a survival advantage. But eagles that are flexible in the use of all three foraging modes are most adaptable to changes in their prey base.

Stealing   Pirating (stealing from other eagles) or kleptoparasitism (stealing from other species) has been viewed anthropomorphically as one of the bald eagle's most ignoble attributes. Benjamin Franklin wrote:

> He is a bird of bad moral character; he does not get his living honestly; you may see him perched on some dead tree, where, too lazy to fish for himself, he watches the labor of the fishing-hawk [the osprey]; when that diligent bird has at length taken a fish, and is bearing it to his nest for the support of his mate and young ones, the bald eagle pursues him and takes it from him. (Quoted in 31.)

Franklin's field observation was correct, but his anthropomorphic interpretation was lacking in insight. In actuality, bald eagles have developed a behavioral trait that enables them to exploit an entirely new range of prey, which they themselves may not be able to catch, and they conserve energy by letting others do the work. As for the osprey, its life would be easier without the eagles' harassment.

Another story supporting Ben Franklin's feelings regarding the ill-mannered feeding habits of the national bird is told by John James Audubon:

> Many vultures were feeding on the carcass of a dead horse when the sudden appearance of an eagle put them all to flight, one among the rest with a portion of the entrails partly swallowed, and the remaining part, about a yard in length, dangling in the air. The eagle instantly marked him and gave chase. The poor vulture tried in vain to disgorge, when the eagle, coming up, seized the loose end of the gut, and dragged the bird along for twenty or thiry yards, much against its will, until both fell to the ground, when the eagle struck the vulture, and in a few moments killed it, after which he swallowed the delicious morsel. (33)

Audubon's story aptly describes the foraging preferences of the bald eagle. The eagle preferred to steal food from the vulture rather than feed on the horse carcass, and after killing the vulture, it preferred to consume the

Fig. 8.2 Bald eagle stealing a fish from one of its favorite victims, the osprey.

horse entrails taken from the vulture instead of eating the vulture itself. It did not kill the vulture as prey, but as part of its effort to steal food.

Stealing fish from ospreys is the eagle's best known foraging ploy. After the osprey has made a successful catch, the eagle takes to wing in hot pursuit. The fish hawk is repeatedly harassed until, fearing injury or tiring of such ill-treatment, it releases the fish from its talons and lets it fall (Fig. 8.2). If quick enough, the eagle will descend on the falling fish and snatch it before it lands. Sometimes the fish lands in water and swims off, leaving both birds without a meal. In one study, 1 to 2 percent of all foraging attempts by ospreys were interrupted by kleptoparasitic forays from eagles, but in another study, ospreys were robbed of all fish on several occasions. (3, 53, 41)

The osprey is not the only victim of the thieving eagle. There are many accounts of eagles stealing prey from sea gulls, loons, many waterfowl species especially mergansers, vultures, harriers, peregrine falcons, red-tailed hawks, golden eagles, and many other birds. (15, 31, 74, 61, 2, 60, 65) One mammal that is commonly robbed is the sea otter. As an adult sea otter is floating on its back and eating, an eagle will approach from behind, glide over its chest, and snatch whatever the otter is eating, much to the surprise of the unsuspecting victim. (37, 60) River otters also are kleptoparasitized. (18) But the most common dupe of this piratical onslaught is the bald eagle itself. Eagles seem habitually compelled to attack and steal from their own kind. They have been seen to drop prey and walk over food carcasses in their attempts to steal from other bald eagles. (68) In the Pacific Northwest, instead of scavenging on any number of available salmon carcasses, most birds arriving at feeding grounds try to rob the eagle that is feeding. Such thefts are particularly common when eagles feed together in large flocks. (67, 68) At a garbage dump on Amchitka Island in Alaska, feeding groups are fiercely aggressive whenever an eagle finds a food item. As many as fifteen birds will pursue and harass an eagle that has found a piece of food. (60) When a large assemblage of eagles is feeding on a limited amount of food, there is almost constant squabbling over feeding rights. And as more birds join the feeding flock, tensions seem to mount and fewer birds find a meal. The pandemonium that exists at these feeding frenzies is hard to describe; it is one of the most exciting and intricate facets of eagle behavior.

Eagles use numerous methods to steal food. *Aerial chases* have been mentioned; a bird carrying food is chased and either harassed or physically abused into dropping the prey. Sometimes, the pursuing eagle will twist underneath its quarry, reach out with its talons, and snatch the food away. An eagle swooping down at another bird on the ground in a *flying attack* can be an awesome foe, because a furious and speeding eagle with outstretched talons can cause great injury. Many times the attacker purposely misses its target; eagles may use these *mock attacks* to test the will of the defending opponent. Eagles sometimes attempt to steal using a *running* or *walking attack*; they trot toward the defender with wings drooping and head extended. A *leaping attack* involves jumping from the ground onto a feeding bird. Raising and outstretching the wings (*wing display*—Fig. 8.3A) is very common, but thrusting the talons up in defiance (*talon display*) may terrify the bird into relinquishing the food item. Sometimes eagles will momentarily lock their talons together (*talon lock*—Fig. 8.3B) and joust for feeding rights, but physical contact such as this is less common than ritual displays. While on the ground, an eagle may grab a food carcass that another is eating, and drag or fly away with it; this is known as *taloning* (Fig. 8.3C). Sometimes both birds will engage in a tug-of-war and rip the carcass in two. One eagle might strike with its beak at another (*beaking*—Fig. 8.3D) to chase it away, or, less frequently, it might steal bits of food with its beak. If it uses its beak for stealing, the thieving eagle will hold its head and body lower than the feeding bird; this submissive posture seems to reduce attacks from the food holder. A bird resisting a robbery attempt may cover the food with outstretched wings. This behavior of predatory birds is known as *mantling* (Fig. 8.3E). Often, birds will defend their food in the same manner used by the birds that are trying to steal it. Defensive birds raise the hackles on their head and neck and voice their intentions with shrill calls. Screaming, opening the beak, jabbing with the beak, feather fluffing, and thrusting the wings forward are all signals of defiance. Other means of defense against a pilfering eagle include: (1) feeding apart from others, (2) eating fast and selecting small prey that can be ingested quickly, (3) selecting a concealed feeding perch, and (4) mimicking a foraging flight to convince other eagles that it is still seeking prey even though the crafty bird has a piece of food concealed in its talons and hidden among its tail feathers. (19, 25, 38, 67, 17, 49)

a

b

c

Fig. 8.3 Pirating behavior displays during communal feeding activities: (a) wing display, (b) talon lock, (c) taloning, (d) beaking, and (e) mantling. (19, 38, 67)

The success of robbery attempts is influenced by many conditions, including the type of attack, type of defense, age, body size, sex, and degree of hunger, but other circumstances undoubtedly exist. Social interactions during feeding are very complex, and biologists are only beginning to unravel the significance of the bald eagle's many behavioral patterns. A flying attack on an eagle that is feeding on the ground is more likely to be successful than any other robbery method. (68) Because the potential for injury from a flying bird is so high, defenders often defer to those that use this technique. Birds that aggressively defend themselves and their food are less likely to be supplanted. (25) Age sometimes influences success; older eagles may be more adept at stealing from younger eagles, but this is not always true. (27, 68, 17, 25) Juveniles seem particularly susceptible to robbery. Because young birds are often subordinate, they spend more time foraging, fighting, stealing, or waiting to eat, in order to meet their needs for food. Consequently, young birds may experience more food stress. (68) When a size difference between two combatants is apparent, the larger foe wins 85 percent of the contests. (25) This implies that females are more successful at stealing because they usually are larger than the males. Will and determination also affect success rates: a hungry eagle is more likely to win a food fight than is a satiated one, and it will more aggressively defend its food. In one study, pirating success of hungry birds was 92 percent compared to 67 percent for well-fed birds. (25) Whether or not the abundance of food alters stealing success is still being debated.

Scavenging Bald eagles forage in a manner similar to that of vultures and other carrion-feeding birds (Fig. 8.4). They will scavenge on dead flesh whenever possible and seem to locate it just as vultures do. (39)

Bald eagles tend to dominate the scene at a food carcass. Along the rivers of the Pacific Northwest, they consume over 90 percent of all salmon carcasses, even though many other scavengers also use this food source. With the possible exception of the golden eagle, all other bird species that feed with eagles are subordinate to them. As long as carrion is available, eagles rarely show interest in their scavenging associates, though they may kill them at other times. Crows and sea gulls often feed with eagles; they pick up leftover food scraps or wait as the mighty eagle rips open a carcass making the contents available to all. When particularly bold, a crow will pull at the tail of a feeding eagle, and while the eagle is momentarily distracted, a second crow will jump on the food carcass, steal a tidbit, and flee. Coyotes sometimes drive eagles away, but these and domestic dogs are the only mammalian competitors known to challenge the bald eagle. (68)

Scavenging may be most common in winter. This is the season when many birds have migrated south and when lakes and rivers are covered with ice, making fishing impossible. Large mammals, such as deer and

Fig. 8.4 Bald eagles scavenging on a black-tailed deer carcass.

elk, are now vulnerable to starvation and cold stress. Eagles feed on their carcasses in many areas, and since cold temperatures prevent decay, a carcass may provide food for a long period. Sometimes, however, food is frozen solid during winter and is not edible until early spring. (67)

Domestic livestock can supplement the eagles' diet in many areas. Most, if not all, are eaten as carrion; there are few verified accounts of bald eagles killing domestic stock. Cow and sheep carcasses are scavenged. In one area, eagles eat the placenta of sheep, but ignore the ewe and newborn lambs. Nearly all accusations that eagles kill stock are unfounded and are based mainly on observations of birds feeding on animals that were already dead. This generally false assumption has led to the killing of many eagles by stock owners (also see Chapter 12). (66, 24, 40)

Hunting and Killing When stealing and scavenging food is not possible, eagles will resort to hunting and killing. Although this may not be their favored method of obtaining food, eagles can be skillful and formidable hunters. They use five basic methods: (1) hunting in flight, (2) hunting from a perch, (3) wading in water, (4) hunting on the ground, and (5) cooperative hunting.

Hunting in flight is a common foraging method. This technique allows the hunter to cover a large area, but the eagle expends considerable energy searching for and killing prey. Eagles will fly or soar above the area, watch for an opportunity to make a kill and, once they spot prey, they will "stoop" down and strike with their talons. When fishing, an eagle will skim the surface of the water, immersing only its talons, and snatch a fish into the air (Fig. 8.5). Rarely, a bird will plunge into the water, much like the osprey. If successful, the eagle may not be able to take flight from the water with its prey, especially if it has snared a large fish. In such an instance, it will tow its victim ashore, swimming in a most ungainly manner—stroking the surface of the water with its wings and pulling the prey along in its talons. (46) Some tows cover up to 150 meters, but most swims are shorter. (6) Waterfowl will try to elude the eagle by flying off or swimming underwater. If the water is shallow, the eagle will circle above and follow the movements of the submerged bird; once it surfaces for air, it is an easy mark. (31) Other waterfowl, particularly coots, might huddle in a dense pack and flap their wings wildly to thwart any predatory attempt, but once the eagle has singled out a victim, it will chase it until either the coot or the eagle is exhausted. (47) Bald eagles kill mammals in much the same manner, chasing them down and striking them with talons. Eagles are rarely able to take a bird on the wing, but when they do so, they turn upside down and thrust their talons into the belly of the beleaguered victim. A particularly cunning trick involves flying low over the ocean and pouncing on unsuspecting prey. In Alaska, eagles drop out of view in the troughs of ocean swells and surprise seabirds that are swimming about. (60) They also take

Fig. 8.5 While hunting in flight, eagles can snatch fish from water, using only their talons.

fish this way and mammals, too, if undulating terrain allows them to approach unseen.

Hunting from a perch is another common method, possibly because it costs little energy. An eagle will perch in a tree, and when prey moves within range, it will lunge at its quarry (Fig. 8.6). The eagle will either yank its victim into the air or pin it to the ground until it dies. This sit-and-wait hunting strategy is especially common with large birds of prey.

Fishing by *wading in water* is less common, but eagles will employ this technique where small fish are available. An eagle will wade in up to its belly, submerge its head, and strike with its beak (Fig. 8.7). Sometimes eagles will run in circles in shallow ponds, creating a ruckus, only to capture a fish the size of a minnow. They will also wade in shallow water to

Fig. 8.6 Hunting from a perch, or ambushing, is a common foraging technique.

seize a submerged carcass and then drag the food to shore and eat it. (62, 58, 67)

Hunting on the ground is a technique employed only in a few areas. Eagles will either stand and wait for prey to come close or walk around and try to flush hiding animals. They will stand on the banks of some rivers and bite or grab fish as they float or swim by. In southern Utah, eagles have been seen walking through sagebrush deserts trying to flush black-tailed jackrabbits from hiding. Once the rabbits are on the run, the eagles strike them down from flight. In Oregon, eagles walk along the edge of rising flood waters and grab mice and other small rodents as they emerge. (62, 63, 14, 36)

The last method of killing is by *cooperative hunting.* Birds hunting rab-

Fig. 8.7 Eagles sometimes wade to catch small fish.

bits on the ground are more successful when two or more eagles cooperate in the stalking process. One eagle will stand, walk, or fly in an effort to flush rabbits, while another waits nearby for the prey to expose itself. (14) About half of all rabbits are killed before they have run more than 30 meters when two birds cooperate in the hunt. Forays by single birds are not as effective. Many eagles cooperate to kill ducks or other waterfowl. They take turns stooping on the ducks as they surface for air and, in this way, do not tire as fast as their prey animals do. Up to five eagles have teamed up in this fashion. (60) It is not yet known if many cooperative hunts are actually beneficial to all participants. Some birds undoubtedly steal the prey from others, and once a kill is made, all participants may not share the spoils.

Other Accounts   A most unusual foraging ploy takes place in Alaska. Eagles excavate seabirds from their burrows by digging in the ground and yanking the nesting birds out. Few animals seem safe from the hungry eagle. (9)

Sometimes the bald eagle mistakes an inedible object for an easy food source. An eagle once snatched a rubber goose decoy from a hunter only to realize its mistake and drop it shortly thereafter. (76) And some prey fight back. One researcher witnessed an incident in which an

> eagle picked up a cat and discovered he had made a bad mistake as the cat began tearing at his vitals. The cat showed fight the moment he recovered from his astonishment at being snatched up so unceremoniously, and he made such an impression on the neck and breast of his captor that the latter would fain have dropped him without more ado; but Tom, it seems, held on, until the eagle, with feathers flying in every direction, descended to the ground and shook himself free of the outraged animal. (31)

But another eagle, this one in captivity, had an affinity for killing cats. Still another bird was found, shot dead, with the bleached skull of a weasel dangling from its neck, its teeth firmly set in the eagle's skin. In a few cases, eagles do not kill prey at the time of capture. Many fish brought to a nest in Ohio were alive, and one almost flopped out. (31) Decapitation is often the means to kill prey.

Hunting Success Success of hunting forays depends on the type, abundance, and vulnerability of prey sought, the hunting methods used, and many other details. Prey that are not alert to the eagle's approach are most vulnerable. Not surprisingly, bottom-feeding fishes make up much of the eagle's diet in many areas; these fishes orient their sight downward rather than keeping a watchful eye above. Birds that have difficulty taking off, such as coots, are more easily killed by eagles. Generally, the young, sick, and weak animals in prey populations make up a large proportion of a raptor's diet. When visibility is optimal, such as when waters are calm allowing the eagle to see fish below the surface, hunting success is higher. It is difficult to generalize on killing success without knowing the type of prey sought and the exact hunting conditions, but it seems the bald eagle has a respectable record as a predator. As examples, success rates have been recorded as 28 percent, 41 percent, 48 percent, 72 percent, and between 50 and 100 percent. (30, 32, 56, 27, 17, 35)

In a study of a nesting pair, the hunting success of the female (46 percent) was higher than that of the male (32 percent). But age seems to affect success even more. Young eagles are less effective than adults at hunting and killing. On the coast of Maine, adults easily snatch squid from the ocean as they fly, but the clumsy youngsters fall into the water during their attempts. (74) In Montana, juveniles and subadults resort to scavenging on salmon while adults take mostly live fish. When these young eagles tried to take live fish, they were successful 64 percent of the time, compared to an 84 percent success rate for adults. (58) In other studies, foraging successes of young and old eagles were 65 and 78 percent and 61 and 74 percent, respectively. (27, 17) In Washington State, young birds congregate in areas where prey is most abundant, possibly indicating that they are less adept at finding scattered food sources. (66) In general, adults are more likely to hunt and kill while juveniles and subadults rely on scavenging, piracy, and kleptoparasitism to get their daily meal.

9

Energy, Food, and Prey Requirements

The energy in food probably is the most important resource influencing the life and evolution of the bald eagle. Eagles require large quantities of food energy by virtue of their great size. Scarcity of energy may have been a frequent hardship during the course of their evolution; this may have forced eagles to adapt in many ways. Individuals who developed behavioral, morphological, and physiological traits that helped them acquire and use limited food sources were the ones that survived, perpetuated their kind, and passed along these adaptations. The present-day habits of the eagle are products of millions of years of evolution in which the ability to exploit energy from the environment has been keenly refined.

Describing the energy, food, and prey requirements of the bald eagle is like solving a puzzle; if all of the pieces are in logical order and in their proper places, then it is a simple subject to understand. In this chapter, three topics will be summarized: (1) energy requirements, (2) food consumption, and (3) prey use; circumstances affecting each will be described. Figure 9.1 illustrates this order of thought and outlines this chapter.

ENERGY REQUIREMENTS

All animals need a constant source of energy, and the bald eagle is no exception. Recent studies indicate that their daily energy needs range

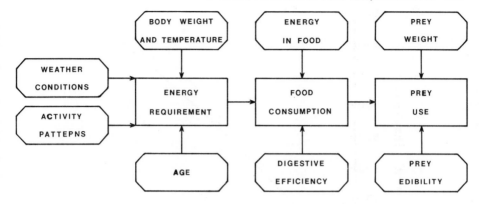

Fig. 9.1 Summary of Chapter 9.

from approximately 450 to 550 kilocalories for a full-grown bird. (A kilocalorie is the same as a "calorie" in popular usage.) Eagles require 15 to 25 percent of the amount of energy a human would need (2,000 to 3,000 kilocalories each day), but they are only about 5 to 10 percent of the weight of the average human. This energy consumption rate, however, is what would be expected from an animal of this size. (8, 11, 12)

Before we can understand how much food and prey an eagle needs to survive, we must examine some physiological and environmental variables that affect the eagle's energy budget. These include body size, body temperature, weather conditions, activity patterns, and age.

Body Size As one might expect, larger eagles need more energy than smaller eagles, but this relationship is not linear (Fig. 9.2). As body weight increases, energy requirements increase at a somewhat slower rate. (5) This pattern occurs because of differences in the surface-to-weight ratio. As body size increases, there is less surface area in proportion to body mass, and this tends to lower the amount of energy used to maintain proper body temperature. Thus, although large eagles require more energy than smaller ones, they use this energy more efficiently. This is true of females because they generally weigh more than males. Predictably, bald eagles in northern latitudes, being larger than those in southern latitudes, require more energy. The difference in weights of Alaska and Florida eagles is great, but there is a gradual increase in size as one proceeds north in the eagle's range. This phenomenon, known as Bergmann's rule, is exhibited by most warm-blooded animals. Eagles exposed to greater cold stress, as in Alaska and Canada, have evolved a larger body size for more efficient maintenance of bodily warmth.

Bergmann's rule applies not only to variations among bald eagles but also to differences among members of the sea eagle group. Sea eagles living in northern latitudes generally are larger than those in southern

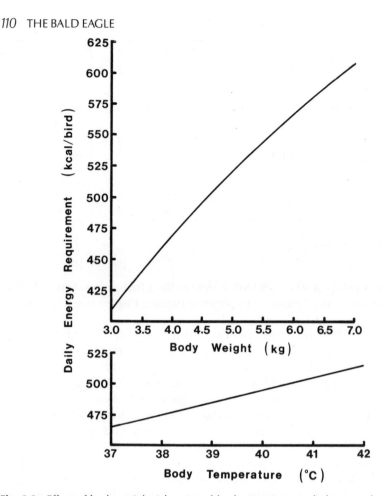

Fig. 9.2. Effect of body weight (above) and body temperature (below) on the daily energy requirements of bald eagles. (9, 10)

latitudes, presumably for the same reason (Fig. 9.3). The immense Steller's sea eagle, which weighs up to 9 kilograms and inhabits northeast Asia, is several times the size of the white-bellied sea eagle of Australia and southeast Asia, which weighs only 2 to 3 kilograms.

Body Temperature The eagle's temperature also affects energy needs (Fig. 9.2). Animals with high body temperatures require more energy than those with low temperatures. The burning of energy stores is doubled with every 10-degree-centigrade increase in body temperature.

Not all warm-blooded animals have body temperatures that remain constant. Bald eagles fit into a category known as "regulated heterothermy," a condition in which temperatures fluctuate within a narrow range. Body temperatures of bald eagles range from 38.8 degrees

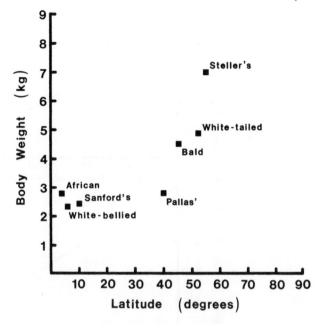

Fig. 9.3 Relationship between the latitudinal distribution of the sea eagles and their body weights. (1)

centigrade at night to 40.7 degrees during the day to 41.2 degrees during flight. (8)

Because their body temperature is lower at night, eagles are able to conserve about 5 percent of their total daily energy rations, since heat loss is reduced when eagles shift their metabolic machinery into a slower pace. Reducing temperature is a clever physiological trick used by many animals to minimize their loss of heat energy. (12)

Weather Conditions Energy requirement is affected by several environmental conditions. Radiation, air temperature, wind, and rain all contribute to energy loss (or gain) thereby altering the amount of food and prey that an eagle needs. Eagles constantly adjust their metabolic processes to counter the effects of weather. By thermoregulating, they keep warm by burning energy stores or keep cool by dissipating excess heat.

As thermal or long-wave *radiation* from the environment increases, eagles lose less heat (Fig. 9.4). They often benefit from this radiative effect by roosting in dense foliage where energy exchange with vegetation is high and exposure to the clear, cold sky is low. Vegetation is relatively warm compared to the sky; the warmer the object, the more radiation it emits and the greater benefit to the eagle. (8, 12)

Radiation from the sun, called short-wave radiation, also can reduce heat loss in eagles. By basking in sunshine, they lower the amount of energy

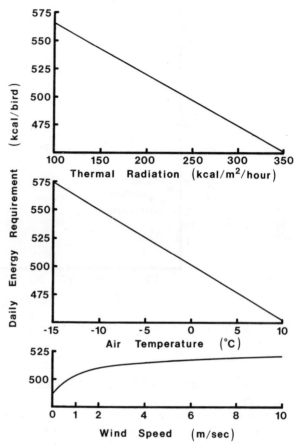

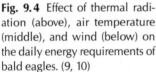

Fig. 9.4 Effect of thermal radiation (above), air temperature (middle), and wind (below) on the daily energy requirements of bald eagles. (9, 10)

they expend maintaining a proper body temperature. This has been studied for golden eagles; the effects to bald eagles are presumably similar. (5) During summer, however, excessive sunshine may cause heat stress.

When *air temperature* drops, heat loss by eagles increases in a linear fashion (Fig. 9.4). For every 1 degree centigrade drop in temperature, daily needs increase by about 5 kilocalories or approximately 1 percent of the daily energy budget. Eagles respond to cold by two means: they shiver to generate additional body heat, and they fluff their feathers to increase the depth of the warm blanket of air surrounding their bodies. Heat stress begins when temperatures are too high; when this happens, panting is the eagle's best defense against overheating. Also, they may seek habitats that are warm in the winter and cool in the summer whenever temperature stress becomes severe. (10, 8, 12)

Wind is the third element that can rob the eagle of its precious heat stores. The effects of wind are most pronounced at low velocities; fewer overall effects occur if moderate winds keep increasing (Fig. 9.4). Wind alone can drain energy, but windblown rain and snow, known as scud, can penetrate the protective feathering and chill the eagle even faster. The effect of wind and low temperatures combined is similar to the effect of the familiar wind-chill factor on humans; exceptional cold stress can result. Eagles tend to avoid chilling winds by seeking protected microhabitats, such as densely foliated trees, canyons, and leeward slopes. They may also face into the wind so that their feathers are not ruffled. (5, 9, 12)

Many eagles, particularly those in the seacoastal areas of the Pacific Northwest, are subjected to relentless rainstorms. What effect does *rain* have on energy loss? This question was answered by a study in which captive eagles were placed under artificial rain and their metabolic responses measured during simulated storms. The results show that energy loss does increase with rain stress, but at a nominal rate. Apparently, the plumage sheds water quite well. Clouds that bring rain play a compensating role: the "warmth" that cloud cover provides overrides the small energy loss due to wetting by rain. Thus, eagles are likely to lose less heat energy in a cloudy and rainy environment than in a clear and dry one. (8, 12)

Activity Patterns Activity can be a particularly important drain on heat and energy reserves. Although no study has determined exactly how much energy an eagle uses in various activities, information on other bird species may be comparable. The best estimate for the cost of flapping flight is about 156 kilocalories each hour; soaring or gliding flight costs 44 kilocalories per hour. An eagle that migrates in flapping flight for eight hours a day would burn some 1,248 kilocalories each day in flight alone. This is about three times the usual daily expenditures. If this eagle were to fly at 45 kilometers per hour, it would cover a distance of 360 kilometers. The cost of energy to travel at this speed and distance is approximately 3.5 kilocalories per kilometer. Soaring and gliding flight costs much less and would require only 352 kilocalories for this same excursion. (8, 9, 10, 12)

With energy costs as high as these, one can understand why eagles are often inactive. In winter, they fly during only 1 percent of the twenty-four-hour day and spend most of their time roosting and perching. Eagles fly only when the need arises, and they soar and glide rather than engage in costly flapping flights; less energy used is more conserved. Eagles further economize on their energy budgets by becoming active only to acquire energy or save more of it; flight is used for hunting prey (acquiring energy) and in seeking protected habitats where expending energy for thermoregulation is minimzed (conserving energy). Because eagles may be limited in number by the availability of energy and because a lack of food can cause starvation, conserving energy may help reduce mortality and might improve reproductive success. The "laziness" of the bald eagle, which Benjamin Franklin observed, is in reality a clever and efficient means of conserving energy. (12, 8)

Age Young bald eagles are voracious eaters, and sometimes need more food than their parents. Surprisingly, the energy needs of bald eaglets have been little studied; the following information is based on only one bird held in captivity. A bald eaglet between seven and fourteen days of age consumed up to 50 percent of its weight in food each day. This amounts to 150 to 200 grams per day. At this age, it gained 1 gram of weight for every 5 grams it ingested—a 20 percent growth efficiency rate. When it was three weeks old, the eaglet consumed up to 672 grams every day. As it approached fledging age, its energy needs were about the same as those of an adult bird. (13)

An active nest with parents and young present can require large amounts of energy from the environment. Approximately 120 days elapse from the start of egg laying until fledging. During this period, roughly 160,000 kilocalories are needed to provide for the parents and two young, based on information from golden eagles. (3) Obviously, reproduction is a costly proposition that can occur only in an energy-rich environment; without sufficient food and energy resources, reproductive efforts may falter or fail altogether.

FOOD CONSUMPTION

There are many exaggerated accounts of the amount of food that bald eagles eat. Eagles are not the ravenous gluttons that many people believe them to be, though rapidly growing eaglets can ingest a surprisingly large quantity of food. The food needs of full-grown birds are what would be expected from an animal of their size and weight. Normal daily food requirements range from 250 to 550 grams for a 4.5-kilogram bird (Fig. 9.5), or 5.5 to 12.2 percent of body weight, depending on the type of food eaten and the temperature of the air. (11) Another study documented food consumption at 4.9 to 6.4 percent of the eagle's weight with females eating more than males, but these birds were losing weight because of DDT poisoning. (2) In order to be more precise, one must know the eagle's energy requirements, the energy value of the food, and the eagle's digestive efficiency (see Fig. 9.1).

Food Energy Content As the amount of energy in the food increases, consumption decreases and vice versa. This relationship is curvilinear (Fig. 9.6). When the energy content of food drops much below 1 kilocalorie per gram, the need for food increases rapidly, and when the food energy content is above 3 kilocalories per gram, food consumption plummets. Some foods, such as spawned salmon or decomposing carrion, fall into the low-energy category; large quantities are needed to meet energy demands. Fatty foodstuffs are at the other extreme. An eagle eating whale blubber, as might occasionally happen, needs less than 100 grams a day to meet its needs. (11)

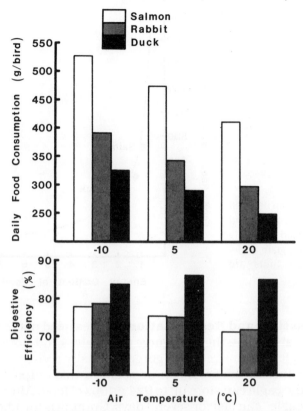

Fig. 9.5. Average daily food consumption by a 4.5-kilogram eagle on a diet of salmon, rabbit, and duck at several temperatures (above), and digestive efficiency of each of these diets (below). (11)

Digestive Efficiency Not all of the food that an eagle eats is digested and assimilated into the body. Some of it passes through in the form of waste, and other materials are regurgitated; these indigestible portions never enter into the metabolic processes of the body. Animals that are more efficient at assimilating food derive more energy from each meal and need to eat less often.

The digestive efficiency of bald eagles is not unlike that of other animals. It ranges from 70 to 85 percent depending on the composition of the food and sometimes on the air temperature (Fig. 9.5). Digestion of fattened waterfowl or other prey with high fat content is most efficient. Prey with high fat levels raise the overall digestibility of the food. Prey low in fat, such as spawned salmon or lean rabbits, is digested with an efficiency of 70 to 80 percent. Interestingly, the efficiency of digestion of some prey animals increases when air temperatures are low. Thus, eagles are more effective at using the energy contained in food when they need it most, during cold stress. (8, 11)

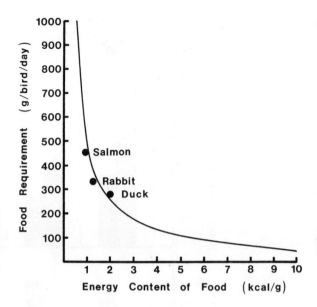

Fig. 9.6. Relationship between the energy content of prey and the amount needed for a daily meal by a 4.5- kilogram eagle. Three common diets are plotted. (11)

Gorging, Fasting, and Regurgitation Eagles need not feed every day. When food is abundant, they will gorge themselves and store food in their crops. An eagle that has recently gorged is easily recognized; a distinct bulge in the throat, the crop, can be seen. In this outpocketing of the esophagus the eagle can store up to 924 grams of food. After storing food in the crop, eagles can fast for several days. Gorging is an adaptation that allows them to survive when prey are difficult to find or when feeding is interrupted for some reason. (13)

Eagles can, however, fast for long periods. A captive bird was purposely starved for sixteen days to determine what ill effects would occur. During this fast, the eagle lost 28 percent of its body weight; 60 to 90 grams were lost each day. No apparent harm was evident, but after food was once again provided, body weight increased at only half the rate at which it was lost. Another captive bird was kept alive for thirty-two days without food, but the consequences of fasting for wild birds are difficult to assess. An eagle in a starved, weakened condition may be less able to lead a normal life. Like other birds, eagles will store energy as fat and use it as the need arises, such as during migration. When their food supply is irregular and un-predictable, the ability to survive with little nourishment has obvious advantages. (13, 7)

Bald eagles, like most raptors, regurgitate pellets after feeding. This usually occurs the morning after a meal. Pellets are formed in the gizzard, passed from there to the mouth, and then vomited or "cast." The pellets are made up of the undigestible portions of the food; they usually contain feathers, fur, and an occasional bone. Pellets rarely show any evidence that fish were eaten. Bald eagles are exceedingly adept at digesting bone

8 cm

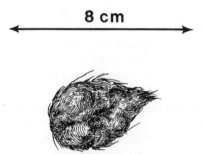

Fig. 9.7. Typical cylindrical (above) and spherical (below) pellets regurgitated by bald eagles. (6)

because of their strong stomach acids. The calcium obtained from digesting bone helps promote their own bone development and aids in the formation of eggshells. (8, 4)

Pellets can be many shapes and sizes. Of twenty-nine examined in Illinois, twenty were cylindrical and averaged 7.1 centimeters in length and 2.5 centimeters in diameter. The other nine were spherical and about 2.1 centimeters in diameter (Fig. 9.7). (6)

PREY USE

A meaningful estimate of the amount of prey that eagles need can be made only once energy and food requirements are known. But two additional factors also must be considered: weight and edibility of the prey animals (see Fig. 9.1).

Prey Weight   Obviously, a large carcass will provide much more food for eagles than a small prey item will. A carcass of a beached whale, for example, would provide hundreds of meals, but a small seabird might not satiate a hungry eagle. Every year, an eagle would need to eat 57 salmon, 87 rabbits, or 135 ducks. (11) One reason why these prey are needed in different quantities is because each type is a different size.

Prey Edibility   Another factor that influences the amount of prey needed is the portion of prey that is edible by eagles. Edibility is expressed as a percentage of a prey animal that is eaten; intestines, bone, fur, and feathers are commonly refused by a fussy eater. Salmon have much edible flesh (79 percent) compared to rabbits (71 percent) and ducks (68 percent), and this means that eagles need to take less salmon. Sometimes eagles are unable to consume an entire prey animal and waste the remaining portion. This wastage factor tends to be higher for large prey and when only one or a few eagles feast on the carcass. But because bald eagles often forage in groups, the amount of leftover food tends to be small compared to the wasted prey from other raptors; the birds that feed last clean up the remains. (11)

Impact on Prey What are the effects of eagles on their prey populations (Fig. 9.8)? This is an especially difficult question to answer because a myriad of factors influence predator-prey relationships. It is likely, however, that for several reasons sea eagles do not affect their prey populations as much as other raptors do. First, bald eagles prefer to scavenge rather than kill their own prey. Second, by stealing food from other predators, eagles distribute their effect among the prey populations of other predators. Third, the eagle's diet is so diverse that few prey are taken from each of the many populations that eagles use. This "buffering" effect minimizes the predatory effects to any one prey type.

In many cases, prey populations are not thought to be regulated by predation. In fact, the reverse may be more common; predator populations are controlled by changes in their prey. If this premise is accepted, then the diverse diet of the bald eagle also acts as a buffer to protect it against any dramatic changes in its prey sources.

Fig. 9.8. Compared to other raptors, bald eagles have less effect on the size of their prey populations.

10

Habitat Use

Bald eagles have a well-defined preference for certain environmental features. They need special areas for nesting, perching, roosting, and foraging. This chapter describes, in detail, the characteristics of these habitats that bald eagles need to exist.

NESTING HABITAT

Nest Location   Nest sites of bald eagles are invariably located near water. Whether along the windswept seacoasts of the Pacific Northwest, the glacier-carved lakes of central Canada, the cypress swamps of the Southeast, or the southwestern deserts, the eagle's nest is not too distant from a shoreline. When the some 900 eagle nests on Admiralty Island in southeast Alaska are plotted on a map, this propensity for selecting waterfront nesting areas becomes quite apparent (Fig. 10.1). These nests form a near-perfect outline of the island. (42)

Of the 2,732 nests surveyed in southeast Alaska, 99 percent are within 200 meters of water and average only 40 meters from the shoreline. (42) Similar distances are apparent in Washington, Saskatchewan, Manitoba, Maine, and in just about all other areas in the eagle's range. (18, 58, 56) A few eagles nest farther from water in Minnesota and Florida. Only about half of 43 nests surveyed in Minnesota were within 500 meters of water, and an average distance of 600 meters was recorded. (13) Selection of nest sites far from water in this area is explained by the lack of suitable trees along the shores of lakes. Nests in one area in Florida average about 1

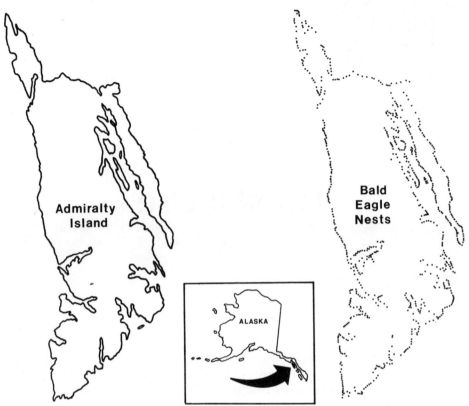

Fig. 10.1 Distribution of bald eagle nests on Admiralty Island in southeast Alaska. (42)

kilometer from water for the same reason; suitable nest trees are not always available near water. (37) Ostensibly, the eagle's preference for a nest substrate is more critical than its need to be close to water.

Although a preference probably does not exist, most nests are along marine seacoasts. Most of these are in the Pacific Northwest, but there are many on the eastern seaboard, too. Lakeshores are also used for nesting. Eagles abound in central Canada where glaciers have carved innumerable lakes and ponds. The banks of rivers and streams seem to be used less than seacoasts and lakeshores. Rivers are, however, common nesting areas in the arid region of the eagle's range, such as in the southwestern deserts.

Nest Tree Species and Types Except in a few unusual situations, bald eagles nest in trees. There seems to be little preference for a particular tree species; eagles select nest trees on the basis of appearance and form. In many areas, they use coniferous trees more often than deciduous trees, but it is not known if conifers are actively selected.

Eagles use a wide variety of nest structures (Table B, Appendix 1). Various species of pines are used in the eastern states, the Great Lakes states, and the inland areas of the western states. White pine, aspen, and birch are commonly used in Maine as is loblolly pine in Virginia, and pines and mangroves are the most important species in Florida. Lofty white and red pines are favored in the Great Lakes states, but hardwoods also may be used. Nests are often located in ponderosa and lodgepole pines and other evergreen trees in the inland western states. In the western coastal areas, stately Douglas fir and Sitka spruce are preferred, but western hemlock is used to a lesser extent. On Kodiak Island in Alaska, the deciduous black cottonwood is a favored place to build a nest.

Where suitable trees are not available, eagles may nest on other objects. On treeless Amchitka Island in Alaska, nests are placed on rock pinnacles, steep ridges, hillsides, or small islets off shore. In Baja California, one nest was placed in a large cactus, but in Arizona and in one area in Alaska, nests are located on the face of steep cliffs much like the nest sites of golden eagles. Ground nests are used in the treeless tundra of northern Canada. (7)

Nest Tree Characteristics   There is one consistent characteristic of the nest tree; it usually is one of the tallest in the forest stand. Selecting a tall tree ensures a structure that will adequately support a large nest, provide an open flight path to and from the nest, and have a panoramic view of the surrounding terrain. These characteristics are preferred components of the nest site (Fig. 10.2).

The actual height and diameter of the nest tree vary greatly depending on the species, but surrounding trees seem like dwarfs compared to most

Fig. 10.2. Typical nesting habitat showing a nest below the top of a tall tree, a snag nearby for perching, and an alternate nest close by.

nest trees. In most instances, the nest provides a view high above the tops of adjacent trees. Nest trees in fourteen areas range from 20 to 60 meters in height and from 50 to 190 centimeters in diameter (Fig. 10.3). Although height can vary, the nest tree is almost always taller than the forest stand (Fig. 10.4). In Virginia, seventy nest trees are an average of 29 meters in height, and the surrounding forest averages 24 meters. In the Pacific Northwest, where trees grow to enormous heights, nest trees are from 30 to 96 percent taller than adjacent stands. In ponderosa pine forests, nest trees average 40 meters in height compared to about 27 meters for surrounding trees. Similarly, nest trees in Sitka spruce and western hemlock forest are 44 meters high, but nearby trees are only 26 meters tall.

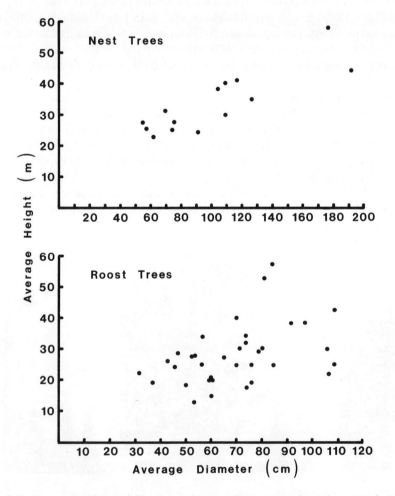

Fig. 10.3. Average heights and diameters of nest and roost trees throughout North America. (1, 2, 4, 8, 10, 17, 23, 27, 32, 36, 51, 54, 59)

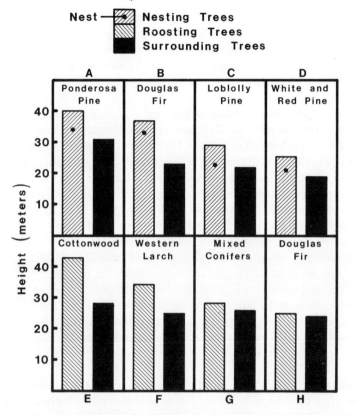

Fig. 10.4. Comparison of the heights of nest trees (above) and roost trees (below) to the heights of the surrounding forest canopies. (2, 4, 18, 27, 31)

Probably the highest nests are situated in giant Douglas fir trees in the temperate rain forests of the Pacific Northwest. One such tree in Oregon is 87 meters tall. Douglas firs used for nesting average about 47 meters in height, compared to 23 meters for the surrounding forest, so that these trees are more than twice the size of those nearby. Nest trees also are larger in diameter than other trees in the stand. (2, 4)

Several hypotheses attempt to explain why eagles nest in such tall trees. A tall tree provides unobstructed flight paths to the nest; this is a necessity because an eagle has difficulty becoming airborne and has trouble maneuvering in dense forest. In fact, it has been suggested that if a fledgling falls to the ground in dense underbrush, it may be unable to fly out because the foliage will trap the bird on the ground. The parents can alleviate this problem by nesting near large openings and on a tall tree so that the first critical flights by young eagles do not end in disaster. Another hypothesis suggests that a prominent nest in a tall tree acts as a signal to unwanted visitors that the territory is occupied, but it also serves as an observation post to help the territorial pair watch for intruders. A tall nest tree provides the needed support for the large nest. Also, the stoutest trees may be more resistant to destruction by violent winds, as may be true of Sitka spruce nest trees in Alaska. Interestingly, nests that are higher above the ground are more likely to contain eggs or young, at least in Alaska. (13, 9, 25, 42)

Many nest trees have damaged tops or a structural peculiarity that provides a site for the nest. Of 218 nest trees surveyed in Washington, 44 percent had broken tops. If not placed on top of the broken tree, nests can be built in the crook of a diverging trunk or, more commonly, against the trunk on stout branches. Nests are usually not located directly on top of the tree, but are placed a short distance below. The distance of the nest from the treetop varies from 3.5 meters in Washington for 218 nests, to 5.4 meters in California for 65 nests, to approximately 6 meters in Virginia for 70 nests. In this propensity for constructing nests below the treetop, eagles differ from ospreys, which build their nests on top. (18, 31, 2)

Because eagles nest below the treetop, some tree foliage and branches are present above the nest. Eagles may actively prefer to nest below such foliage. Perhaps a mild microclimate develops there; this cover could protect adults and their young from rain and sunlight and could reduce radiative cooling of the birds when the sky is clear at night. Also, cover may protect the unoccupied nest so that fewer repairs are needed. (18)

Forest Stand Appearance Bald eagles prefer to nest in forests that are old or that appear to be old. These forest stands typically have many tall, aged, dying, and dead trees, and a canopy that has many layers, created by the presence of many trees of different species, ages, and heights. These mature or overmature forests often are of overwhelming stature. Eagles completely avoid young forest stands, especially those with a dense complement of trees of similar age, such as many cultured stands. They desire many openings in the forest canopy, such as those created by lakes, rivers, meadows, or open fields, and a diverse appearance. Because the largest trees usually are the oldest, eagles distinctly prefer to nest in old-growth forest. (4, 49)

Forest stands with these characteristics are rapidly dwindling in North America. Not only do they take several hundred years to develop, but they are highly valued by the forest products industries. It is for this resource that bald eagles and humans often are in intense competition.

PERCHING HABITAT

Bald eagles spend over 90 percent of the daylight hours perching, in both winter and summer. One bird with an attached radio transmitter was monitored for more than eighteen hours; during that time it did not move from its perch. Because of their affinity for this activity, perching habitat has special significance to eagles. In general, however, eagles are more flexible in selecting perch locations than in choosing nesting, roosting, and foraging habitats. (48, 15)

Functions of Perches   Perches serve the eagle in many ways. Eagles may *loaf* or *rest* on perches rather than engage in more active endeavors. They may *forage* or *hunt* from perches, as when they ambush unsuspecting prey that come nearby, and afterward they may *feed* or *eat* while perching. Eagles use *sentry* or *guard* perches as lookout points while watching the nest, food, the territory, or an offspring. Perches also provide a means for *displaying* some message, usually to other eagles, about occupancy of a territory, location of food and roosts, or receptivity for mating. Sometimes, a perch provides a *thermal* benefit; it is a place to keep warm or cool by basking in the sun, seeking shade under leaves, or avoiding wind and rain in sheltered foliage. A tall perch near the nest might, at different times, serve all six purposes for the eagle. And this may be only a partial list of the functions of a perch.

Perch Location   Eagle perches, especially those used for foraging and feeding, are close to water. Nearly all birds will perch within 50 meters of a shoreline, because fish, waterfowl, seabirds, and other prey can be acquired there. (26, 50, 53) But eagles will also loaf near water. Sentry perches are close to the nest or in an area where the nest can be seen, usually in the closest tall tree, often a snag, and rarely more than 50 meters from the nest. (12) Display perches are not necessarily along a shoreline; they can be in a territory, along favored flight paths, or at winter staging areas where eagles "invite" other eagles to join them at a sheltered roost or a food source. (22, 48) The feeding perch is sometimes a thickly vegetated tree where flight paths and views are restricted. This could be an adaptation for preventing other eagles from stealing their food; the feeding bird may actually be hiding from potential thieves. (23, 29) But most eating perches are on exposed limbs close to, or even overhanging, water.

Perch Tree Species and Types   Eagles choose more varieties of perch trees than nest or roost trees. Nevertheless, they prefer some types. Snags of any species seem to be the favored perch. Where snags are not available, cottonwoods are widely used. Eagles select large maples in some areas. Where deciduous and coniferous trees grow together, most birds will choose the deciduous species and avoid the conifers, perhaps because the dense foliage of the latter obstructs both vision and flight. They do use conifers where they are abundant, especially ponderosa pine and Sitka spruce in the West. Additionally, bald eagles will perch on rocks and riprap, cliffs, logs, pilings, driftwood, ice, gravel and mud bars, haystacks, poles, beaches, fence posts, and even powerhouses, but natural perches are preferred. (5, 11, 16, 20, 21, 23, 30, 32, 50, 51, 52, 53, 59)

Perch Tree Characteristics Eagles prefer to perch on trees, but they select a particular tree on the basis of the growth form, not the species. They will most often choose the tallest tree along a shoreline, a tree that has a panoramic view and open exposure on at least one side (Fig. 10.5).

Measurements of perch trees have been made only in a few areas. The average height and diameter of cottonwood perch trees are 21.7 meters and 42.0 centimeters in South Dakota, and 31.5 meters and 108.0 centimeters in Illinois. A variety of species in South Dakota average from 12.8 to 16.4 meters in height and 28.4 and 55.5 centimeters in diameter. Ponderosa pines used in Washington are 19 meters tall and 51 centimeters in diameter. These perch trees are all taller than the surrounding forest. (53, 23, 59)

Eagles select the highest perch that can support their weight. They nearly always perch on the upper half of trees, and if branches are strong enough, they prefer the upper quarter. More important, though, is the height of the perch relative to the forest canopy; it usually towers above the surrounding trees. But height of the perch can be influenced by other circumstances as well. A bird will use a lower perch if it has just fed, if the weather is harsh, or if the eagle has just flown there from a ground perch. Branches that are horizontal, thick, and easily accessible are most widely used. With their large wing spans, eagles need open avenues for landings and takeoffs. (50, 43, 32)

ROOSTING HABITAT

A roost is an area where eagles rest and sleep during the night. Although they often gather at large communal roosts during the evening, some birds may remain at their daytime perches throughout the night. And during particularly inclement weather, eagles may remain in sheltered roosts during daylight hours. Although the distinction between perching and roosting habitats is not always apparent, roosts often have a number of special characteristics. (28, 32, 40, 49, 51)

Roost Location and Size Unlike nesting and perching sites, roosting habitat is not necessarily close to water. Prey sources are in the general vicinity, but close proximity to food is not a critical need. More important is the shelter that a roost affords. Eagles will choose a roost that has a protected microclimate, tall trees that extend above the forest canopy, and locations that provide clear views and open flight lanes (Fig. 10.6). In winter, the company of other eagles also is a desired feature.

Roosts can be located near a river, lake, or seashore, or be as far away from water as 29 kilometers or more. Normally, however, they are within a few kilometers of day-use areas. Of twenty communal roosts that have been studied throughout the states, 40 percent are within 1 kilometer of water, but the remaining 60 percent are scattered between 1 and 29 kilometers

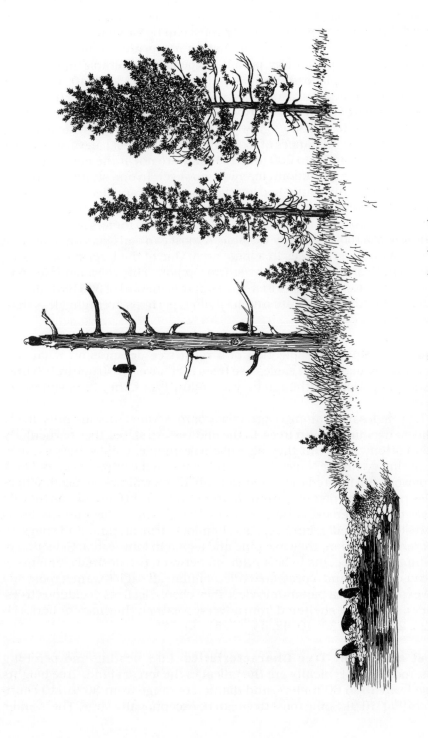

Fig. 10.5. Typical perching and foraging habitat with tall trees, especially snags, near a shoreline where the birds can acquire food.

away. These roosts are an average of 8.4 kilometers from water. The distance of a roost from water depends on the availability of suitable habitat. If the preferred elements of a roost can be found in stands close to day-use areas, then long flights to distant roosts are not necessary. But eagles may go out of their way, perhaps expend considerable flight energy, to find a sheltered place to sleep each night. (55, 22, 23, 28, 40, 44, 53, 59)

During the breeding season, roosts of nesting adults are located within the boundaries of the territory. Roosting is common in the nest or at the nest tree, but as the nestlings grow, the adults gradually roost farther away from the nest tree. Distances of roost sites from the nest can vary, but they usually range from 50 to 200 meters if they are not at the nest tree itself; they can be as far as 1 kilometer away, however. In one study, during the first month after the young had left the nest, adults and fledglings roosted an average of 595 and 175 meters from the nest, respectively. After a month, they roosted an average of 1,270 and 1,090 meters away. (41)

The size of a roost is highly variable. A roost can consist of only one tree or many hundreds of trees in a large area. One of the largest communal roosts is in Bear Valley in south central Oregon. This roost contains 645 trees, encompasses 254 hectares, and supports upward of 300 birds during winter. Most other roosts are much smaller, perhaps averaging less than a few hectares. (29)

Roost Tree Species Selection of a roost tree depends on what tree species are available, but eagles use trees that have the structural characteristics they desire. Although they use many types, they favor some over others.

When eagles roost along rivers, lakes, or reservoirs, they are most likely to choose deciduous roost trees. In the midwestern states, they particularly prefer cottonwoods, but they also use oak, maple, willow, hickory, ash, pecan, elm, sycamore, aspen, birch, and snags. In the western states, black cottonwood is a favored roost tree. In Utah, black willows are used. Where eagles roost some distance from riparian (waterfront) habitat, as they do out west, they often use coniferous trees. Douglas fir is a favorite species as are western red cedar, larch, spruce, hemlock, true fir, pine, and snags. In the breeding season, they use pine and aspen in Minnesota. Selection of roosting habitat seems to be a trade-off between two desired elements: a wide visual field and a protected microclimate. If eagles want a roost site with exposure and a panoramic view, they choose leafless deciduous trees. If they desire a site sheltered from adverse weather, they use conifers. (11, 16, 22, 23, 29, 32, 33, 40, 42, 44, 45, 51, 53, 59)

Roost and Roost Tree Characteristics Like nesting and perching trees, roost trees typically are the tallest in the forest stand. Tree heights range from 15 to 60 meters, and diameters range from 30 to 110 centimeters (Fig. 10.3). Some roost trees can be exceptionally large. The average

Fig. 10.6. In many areas, eagles prefer a sheltered communal roost with tall conifers, easy flight access, and clear views.

height of Douglas firs in a roost in Washington is 58 meters, but some individual trees are much taller. Diameters are exceedingly large, too. (22)

Trees having these characteristics are mature or old. Coniferous roost trees in the Klamath Basin of Oregon and California range from 100 to 535 years old and average 236 years of age. Trees in a western larch roost in Glacier National Park in Montana are older than 300 years. (29, 4)

An important feature of a preferred roost tree is its height in relation to the surrounding forest. Like nest and perch trees, roost trees tower above the adjacent forest cover, no matter what species they are (Fig. 10.4). This allows easy access and provides wide views. Snags and deciduous trees provide open branching as do dead and widely spaced branches on conifers. Where exceptionally tall trees are not available, eagles may roost on the edge of the forest stand. On steep slopes, trees that are naturally layered above one another are used; they allow a downslope view, and their foliage does not obstruct the eagle's cumbersome flight. The birds prefer stout lateral branches that they can easily grasp with their feet.

Roost Microclimate A microclimate is a condition in which the overall weather patterns of an area are modified in some way. This can be caused by many habitat features and landform characteristics. Eagles seem to seek microclimates that protect them from harsh weather. They will often select sheltered sites when weather is extreme or threatening; during mild conditions, they use a variety of roosts.

How are these protected microclimates created? Winter roosts can be sheltered when they occur in depressions, in steep-sided valleys, or on slopes in the lee of prevailing winds. Vegetation also can ameliorate harsh weather. Conifers provide a milder microclimate than do deciduous trees or snags. Often, eagles will select a combination of protected landforms and sheltered trees in order to obtain as much protection as possible. (22, 29, 48, 28)

Protection from wind may be the most important feature of a roost microclimate. This is particularly true in deciduous roosts or in roosts that are sheltered by landforms. High winds can increase the wind chill, and can also flush warm air from the roost, thereby lowering the air temperature. In coniferous roosts, wind, temperature, and thermal radiation all play an equal role in terms of energy savings for the roosting bird. Protection from rain and snow is less important; precipitation has a small effect on an eagle's energy loss. (53, 48)

Studies have shown that eagles conserve energy by roosting in protected habitat. If the energy costs of flight to and from a distant roost are not too high, an eagle can conserve about 5 percent of its daily energy budget by being protected from adverse weather. In one study, the cost of flight to and from a roost 4 kilometers away just equaled the energy that was saved by staying there throughout the night. The death of eagles as a result of severe weather seems uncommon, but cold stress does increase energy demand and the need for food. If food is readily available, the energy-stressed bird simply eats more, but if prey are difficult to obtain, cold stress as well as food stress can occur. Thus, eagles that save energy by roosting in mild microclimates need less food. (28, 47, 48)

FORAGING HABITAT

A foraging area is the most essential component of the habitat used by bald eagles. (49) Foraging areas must provide an adequate amount of food in a more or less consistent fashion, and they must have a minimal amount of disturbing human activities. Nesting, perching, and roosting trees in the vicinity will enhance the suitability of the foraging area (Fig. 10.5).

The most important element of foraging habitat is the presence of large open areas where prey can be killed and eaten. This includes lakes, rivers, oceans and their shorelines, beaches, gravel, sand and mud bars, and associated physiographic features. On occasion, open deserts, grasslands, and alpine or arctic tundra also serve as foraging sites. Eagles need open foraging areas because they are unable to fly through or become airborne in thick forest, and because they prefer a wide visual field while they are pursuing or eating prey.

The size of foraging habitat has not been measured, but it is assumed to encompass a very large region. Eagles will forage at least several kilometers from their nest. In winter, they will wander about from one foraging place to another, sometimes traveling thousands of kilometers.

These birds require a large amount of food, so prey must be abundant, especially in areas where eagles feed communally. But access to food is another concern; many environmental influences can alter the availability of prey. Ice covers lakes and rivers in winter, totally eliminating access to fish and causing waterfowl to migrate south. Flooding on rivers can wash away carcasses of fish, such as spent salmon. Shallow waters, on the other hand, may provide easy access to fish, and fish that swim near the surface or those stranded by low waters are most easily captured. Natural or human-caused catastrophes that create mass die-offs of potential prey animals are beneficial to eagles, at least temporarily. Dams provide open water below their spillways in winter, and fish sometimes are killed while passing through the turbines. They float downstream and are scavenged on by eagles. Fish kills, due to oxygen depletion, pollution, or other causes, can provide considerable forage at times. Even animals that have been killed by accident can serve as much-needed carrion for eagles. Disabled waterfowl, such as those that die from avian cholera or botulism, can be a feast for eagles. Foraging habitat, therefore, can be found in many different areas where prey or carrion are abundant, vulnerable, and accessible to eagles.

11

Reproduction and Survival

Wildlife biologists have spent considerable time and effort determining what factors influence the size of animal populations, particularly those that have economic importance to humans. Today researchers need to understand the population characteristics of endangered species if these animals are to be saved from extinction. The endangered bald eagle has been the subject of many population studies throughout its range, but the actual ecological mechanisms that regulate its numbers are still not fully understood.

The reproductive biology of the bald eagle is being studied in most states and some Canadian provinces. Nearly all population studies of bald eagles have focused on the rate of reproduction, or *natality;* there has been comparatively little research on the rate of death, or *mortality.* Thus, we have only half of the population picture for this species, and more research is urgently needed if we are to understand all of the variables that affect survival.

NATALITY

Assessing Reproduction The terminology used in discussing reproduction has been standardized, but breeding information is complex, confusing, and sometimes not comparable among studies. Before discussing reproductive patterns, it is necessary to define the terms used. (46) A *territory* is an area occupied by one mated pair of eagles during the breeding season; the eagles will nest within this area and defend it. Sometimes the terms "breeding site," "breeding area," and "breeding territory" are used instead of "territory." A pair may have more than one nest in the territory; the "alternate" nests will be close to the occupied nest. An *occupied nest* is one in which evidence indicates that a pair of eagles is present. Such evidence might include fresh nest material, droppings, feathers, or prey remains in or below the nest, or the birds themselves. An *active nest* is an occupied nest in which eggs have been laid or young are present, indicating that the mated pair are actively attempting to produce young. A *successful nest* is an active (and occupied) nest where young have been successfully raised and in which they have fledged or are expected to. Successful nests are also called "productive" nests, because young are produced there.

To determine the reproductive rate of a bald eagle population, a researcher will usually conduct two surveys during the breeding season. The first survey is often made by flying low over each nest in a light airplane or helicopter; the second survey is sometimes made by climbing to the nest. The first survey, taken during the egg-laying or early incubation period, determines the number of nests and territories present and the number of nests that are occupied or active. The second survey is made just before the young leave the nest. This survey determines the number of nests in which young were successfully produced and the number of young raised. Because this survey is done just before fledging, it is assumed that all young counted will leave the nest in good health.

This technique for assessing reproduction can be easily understood by examining Figure 11.1. The information presented is from a study in Washington in 1975. (24) The larger boxes contain the data collected from the two surveys; all values in the smaller boxes are calculated from figures in the larger boxes. Aerial surveys in April and May showed that 218 nests were present. Because of the clumped distribution of the nests, it was estimated that 144 territories existed. A simple calculation showed that each territory contained an average of 1.5 nests. This first survey also revealed that 114 of the nests were occupied by eagles. Therefore, 79 percent of all territories were occupied. Of these 114 occupied nests, 100 were active, which means that 88 percent of the mated pairs were attempting to reproduce. Thus, eggs were laid in only 69 percent of all territories. The second survey conducted in June showed that 63 nests had young present; thus, 63 of 100 (63 percent) active nests were successful. Because 37 pairs did not raise young, a 37 percent failure rate was recorded. An important index that is widely used is variously referred to as "percent nest success," "nest success," "success of occupied nests," and, in the diagram, "occupied nests successful." This was calculated as 55 percent. Only 44 percent of the territories were successful. Because 86 young were raised that year,

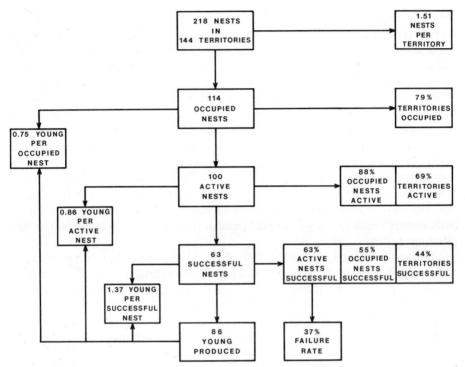

Fig. 11.1. Terminology used in reporting the reproductive patterns of nesting bald eagles. Information gathered during aerial surveys is contained in the larger boxes, which allow the calculation of the statistics contained in the smaller boxes. The values presented are actual data from a study in western Washington in 1975. (24)

1.37, 0.86, and 0.75 eaglets were produced in each successful, active, and occupied nest, respectively. The number of young in each successful nest also is the average brood size. The "reproductive rate" or "productivity" is the number of young raised in an occupied nest (0.75 in the example). Because it is the product of both nest success and brood size, "reproductive rate" is the most useful statistic for assessing the degree of breeding success. The number of young per active nest also is used, but less frequently.

Reproductive Patterns Formalized studies of the bald eagle did not begin until the 1920s, and reproductive patterns were little studied before the 1960s. Only two studies have given us detailed information regarding reproduction prior to the 1960s, and these were both done in Florida. Their results sparked the beginning of widespread work to evaluate reproductive rates. (8, 33)

It was in 1947 when Charles Broley first voiced concern that the national symbol was not reproducing itself at a rate to maintain a stable population.

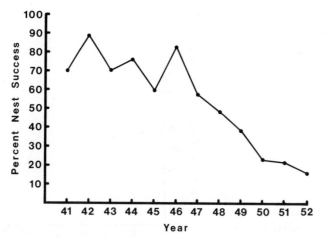

Fig. 11.2. Percent of nests that successfully produced young in a population in Florida from 1941 to 1952. (8)

His work, between 1941 and 1958, showed a dramatic drop in the ability of eagles to nest successfully (Fig. 11.2). From a high of 89 percent in 1942, nest success declined to only 14 percent in 1952; the most rapid drop occurred between 1946 and 1952. In 1958, Broley could find only three successful nests compared to his usual 125. (6, 7, 8) Broley was the first to observe the precipitous decline in reproduction and to correctly identify the reason. In 1958, he suggested that pesticides, particularly DDT, were responsible for the nest failures. His insight into this problem started a myriad of studies that eventually identified DDT and other pesticides as the culprits in the demise of many birds of prey. But Broley was not a biologist by training, and his work had to be verified by a specialist. Joseph Howell, a professor of zoology, also was studying the reproduction of eagles in Florida, even before Broley. His surveys, which started in 1935 and continued at five-year intervals, confirmed what was suspected. Astounding drops in nest occupancy started in the early 1950s and continued into the 1970s (Fig. 11.3). (33)

It was not until 1960 that a widespread effort was launched to determine the reproductive rates of bald eagles. Alexander Sprunt IV, a research biologist with the Audubon Society, became the leader of the Continental Bald Eagle Research Project. During the 1960s, Project researchers surveyed thousands of nests. Sprunt's findings in the early 1960s again depicted a poor level of reproduction. (58, 59, 60) The culmination of this effort showed that some populations were reproducing at a reasonable rate whereas many were not (Fig. 11.4). Those nests on the fringes of the Great Lakes, in Maine, and in Michigan were not faring well.

From the early 1960s to the Year of the Eagle in 1982, population statistics have been gathered in many areas. In ten populations that have

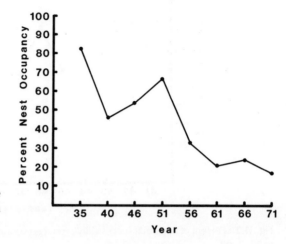

Fig. 11.3. Percent of nests that were occupied in a population in Florida from 1935 to 1971. (33)

been intensively studied, the trend from the 1960s and 1970s to the early 1980s is clear (Figs. 11.5, 11.6, 11.7, 11.8). Most populations continued to falter, or at best remained at status quo, until the early 1970s. Thereafter, nest success and productivity increased, sometimes dramatically, sometimes slowly, into the 1980s. Surprising to many, the last decade before the national bird's two hundredth birthday was one of cautious optimism, as the species finally reversed its long downward trend in reproduction. (47)

Although the general trend is toward improvement, some populations are still reproducing at marginal or poor levels. The populations in Wisconsin and Minnesota have reproduced well, but in neighboring Michigan,

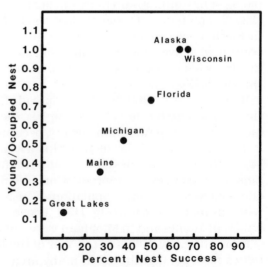

Fig. 11.4. Percent nest success and number of young produced in six populations in the early 1960s. (61) Compare to Figure 11.9.

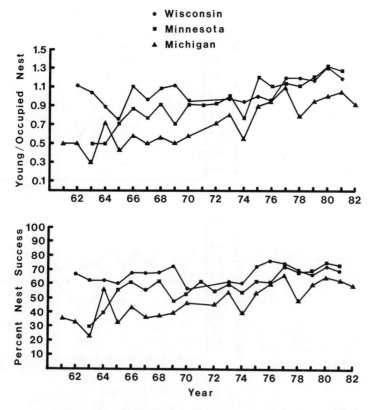

Fig. 11.5. Young produced per occupied nest (above) and percent of successful nests (below) in Wisconsin, Minnesota, and Michigan. (38, 61, 39, 48)

rates are lower, though an upward trend is evident (Fig. 11.5). In central Canada, a Saskatchewan population has enjoyed impressively high success and productivity in the past decades, but in Ontario, production and success have lagged behind (Fig. 11.6). In Florida, a gradual improvement is apparent, and in the Chesapeake Bay area and the state of Maine, major increases have been made from staggering lows in the 1960s and early 1970s (Fig. 11.7). Nest success and productivity have increased in Washington, but in Yellowstone National Park the trend is less certain (Fig. 11.8). In 1975, no known nests produced any eaglets in the park. Overall, bald eagles enjoyed improved breeding success during the 1970s and early 1980s throughout North America (Table C, Appendix 1). Compared to success and reproductive rates for the 1960s (Fig. 11.4), these more recent studies show substantial improvements, though there still are problem areas (Fig. 11.9).

Alaska is regarded as an area where bald eagles have been reproducing free from human influence since the eagle bounty was eliminated in 1952.

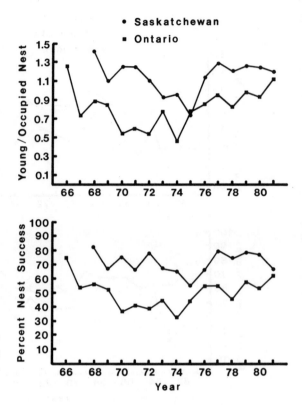

Fig. 11.6 Young produced per occupied nest (above) and percent of successful nests (below) in Saskatchewan and Ontario. (18, 23)

Reproduction has always been high in Alaska. But during 1979, 1980, and 1981, the activity of nests dropped from an average of 34 percent to 20 percent. It is thought, but not known with certainty, that the Alaskan population is now so high that not enough resources are available to allow the population to expand. (27, 31) After fifty years of bounty killings (about 150,000 killed; see Chapter 12), it is thought that the population has returned to near its historic number.

By analyzing the data in Table C, Appendix 1, and calculating it according to the technique outlined in Figure 11.1, the status of the entire bald eagle population in North America in the 1970s and early 1980s can be estimated.

Figure 11.10 shows the status of thousands of territories. Overall, a large number are not used every year. This low occupancy rate could suggest that many populations are so low that not all available breeding areas are filled. It could also mean that many old territories are no longer suitable for breeding and are now abandoned. On the average, a territory will have eagles there attempting to breed two out of every three years. (11)

Figure 11.11 provides specific information on nests. Eighty-nine percent of all eagle pairs at a nest attempt to breed, but only 58 percent successfully raise young; 11 percent do not lay eggs. At nests where they do lay

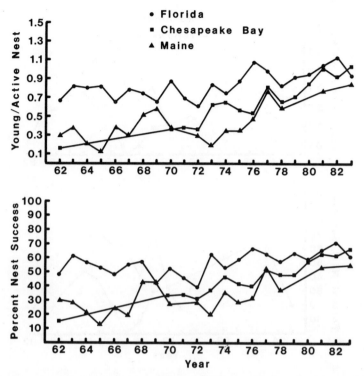

Fig. 11.7. Young produced per active nest (above) and percent of successful nests (below) in Florida, Chesapeake Bay in Maryland, Delaware, Virginia, and Maine. (44, 61, 1, 13, 65) For Maine (1962–70) and Florida (1962–72) values are for occupied nests.

eggs, only 62 percent are successful. Thus, there is an overall 38 percent failure rate for those trying to reproduce.

Figure 11.12 presents the number of young produced by the bald eagle population during the same period. There was an average of between 0.92 and 1.61 young raised for every nest, depending on the nest status. (This later statistic is the brood size discussed in Chapter 5.)

Of nearly four thousand occupied nests surveyed in the 1960s and 1970s in North America, there was a nearly equal chance of an occupied nest being barren or productive, and of successful nests, there was nearly the same chance that either one or two eaglets would be raised, but rarely three (Fig. 11.13).

Factors Affecting Reproduction Between the mid-1940s and mid-1970s, a dramatic depression in eagle nesting success and production occurred. It is no coincidence that this was the period of heavy use of the insecticide DDT. From the end of World War II until 1972 when its use was banned, DDT was widely used throughout North America to control in-

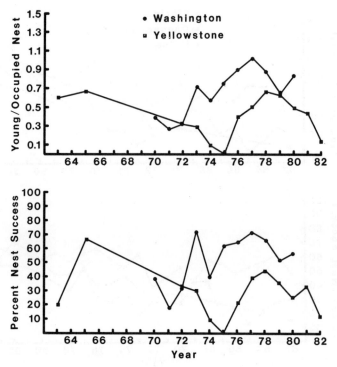

Fig. 11.8. Young produced per occupied nest (above) and percent of successful nests (below) in Washington State and Yellowstone National Park in Wyoming. (43, 2, 64) For Washington (1970–75) values were reduced 3.5 percent to convert from active to occupied nest status.

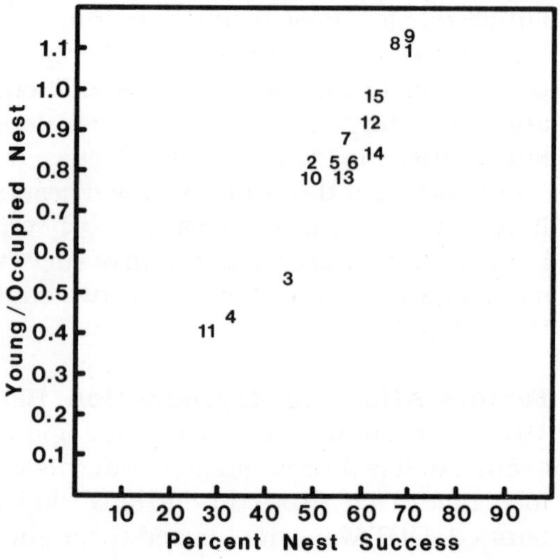

Fig. 11.9. Percent nest success and number of young produced in fifteen populations in the 1970s and early 1980s (see Table C, Appendix 1, for locations and other statistics). Compare to Figure 11.4.

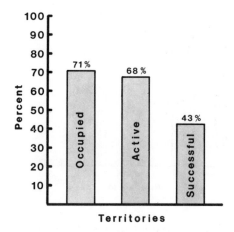

Fig. 11.10. Overall percent of occupied, active, and successful territories throughout North America in the 1970s and early 1980s. Data for occupancy are from seven studies and 2,610 nests; for activity, seven studies and 3,372 nests; for success, eight studies and 3,443 nests (see Table C, Appendix 1).

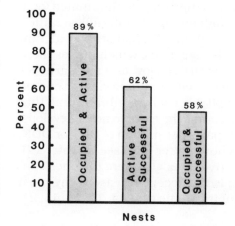

Fig. 11.11. Overall percent of nests occupied and active, active and successful, and occupied and successful throughout North America in the 1970s and early 1980s. Data for occupancy and activity are from six studies and 1,552 nests; for activity and success, nine studies and 3,459 nests; for occupancy and success, fifteen studies and 8,276 nests (see Table C, Appendix 1).

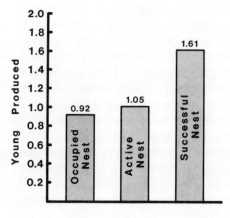

Fig. 11.12. Overall number of young produced per occupied, active, and successful nests throughout North America in the 1970s and early 1980s. Data for occupancy are from fifteen studies and 8,276 nests; for activity, twelve studies and 5,452 nests; for success, seventeen studies and 8,853 nests (see Table C, Appendix 1).

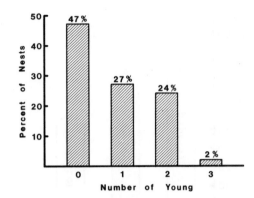

Fig. 11.13 Percent and number of young at 3,893 occupied nests throughout North America in the 1960s and 1970s. (16, 18, 20, 24, 40, 53, 54, 57, 61, 64, 65, 66)

sects. Since it was banned, reproductive levels of eagles have been steadily climbing. (23)

Much has been written on the effects of DDT on eagle reproduction. Although some eagles have died because of ingesting contaminated food, levels of DDT in prey are not normally high enough to kill eagles; rather, they impair reproduction. DDT, or its metabolite DDE, disrupts calcium metabolism, resulting in a thinning of the eggshells, which makes them susceptible to breakage. Levels of DDT or DDE as low as a few parts per million may cause thinning. Sometimes, if contamination is severe, no eggshells are formed at all. Instead, the pliable shell membrane is all that holds the inner contents in place, and of course the embryo never develops. When eggs contain more than 15 to 20 parts per million of DDT or DDE, many shells break, and reproductive efforts falter (also see Chapter 12). Those populations with poor reproductive rates also were the ones contaminated with DDE (Fig. 11.14). This is the accepted reason why most bald eagles have had difficulty reproducing in the past. (4, 12, 14, 15, 21, 23, 35, 36, 37, 42, 49, 51, 62)

There are many other causes of nest failure and reduced production, though none compare to the effects of pesticides. Of 1,136 occupied nests surveyed in Florida from 1941 to 1951, 476 failed. Eggs did not hatch in 31 percent of these failed nests and adults did not attempt to breed in 20 percent. (9) Thirteen percent of these nests were taken over by great horned owls before eagles could reoccupy them the following year. Hurricanes and spring storms were responsible for the loss of 11 percent of nests or entire nest trees. (6) Other reasons for failures include desertion of territories, cutting of nest trees, disturbance to the nest, killing of eggs, young, or adults, and many unaccounted mishaps. (9) Raccoons, bobcats, magpies, crows, and gulls prey on eggs and some of these kill eaglets. (17, 30) Black bears have been observed raiding eagle nests. (41) In the San Juan Islands in Washington, a disease reduced the number of raccoons, and during subsequent years, the nesting success of bald eagles greatly increased. (43) As strange as it sounds, eagles are occasionally killed by lightning while on their nests. (6, 9, 32) Nestlings can die from a lack of food, fighting with nestmates, falling from the nest, hypothermia and hyperthermia, and poisoning. (37, 16, 69) Some have succumbed from being impaled on fishhooks brought to the nest while still attached to fish. When especially frightened, nestlings can even die of "shock syndrome." (16)

Rates of egg and nestling survival were studied in many areas in the 1960s and 1970s. Of 451 eggs surveyed in six studies at various locations, an average of 75 percent (from 62 to 87 percent) successfully hatched and 25 percent (from 13 to 38 percent) died. (11, 18, 26, 29, 30, 54, 57) Once hatched, the nestling has a better chance of survival. Of 433 nestlings surveyed, an average of 85 percent (76 to 88 percent) survived and eventually fledged from the nest; a 15 percent (12 to 24 percent) mortality rate was recorded. (16, 28, 30, 54, 57, 67) But in a study in Alaska in the 1980s, only two of forty-eight nestlings survived. At nests where food was provided by researchers, four of twelve were able to survive. (27)

The chances of a nest failing are greater during the early stages of breeding. Of fifty-two unsuccessful nests in Minnesota, 52 percent failed before eggs were laid, 37 percent failed during the incubation process, and only 11 percent failed while nestlings were present. (16) As an eagle embryo or nestling grows older, and as the adults "invest" more time and energy into the breeding effort, there is a greater probability that the nest will successfully produce young.

MORTALITY

Causes of Death   It is difficult to discuss mortality of bald eagles without implicating human activities (also see Chapter 12). Without question, the

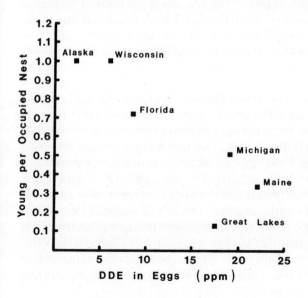

Fig. 11.14. Relationship between the number of young produced at occupied nests and the amount of DDE, a metabolite of DDT, found in eggshells in six populations in the 1960s. (37, 61)

leading cause of death continues to be indiscriminate killing, usually by shooting, by irresponsible persons (Table 11.1). As many as five hundred eagles die because of humans each year. (5) In some areas, over 50 percent of the fledgling birds are shot every year. (52) During 1982, three hundred birds were killed by a group of professional eagle killers. (55) Most eagles are killed by stockmen, especially sheep ranchers who believe that eagles kill lambs, by Native Americans for the profit of selling feathers and parts to other Indians, and by irresponsible hunters who either misidentify eagles or kill them for sport. Of ninety-two bald eagles in captivity in 1975, forty-one (44 percent) were injured because of humans, and at least thirty-one (36 percent) were shot. (56) Of two hundred eagles admitted to a rehabilitation center, 76 percent had traumatic injuries due to shooting, trapping, collisions, and other human-related accidents. (50) In addition, at least 128,273 bald eagles were shot or killed between 1917 and 1952 in Alaska because a bounty was paid for them. (54)

Injuries or deaths caused by impacts and collisions with such obstacles as cars, airplanes, towers, and power lines account for a large number of eagle fatalities each year (Table 11.1). Poisoning also is an important cause of death. Most poisoning deaths are due to indiscriminate use of contaminated carrion for controlling coyotes, the use of pesticides to control insects, and industrial pollution. Electrocution still causes many deaths. When precautions are not taken while constructing power lines and poles, eagles that perch on or near them may be electrocuted. Accidental trapping with leg traps is a problem, and birds can be drowned while being held underwater in one. Surprisingly, emaciation, which results from starvation, accounts for few deaths, but many birds that are weakened by a lack of food probably fall victim to disease or illness. (63) Fights with other eagles can be injurious or fatal. (49) The list of incidental diseases, infections, and other causes of death reads like a file from the *New England Journal of Medicine* (Table 11.1). It is a sobering thought that approximately 80 percent of all known eagle deaths are related to humans (also see Chapter 12).

Survival Rates We know little about the survival rates of bald eagles, and any new information that is obtained seems to cast doubt on previous studies. This is no surprise, because determining how well a cohort of a population is surviving is a difficult task. Two methods generally are used to determine survival rates. First, we can obtain a minimum estimate of survival by banding or color-marking known-age eagles and then recovering the banded birds or resighting the ones that were color-marked. The second method entails counting the number of eagles in each age group and assuming that the death rate of each age group equals the birth or "recruitment" rate. If the number of eagles in each age class remains the same over many years, the mortality rate should be about the same as the percent of birds in each class. Estimating survivorship by collecting

Table 11.1. Probable causes of bald eagle deaths from 1960 to 1977 based on 374 autopsies. (4, 14, 15, 35, 42, 49)

Cause of death	Number	Percent
Shooting	161	43.0
Impact injury	54	14.4
Poisoning*	47	12.6
Electrocution	29	7.8
Trapping injury	12	3.2
Drowning	12	3.2
Emaciation	7	1.9
Pneumonia	7	1.9
Coccidiosis	7	1.9
Bacterial infection	5	1.3
Puncture or laceration injury	4	1.1
Intestine impaction	4	1.1
Nephrosis	4	1.1
Aspiration, asphyxiation, choking	3	0.8
Avian cholera	3	0.8
Peritonitis	3	0.8
Aspergillosis	2	0.5
Septicemia	2	0.5
Enteritis	2	0.5
Hepatic necrosis	1	0.3
Arteriosclerosis	1	0.3
Gout	1	0.3
Myocardial infarction	1	0.3
Hemorrhage	1	0.3
Euthanasia	1	0.3
Total	374	100.0

*Poisoning by dieldrin, 21; lead, 10; thallium, 9; strychnine, 3; endrin, 2; cyanide, 1; and DDE, 1.

carcasses is not possible, because most eagle remains are never found, are quickly eaten by scavengers, or rapidly decompose.

The survival rates of eggs and nestlings have already been discussed, but what happens after the young leave the nest? The first year of life is a difficult one. Survival of juvenile eagles is the lowest of any stage in their life history, undoubtedly because they must fend on their own for the first time. Studies of 165 banded or color-marked nestlings showed that only 28.5 percent were alive less than a year after fledging. (10, 19) Two years later only 14.5 percent were alive, and after three years, a mere 9.1 percent of the original 165 were still alive. Another study estimated that only 10.7 percent survive to about three years of age. Overall, less than 10 percent of the newly hatched eaglets will reach adulthood. (57) Yet another study, involving 107 banded eagles, found that almost 100 percent died before reaching sexual maturity; 78.5 percent succumbed during their first year of life. (10) Because these study methods are imperfect, these survival rates probably underestimate the actual survival ability of young eagles.

Information on fledglings that have been released (hacked) in New York State to reestablish a population there is more encouraging. Of 81 young birds released, at least 50 percent survived to adulthood. (45) Once an eagle has survived the first critical year or two of life, its chances for continued life improve, and by the time it reaches adulthood, it has even better prospects for staying alive. (57) But only a few percent of all eagle eggs will ever produce an adult bird capable of continuing the cycle of reproduction.

POPULATION REGULATION

What Regulates An Eagle Population?   There are two key points to consider when trying to determine how an eagle population is regulated. First, the environment must be able to provide for the many needs of eagles before a population can exist, and second, there is an upper limit on the number of eagles that can inhabit a particular area. It is not enough that only a few of their living requirements are available; eagles need many resources from the environment in order to survive and reproduce. Food is particularly important, especially when young are being raised or when winter cold or long migrations increase the need for energy. Eagles require special habitat for nesting, perching, and roosting. A vacant area that is secure and undisturbed is needed for a nesting territory. And once an eagle population is well established in a region, only a certain number, the "carrying capacity," can exist. This upper population limit can be controlled by numerous factors and may be influenced by the density of the population and other extrinsic conditions. These extrinsic factors, such as harsh weather and killing by humans, occur regardless of the number of eagles in the population: their effects are "density-independent." When eagles are numerous, competition for essential resources can occur. This "density-dependent" regulation can happen when eagles are so abundant as to influence one another and compete for limited resources such as food or nesting territories. As previously discussed, this could now be happening in Alaska because of the large number of bald eagles found there. Those pairs not able to find and defend a territory must wait for an opportunity to acquire one at a later time. And if they are lucky enough to reach reproductive age, find a territory, and begin breeding, it will take many years, perhaps a decade or more, to replace themselves with young that will eventually reproduce themselves.

Eagle biologists are now trying to understand why populations increase or decrease and how populations can be manipulated so that eagles will increase in number and expand their range (also see Chapter 13). Despite their slow level of reproduction, it is imperative that the brood stock be maintained. Thus, it is best to concentrate efforts on increasing survivorship rather than on increasing reproduction. (22, 70) This may seem contrary to common sense, especially because most management efforts have been directed at improving reproduction. And it is not to belittle the

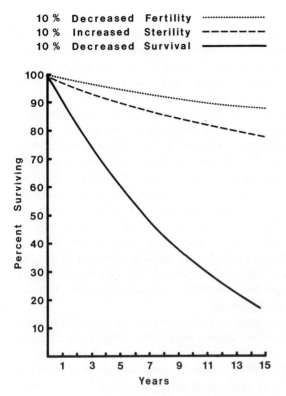

10 % Decreased Fertility ·······················
10 % Increased Sterility — — — — — —
10 % Decreased Survival —————————

Fig. 11.15. Survivorship curves, based on computer simulation, of a hypothetical bald eagle population after 10 percent changes in fertility, sterility, and survival. (70)

need for maintaining adequate breeding, but production of new eagles is secondary to the need for keeping alive those already in the population.

When a hypothetical population of bald eagles is altered by a 10 percent change in fertility, sterility, and survival, the effects are considerably different (Fig. 11.15). (70) A simulation model predicts that reduction in survival will have the most profound influence. In fact, a population may be reproducing at the maximum rate, but if the survival of full-grown birds is poor, the population can rapidly become extinct! (22) It is for this reason that killing of bald eagles, especially the adults, has a much more dramatic impact than does disruption of nesting efforts.

Strategies for Reproducing and Surviving   When we think of an eagle population, we must consider its genetic framework and evolutionary past if we are to appreciate why it behaves as it does. If, through millions of years of struggle in the face of environmental changes, the bald eagle is still present, then some clever "strategies" for reproduction and survival must have developed. We can only speculate on what conditions shaped the life-style that we observe today, but some aspects are clear.

The life history strategy of the bald eagle is one of long-term survival, with reproductive efforts occurring only when conditions are favorable for raising young. Eagles take many years to reach reproductive age, they do not always breed every year, and, even if successful, they raise few young. Because of their low and slow rate of reproduction and their long life span, population fluctuations are dampened; if something upsets the reproductive rate, such as DDT poisoning, the population declines at a slow rate. By the same reasoning, recovery also is slow. Eagles "strive" for reproductive quality rather than quantity. They produce only a few young that have a reasonable chance for survival instead of flooding the environment with eaglets that have only minimal chances for living. To reduce competition, eagles partition their habitat into territories during the breeding season, but in winter they become gregarious. By socializing in large groups, eagles may enjoy improved survivorship. They acquire food more easily by associating with fellow birds even though they are quite adept at scavenging and killing on their own. They also are adept at conserving energy by several means. One very special benefit is learning. When a species such as the bald eagle lives so long, it accumulates a storehouse of information that helps it survive and reproduce. Other short-lived species must rely more on instinct. The bald eagle has, through evolutionary time, become a smart, efficient, and masterful animal.

But it is apparent that these strategies and others are not enough in view of the overwhelming influence of man's activities. Populations have steadily declined since civilization reached North America. Even if eagles and their habitats are completely protected, their numbers will never again reach historic levels. There still exists some potential for increases in many populations, but competition and crowding by humans will set an upper limit on the eagle population. As will be seen in the next two chapters, man is responsible for the demise of many populations, but human activities also are the means by which eagles will be protected and encouraged to expand in number.

Plate 1. Bald eagles are more appropriately called "white-headed sea eagles."
(Buck Miller)

Plate 2. Eagles will hunt and kill many types of prey animals, but fish is the favorite diet. (Jim Simmon)

Plate 3. In winter, bald eagles feed together in large groups. The adult on the left is defending its food from other eagles. (Mark McCollough)

Plate 5. Researchers visit many nests each year to evaluate reproduction, food habits, and many other aspects of the eagle's natural history. (M. Alan Jenkins/USFWS)

Plate 4. Bald eagles have the largest nests of any bird in North America. Here, a parent guards its nest and young. (M. Alan Jenkins/USFWS)

Plate 6. A hatchling bald eaglet, one to two weeks old, has a light gray covering of primary down. (Richard Knight)

Plate 7. A nestling bald eaglet, three to four weeks old, is begging for food. Its secondary down coat is dark gray. (Richard Frenzel)

Plate 8. In the "transition" stage, the nestling starts to develop the black juvenile plumage that will replace its down feathers. These two eaglets are four to six weeks old. (Teryl G. Grubb)

Plate 9. The juvenile plumage (Plumage A) is well developed on this eight- to ten-week-old eaglet. Colored wing markers and a leg band will enable researchers to study its movements and health after it leaves the nest. (Richard Frenzel)

Plate 11. A subadult bald eagle (Plumage C) feeds in the company of ravens. (Mark McCollough)

Plate 13. Food is easier to find in winter when bald eagles live in groups. A subadult on the right (Plumage E) is starting to develop the adult plumage. (Mark McCollough)

Plate 10. Bald eagles in their first year of life (Plumage B) can soar more easily than adults because their wings are wider. (Kent Keller)

Plate 12. A subadult bald eagle (Plumage D) vies with an adult for a favorite perch. (Buck Miller)

Plate 14. A winter communal perching area on the Chilkat River Bald Eagle Preserve in Alaska. Eagles in all stages of plumage development (Plumages A, B, C, D, E, and Adult) are present. (Art Wolfe)

Plate 15. Most bald eagles in the contiguous United States die because of some type of human interference. This adult was electrocuted while perching on a power pole. (Kent Keller)

Plate 16. Only with a strong commitment and special care can we ensure that the bald eagle does not fall into the irreversible state of extinction. (Mark McCollough)

Interactions with Humans

Bald eagles were present before the human species evolved and long before human travelers reached the North American continent. Fossil remains of ancient sea eagles date back some 25 million years, long before the appearance of the first human beings. It was only about 50,000 years ago that humans arrived in the New World. Their journey to North America, across the intermittently passable land bridge between Alaska and Siberia, was the start of a long association with the bald eagle. It was, however, only after Europeans began arriving in North America a few hundred years ago that serious conflicts between bald eagles and man developed.

HISTORIC ASSOCIATION

Unlike the whites, Indians lived in close kinship with all animals. When compelled to kill for subsistence, they gave thanks to nature after taking the life of an animal. They also performed rituals in apology and propitiation to nature. Ceremonies also were held to worship certain animals, and some dances imitated certain creatures that were held in high respect. By performing rituals, or by killing or outwitting animals, Indians believed that they could draw the creatures' spiritual essence into themselves and enhance their own inner power of life. (56)

Among the many birds held in superstitious, religious, and appreciative regard by Native Americans was the eagle. By reason of its majestic, solitary, and mysterious nature, it was an object of worship by many Indian tribes, who admired its courage and envied its strength. The great height to which it flew gave evidence that it could reach heaven, and its plumes were said to carry prayers. The eagle became a symbol for clans and religious fraternities in nearly every tribe in North America at some period in history. The mythology of almost every tribe is replete with eagle beings, and the widespread thunderbird myths relate in some cases to the eagle. (22, 24)

Indians used parts of eagles for many purposes. Wing bones were often employed as sucking tubes with which medicine men attempted to remove disease, as whistles carried by warriors, or as adornments in ceremonies. (22) Eagle talons were donned as amulets and, supposedly, protected the bearer from evil spirits or injury. Feathers were, however, the most prized portion of the eagle. Indians wore them in their hair, on their bonnets, or on shirts, shields, lances, or other possessions. The wearing or display of feathers symbolized exceptional deeds of valor called "coups." With each coup, the Indian could wear another feather. (59) Other applications, to name a few, included the use of fans made of wing feathers for ceremonies and to conjure spirits, the sprinkling of down feathers in various rituals, and feather display for purposes of prestige, recognition, or charms. (22, 49)

Indians acquired eagles and their feathers by several means. Hunting them with their crude weapons undoubtedly was difficult. Often, Indians raided nests, killed the eaglets, and took their feathers. Some southwestern tribes kept live eagles for their feathers; in this way, their supply was constantly replenished. The best known and most dramatic method was to catch an eagle with the bare hands. An Indian claiming to possess secret power would dig a pit to hide in, cover the top, and place a piece of meat as bait on the roof. When the eagle swooped down to take the bait, the brave would quickly reach through the roof, grasp the eagle by its feet, pull it into the pit, and wring its neck. (9) Catching and killing eagles by this method was more than a way of obtaining feathers; it was also believed to be a means of acquiring the power contained in the spirit of the bird. This technique was used by the Plains Indians, and golden eagles were the most common victim. But another technique was specifically designed to kill bald eagles, particularly along the Pacific Northwest coast. A Bella Coola Indian would hide in a blind near a river. When an eagle came down to a bait of dead salmon, the Indian would extend a pole with a cord of nettle fiber attached and try to snare the bird by the neck. If he was successful, he would pull the hapless bird into the blind and wring its neck (Fig. 12.1). (49)

It is unlikely that we will ever fully understand the ecological relationship of eagles and American Indians. The association was not beneficial to eagles, but it is impossible to say if ancient Native Americans had any appreciable effect on eagle numbers. The killing of eagles was a common practice; in some middens of Indian villages, eagle bones are exceptionally abundant and are sometimes the most common fossil remains. (34) It may

Fig. 12.1. Ancient technique used by the Bella Coola Indians in the Pacific Northwest to snare bald eagles. (49)

be that feathers of golden eagles, especially tails of the young birds, were prized more highly than those of bald eagles. Nevertheless, both species were frequently killed by the ancient civilizations in North America.

Eagles are still admired by the contemporary Indian, but laws now prohibit killings as practiced by past cultures. Indians are exempted from the law prohibiting the possession of eagle parts, though a special permit is required. In fact, the federal government maintains a nationwide supply of dead eagles and feathers, which are distributed to those who use eagle parts in religious ceremonies. Some Native Americans are still responsible for the deaths of many eagles each year. In fact, federal courts have debated the legality of eagle killing by Indians as recently as 1986. Most birds are sold on the black market to other Indians who use the feathers and parts to adorn costumes and other ceremonial garb. Although Indians still kill eagles today, white men have been a much greater cause of destruction to the bald eagle and its habitat.

RECENT INTERACTIONS

The early Europeans brought with them an attitude toward nature much unlike that of the American Indian. These newcomers considered the natural world as a threat, but recognized its wealth of natural resources waiting to be exploited. Perhaps out of fear, disregard, indifference, greed, or even contempt, they wantonly destroyed wildlife to benefit themselves. Some white men view the bald eagle with high esteem, as most past cultures had, but because other whites regard this bird as a verminous menace to their own interests, they have recklessly persecuted it. Only recently, late in this century, have the tides turned in favor of the eagle. Renewed interest in their fate has forced us to reexamine our attitudes and reassess the many ways in which civilization threatens the existence of the eagle. Many Americans are now sympathetic to the plight of the eagle, but much of the damage done during the early colonization and settlement of North America can never be repaired.

The actual number and distribution of eagles prior to the arrival of white men will never be known, but eagles probably were once widespread thoughout the continent. The few historic records available indicate that bald eagles formerly nested in at least forty-five of the forty-eight contiguous states. As of 1982, however, occupied nests were known in only thirty-one states, and about 90 percent of these were in just ten states. Thirty-one states have fewer than ten nesting pairs or have lost their entire nesting population (also see Chapter 4). (14, 17)

The reasons for the eagle's demise are both circumstantial and implicative. There has been a gradual reduction in the eagle's breeding range and nesting success along with a loss of habitat, reduction of prey populations, and disturbances by humans, but direct links between these causes and effects are often difficult to show. In contrast, many activities of man have had an unequivocal impact. Direct and indirect killings, poisoning, and destruction of nest trees have been widely documented as having immediate adverse effects. In general, there have been and continue to be five major causes of the decrease in the eagle population: (1) killings, (2) poisoning, (3) habitat destruction and alteration, (4) prey base changes, and (5) disturbance by humans.

Killings Human-related killing is the most common source of mortality for bald eagles today. Four causes of death—*shooting, electrocution, trapping,* and *collisions*—account for about two-thirds of all deaths reported (see Table 11.1).

The first documented massive eagle shootings took place in Alaska. The magnitude of the killings that occurred during the Alaskan eagle bounty, from 1917 to 1952, is difficult to comprehend. Over 128,000 birds, or their talons, were turned in to officials for bounty payment. (42) Compare this number to the current estimated eagle population of North America, which is 70,000 to 80,000; to the wintering population of the forty-eight contiguous states, which is 13,000 birds; and to the scant 1,400 nesting pairs left in the contiguous states. Furthermore, we will never know how many eagles were shot, crippled, and never retrieved. Eagles are difficult to kill because of their size, and a wounded bird might easily elude its hunter. Thousands of deaths may have gone unreported. A more reasonable estimate of the death toll is closer to 150,000. (28)

The war on eagles in Alaska was not the only battle; skirmishes also raged in the lower states. In the 1930s, sheep ranchers in California shot hundreds of eagles each winter. Though the intended quarry was the golden eagle in most circumstances, many of those shot were bald eagles. (8) Throughout the 1940s, ranchers in Texas also hunted the eagle, often with dramatic "success." One eagle hunter proudly reported a daily tally of twenty-eight birds and, in one year, is said to have killed over a thousand, mostly golden eagles. His stated lifetime total was twelve thousand eagles. (30) One can only guess at how many eagles were killed in secret by the many other professional eagle hunters. One reason why these hunts were so devastating is because eagles were chased and shot from airplanes.

In 1970, a systematic effort to exterminate eagles on several Wyoming ranches was instigated by livestock owners. Both bald and golden eagles were indiscriminately killed with shotguns from helicopters and, on some days, thirty to forty birds were shot by one gunner. Although the precise number of deaths will never be known, some records were kept because the pilot and gunner each received a $25 fee for each eagle killed. A total of 770 birds are known to have been killed; the actual figure probably is higher. (30)

In 1975, 1976, and 1977, several sheep ranchers in Texas shot an estimated seventy-five eagles during helicopter hunts; several of these were bald eagles. (45) These killings occurred because ranchers thought the birds were killing lambs, but this was not true of the bald eagle.

Now a new affliction has brought trying times to the eagle. Today more than ever, eagles are being shot for parts and feathers, which are sold or traded on the black market. Indians as well as whites are harvesting valuable eagle feathers at the cost of the birds' lives. In 1981, twenty-two people were indicted for eagle killings in Washington State. (3, 37) At least fifty-seven birds were killed and their parts sold to undercover agents working for the U.S. Fish and Wildlife Service. Feathers and parts can bring astounding prices on the black market. A whole carcass costs up to $1,000, an eagle tail-feather fan sells for $500, the talons and wings cost $200, and individual feathers bring about $25. A war bonnet adorned with many tail feathers costs over $5,000. The incentive for killing is certainly great, but the costs also are high. One five-year sentence was handed down, another eagle killer received two years, and several other sentences ranged from six months to one year in jail.

Also in the early 1980s, two to three hundred bald eagles were killed in South Dakota by shooting and trapping. (1) These eagles also were killed for profit, their feathers and parts collected for ceremonial use by Native Americans. An undercover scam, known as "operation eagle," revealed the inner workings of a widespread conspiracy to kill eagles and market their parts. The operation, conducted by the U.S. Fish and Wildlife Service, culminated with the arrest and indictment of over fifty people.

Some eagles continue to be shot one at a time by many irresponsible people. It seems that every month another incident is reported. Despite public outcry, shootings continue to this day and, if the past is any lesson, they will continue in the future. It is estimated that up to five hundred bald eagles die as a result of direct human intervention every year. (5)

Indirect killing of eagles also is a source of mortality. Eagles can be killed by *electrocution* while perching on high-voltage power poles. Electrocution occurs when an eagle's wings are spread so far that the bird touches a power source and a ground at the same time. If this happens, a current passes through its body and it is instantly killed. Power lines are more dangerous when the eagle's plumage is wet. When electrocution occurs, the cause of death is unmistakable; the bird falls directly below the power pole and usually is scorched on part of its body.

Although golden eagles are killed more frequently in this manner, electrocution of bald eagles continues to occur. On Amchitka Island in Alaska, for example, as many as five dead bald eagles were found under one pole. (47) Today, special precautions are being taken to alleviate this problem, at least in some areas.

Inadvertent *capturing* of eagles in animal traps has caused many deaths. Leg-hold jaw traps, usually set for coyotes, fur bearers, or other mammals, can severely injure an eagle or detain it until it dies. Many eagles survive such trappings, but some lose a leg in the process or are crippled in some way so that they cannot fend for themselves in the wild.

Eagles come to traps for one of two reasons: first, to feed on the bait set for other animals, or second, less commonly, to prey on an animal that has already been caught in the trap. If other traps are nearby, the eagle, too, may be snared.

It is difficult to assess the magnitude of this problem, but it is probably larger than most people realize. Between 1972 and 1976 on the Kenai National Wildlife Refuge in Alaska, an average of 6.5 bald eagles were inadvertently caught in traps each year; 20 percent of them were injured. (4) In one winter, several hundred eagles were accidentally trapped in Nevada, though most were golden eagles. (44) In another study, only twenty-one of fifty-two eagles, both bald and golden, caught in steel traps survived, though most lost one or more toes; the remaining thirty-one died or were so badly crippled that they had to be put to sleep. (41)

Impact injuries, usually caused by *collisions* with man-made objects, also account for deaths. Eagles have been killed or severely injured by flying into towers, buildings, power lines, vehicles, and other obstructions. The eagle's eyesight is keen enough so that it can avert many collisions, but accidents still befall even the most cautious and experienced birds. Solving this problem, as might be expected, is exceedingly difficult, and collisions undoubtedly will continue.

Poisoning Poisoning of eagles is a recent problem that developed after man started using chemicals for a variety of purposes. This new "chemical age" brought about many benefits to man, but birds of prey suffered immensely. Poisoning is the main reason why bald eagle reproduction declined in the mid-1900s (see Chapter 11), and it is a widespread problem. Americans use many types of chemicals from a number of sources, and they can have myriad effects on the eagle during any stage in its life history.

There are two major forms of poisoning. First, eagles can ingest poisons that are placed in bait and meant for other animals, or, second, they can acquire poisons in the form of pollutants or contamination from the environment. The first type of poisoning is fast, and the results are dramatic, whereas the second type occurs gradually and the effects are subtle.

Poisoned bait has been used to kill nuisance animals, particularly coyotes, but such predator-control programs also have killed eagles. In 1971, fifty bald and golden eagles were poisoned to death during an effort by several Wyoming ranchers to eradicate coyotes that were feeding on lambs. (30) This was but one of numerous incidents in which eagles have died from eating poisoned bait meant for other animals. The problem with these programs is that indiscriminate killing occurs; any scavenger that takes the bait is affected. These non-target species, as they are called, suffer a most terrifying death.

The poison used in Wyoming was *thallium sulfate*. Developed as a poison for rodents, thallium sulfate damages the heart, liver, kidneys, and lungs, and causes massive hemorrhaging in the digestive tract. During the several days before death occurs, the victim experiences paralysis, blindness, deafness, muscular pains, and brain damage. (30) Other widely used predator poisons include *strychnine* and *cyanide*, both of which have been implicated in the deaths of eagles. In recent years, use of poisoned bait has been restricted, but it seems likely that this problem will continue as long as predator-control methods do not take adequate precautions to prevent the deaths of non-target species.

The number of poisonings from baited carcasses has been small compared to the effects of widespread environmental pollutants. Man-made contaminants pollute the natural world from a variety of sources and they enter the food chain in several ways. Eventually, these pollutants move through the food chain as animals feed on plants, and as small animals fall prey to larger ones. The concentration of many chemicals increases in each successive animal that is preyed on; this biomagnification reaches its peak when a predator, such as a bald eagle, eats contaminated prey.

Poisoning by chlorinated hydrocarbons is well documented and is thought to have been responsible for many cases of reproductive failure in past decades (see Chapter 11). *DDT* and its metabolites *DDE* and *DDD* have been implicated in many cases of "raptor pesticide syndrome." (27) DDT is sprayed on crops and forests to kill herbivorous insects. Once in the environment, it degrades slowly, is washed away in surface drainage, and accumulates in aquatic ecosystems such as lakes. Here DDT is concentrated in fish, which fall prey to the bald eagle. Golden eagles have not been affected by DDT to the extent that balds have because they do not eat fish as often. Ospreys, which are fish eaters, have had problems similar to those of the bald eagle.

Eagles that ate food containing 160 ppm of DDT exhibited tremors, indicating pesticide poisoning, and eventually died, but DDT can be lethal in concentrations as low as 30 ppm. (6, 35) A lethal dose to full-grown eagles in the wild is rare; rather, DDT causes the death of the embryo in the egg stage of the eagle's life. This occurs because DDT disrupts the calcium metabolism of the egg-laying female. Calcium, a vital component of the eggshell, is deficient during the formation of the egg and only a thin shell is produced. If more than about a 17 percent reduction in shell thickness occurs, the egg may break and the embryo will die. (21) The concentration of DDT or DDE needed to cause eggshell thinning is much less than levels that cause death to adults. Since DDT was banned in 1972, this raptor pesticide syndrome has gradually waned. Prior to this, however, virtually every eagle carcass analyzed for DDE had residues present. (40)

Other pesticides, particularly *dieldrin* and *endrin*, also have caused problems. Many deaths due to these two chemicals have been documented, but as with DDT, sublethal quantities of dieldrin are suspected to upset reproductive efforts by birds of prey. (31)

Recently, PCBs (polychlorinated biphenyls) have been cited in the deaths of some eagles. PCBs are used for a variety of industrial purposes, though not as pesticides. Although they are known to be toxic in high concentrations, the effects of sublethal doses are still unresolved.

Eagles are also poisoned by heavy metals, especially *mercury* and *lead*. Mercury is used as a fungicide, but has many other uses. It accumulates in the sediment of lakes and other waters and eventually finds its way to the bald eagle through the food chain. Some eagles have succumbed after eating fish that contained lethal residues. (50)

Mercury poisoning is rare, but deaths due to lead poisoning are increasing. Eagles acquire lead by feeding on waterfowl that have been shot by hunters and crippled by the lead pellets. Eagles are poisoned after ingesting the actual lead pellets; eating the lead-contaminated flesh has a lesser effect. Each year, about ten bald eagles are known to die because of lead, but the number is undoubtedly much higher. Of 650 eagle carcasses examined, 7 percent probably died of lead poisoning. Although eagles are often able to regurgitate lead pellets before being poisoned by them, as few as ten pellets can kill a bird. One eagle found dead had ingested seventy-five pellets. (38, 10, 23, 39, 25)

Because many pollutants increase in concentration in animals that are higher on the food chain, the bald eagle, which is on top of the chain, may be the first to experience adverse effects. Thus, the well-being of predators can be used as a yardstick to measure the "health" of the environment. Like canaries used by miners to gauge the toxicity of the air, the eagle is a biological indicator that tells us if something is amiss and if a problem exists that conventional methods cannot discern. The eagle and other birds of prey have brought considerable attention to the problem of industrial pollution of our waterways.

Habitat Destruction and Alteration Overt as well as subtle changes in the environment have destroyed habitat so that less living space is available to eagles. Cutting of nesting, perching, and roosting trees has been occurring since humans first arrived in North America, and it continues today. Less dramatic, but nonetheless influential, is the gradual alteration of forested areas which, in most cases, makes the area unfit for habitation by eagles.

Though the eagle itself has long been protected, its habitat was not afforded similar measures until 1978 when this species was declared endangered throughout much of its range. By law, the eagles' "critical habitat" is now protected, at least on public lands. The term "critical" can have many interpretations, but today, destruction of nesting, perching, roosting, and feeding habitat is forbidden by law on public domain.

Development of waterfront property is one of the most destructive activities that humans have inflicted on the bald eagle. Because eagles derive their livelihood from shoreline habitat and aquatic food sources, conflicts with humans are often intense. Nesting eagles have been extirpated in many areas because of commercial, industrial, and recreational activities along shorelines.

Indiscriminate harvesting of timber has also damaged eagle habitat. Cutting of specific trees used by eagles and changes in the overall condition of the forest have left few areas where they can live. When nesting, perching, and roosting trees are cut, some birds may move to undisturbed areas. But over time, this gradual loss of habitat confines eagles to small areas, and the overall population shrinks. The problem is that habitat is slowly being altered; this cumulative impact may have few effects on a local and short-term basis, but because it is so widespread and long-term in nature, the effects to eagles are tremendous. And once altered, forest habitat is rarely allowed to return to the old-growth state that the eagle prefers. In many areas, the last vestiges of old growth are now being removed and replaced with fast-growing, economically efficient forest stands. (7) This loss of old-growth forest habitat presents a most acute and continuing problem, as most eagles will use only old forests for nesting and other activities.

In a general sense, "habitat" can include all of the ecological components of the environment that an eagle needs to survive and reproduce. Habitat means more than just forests and shorelines; it encompasses the amount of prey available, the degree of solitude present, and many other features. We are still striving to understand the intricate needs of eagles, but it is safe to assume that they require a vast array of conditions and components from their habitat and that each of these has a different degree of importance to them. Some components, such as an abundant and nutritious food supply, could well be critical, whereas the type and condition of perch trees could be of minor importance. But any alteration of one or several habitat components can have debilitating effects. It is undeniable that humans have been a significant force in changing some or many features of eagle habitat and have swept the eagle from many of its former haunts.

Prey Base Changes   Largely ignored in studies of the demise of the eagle is the vast reduction of wildlife species that served as a prey base. It is especially difficult to attribute the decline of eagle populations to a loss of food, but a correlation between the two is certainly evident. Recent studies do indeed suggest that survival may depend on the abundance of food and that improved reproductive success occurs when food is abundant. (54, 11, 19) Humans vigorously compete with eagles for this resource, and as humans deplete the aquatic food stocks and other prey sources, the eagle has more difficulty finding an adequate meal. Perhaps because of their diverse diet and opportunistic foraging abilities, bald eagles have been able to adapt to many changes in their prey base. But a paradox exists; this propensity to eat a wide variety of foods has been a cause of the eagle's fate. (36) Because it is sometimes in competition with humans for food, many people regard the eagle as vermin.

With the eagle's large appetite and need to feed its voracious young, any reduction in the *quantity* of the prey base can be detrimental. Many prey populations have been devastated, and examples of this are many. Both Atlantic and Pacific Coast salmon runs have been reduced; these were of great importance to eagles. Loss or destruction of aquatic habitats has reduced both fish and waterfowl populations. Seabirds and mammals, in general, are not as abundant as they once were.

The overall situation, however, is not entirely bleak. Humans have created new prey sources that are now being exploited by eagles. Dams, though destructive to many fish, have provided a new food source. As mentioned earlier, fish are killed in the turbines, float downstream, and are scavenged on. Also, because the waters directly below some dams remain ice-free in winter, waterfowl congregate there as does their predator, the bald eagle. In Glacier National Park in Montana, an introduced run of kokanee salmon now feed the densest concentration of wintering eagles in the lower states. (33)

Food also must contain sufficient energy, nutrients, and vitamins to sustain vigorous health. This *quality* of prey has been little studied, but it is known that prey can vary greatly in their energy contents. For example, dead Pacific salmon have a lower energy content than do rabbits, but neither of these prey can match the high energy levels found in fattened waterfowl carcasses. (53) Nutrition might be particularly important prior to and during egg laying as well as during the development of the eaglets.

Another attribute of the food base is the *accessibility* of carrion and the *vulnerability* of live prey. Prey may be abundant, but if it cannot be acquired, it is useless to the eagle. Accessibility of fish carcasses on rivers can vary depending on water conditions. Humans have altered rivers by damming them or by disturbing watersheds; these changes can diminish the amount of fish carrion available. Many salmon, for example, now return to hatcheries to spawn, making them unavailable to eagles. Vulnerability of prey also is important. Some fish are easier for eagles to catch, and if man selectively eliminates these species, the birds' foraging success may suffer. There are many examples of human activities having either increased or decreased prey vulnerability. In Florida, a channelization project for controlling floods both reduced the quantity of prey available and caused a reduction in foraging success; as a result, the bald eagle population there declined. (52, 56, 46)

The last consideration, *contamination* of prey, has been previously discussed. Prey must be free of environmental pollutants to maintain a healthy and growing eagle population.

Disturbance by Humans The bald eagle is a creature that seeks solitude and all the amenities that a wilderness can provide. Although eagles are able to withstand some human activity without a significant alteration to their lives, some levels of interference will cause reproductive failures and change normal behavioral patterns. Many studies have addressed this problem, and some tentative conclusions have been reached, but much more work is needed before we fully understand what activities eagles perceive as a threat and what effects these are having.

Human disturbances can *disrupt breeding* by reducing the occupancy, activity, success, and/or productivity of nests or by causing total *desertion* of the nesting territory. Parental care is disrupted when parents are frightened from their nest; this can cause the death of eggs or eaglets. (60) Although the first study of this sort (32) failed to show a relationship between disturbance and nesting, other research suggests that such a relationship does exist. (2, 18, 26) When the entire population of an area is considered over a long period of time, the effects of human activities on nest success are readily apparent. (26) Nests closer to the scene of human activities tend to be less productive than those that are secluded. (11, 18) Lower nest success and a reduction in productivity occur when nest sites are adjacent to major roads and recently logged areas. (2) Harvesting of timber along shorelines reduces the occupancy of traditional nesting territories. (7) Desertion of nests due to the presence of humans is sometimes difficult to prove, but it does occur. Even a single visit to a raptor nest during a critical time can cause abandonment. (13) Oologists (those who study bird eggs) collected many eagle eggs in earlier times. Even Arthur Bent, a well-known ornithologist, often enjoyed "eagle eggnog"!

Potentially disturbing activities are most critical during nest construction, egg laying, and incubation. As eaglets hatch and grow older, the same activity has a lesser impact. (32)

Disturbances can *displace* eagles to areas of lower human activity. In California, Oregon, and Minnesota, eagles build their nests farther from shorelines in an apparent attempt to avoid humans. Though they must nest farther from preferred areas, this pattern suggests that they are somewhat adaptable while nesting. (57, 2, 12)

Research is thought to have a minor influence on nesting eagles as long as adequate precautions are taken. Visiting a nest while young are present rarely causes desertion and does not change nest activity in subsequent years. (13, 12, 15) Nestlings have been frightened by researchers and have died or been injured as a result of falling from the nest, but such mishaps are rare. In the past, researchers collected live eggs, nestlings, and even adult birds for museum specimens. Such activities are now illegal.

Sometimes human disturbance can have unforeseen effects. A large number of seabirds such as sea gulls, cormorants, and guillemots nest on an island off the coast of British Columbia, but eagles and crows also live there. On weekends, human visitors frighten the eagles and cause them to fly over the island. The seabirds, frightened by the approaching eagles, temporarily desert their nests. Eager to take advantage of the situation, the crows descend on the unguarded nests and devour the eggs, thereby reducing seabird productivity.

Wintering bald eagles may not have a nest or family to care for and are not bound to a breeding territory, but they, too, can be disturbed by the presence of humans. High levels of human activity adversely affect eagles by causing *disruptions of normal behavior* and by *displacing* eagles to nonpreferred, marginal habitat. (55)

Eagle watching, boating, and other outdoor activities, whether recreational or commercial, can prevent eagles from dining in favored areas, especially if they must eat while on the ground. The lowered intake of food can cause energy stress. Human presence also can alter the complex social structure of foraging groups, and this could lead to poorer feeding success. Disturbance to perched or roosting eagles can cause them to fly off, thus increasing their energy expenditures. (52) Any stress in winter can increase the already difficult task of finding food and staying warm.

A case in point is the Skagit River Bald Eagle Natural Area in northwest Washington. Here, hordes of fishermen and eagle watchers float through the sanctuary in boats and create unrest among eagles. The problem here may become widespread; nature lovers are flooding sanctuaries throughout the United States to observe bald eagles, but they also are disturbing them.

Wintering eagles may be forced to live in areas that provide marginal resources because human activity prevents them from visiting preferred areas. (51) Eagles will not eat food that is too close to human activities, and their use of traditional communal roosts may be impeded if humans are close by. (52) Many eagles can adapt to moderate levels of activity, especially if food is available; less tolerant individuals will seek secluded habitat where resources may be scarce.

Many circumstances influence the degree to which humans disturb wintering eagles. Eagles feeding or standing on the ground are more sensitive to disturbance than are those perching in trees. (29, 55) Apparently, a reduced visual field and vulnerability to ground predators causes this flightiness. Hungry eagles will allow humans to approach closer than will satiated birds. (48) In fact, starving eagles have been known to take food from a person's hand. (47) Older eagles seem more wary of humans than younger birds are, but in other areas, the reverse may be true. (55, 29, 43) Several studies suggest that eagles may become habituated to some activities, at least on a temporary basis. (43, 55) If habituation does occur, it may be beneficial, but in areas where raptors are persecuted, habituated eagles may be more likely to be killed. Eagles may well recognize individuals or situations that pose a threat to them and may be quick to respond. (20) In addition, they are more tolerant of humans when activities are screened from view rather than out in the open, and they are more likely to tolerate humans while alone than while in a flock. (29, 55)

The effect of human disruption depends on the life history stage of the eagle and on whether reproduction or survival is influenced. Reproduction is the most sensitive stage of the eagle's cycle, and slight interferences can cause nest failures, thereby dooming eggs or nestlings. But though reproduction is easier to disrupt, the long-term effects are less serious than if full-grown birds are killed. (16) A reduced survival rate has a greater overall effect on the health of the population. Human interference is most critical to adults and has a lesser impact on younger birds. It is the breeding stock that is most vital.

FUTURE OUTLOOK

How can we predict the future of the bald eagle? Current population trends show a promising increase in reproductive success, but if mortality rates continue to remain high, the actual number of eagles may increase only slightly, stay the same, or even decline. But human populations will continue to expand and will create persistent pressures on the already depleted populations of eagles. Habitats are continually being disrupted or completely destroyed by man's activities, but in some areas, sanctuaries and wilderness areas are being set aside where eagles can exist in their natural state. It is true that some human activities have created new and unusual food sources, but at the same time, many feeding areas and prey populations have been eliminated. Poisoning of eagles by pesticides has slowed, but other problems such as those caused by lead shot poisoning and acid rain may be adversely affecting some populations.

It is a dynamic and complex situation, this confrontation between humans and eagles. As long as both compete for some of the same resources, there will continue to be unresolved conflicts. The likely result of these interactions will be the gradual withdrawal of eagle populations to the few remaining wilderness and protected areas where suitable habitat is still available. In the future, national parks, forests, refuges, and sanctuaries may well be the only areas where eagles will continue to thrive. But the risk of extirpation still lingers for many populations. Only with a strong commitment and special care can we ensure that the bald eagle does not fall into the irreversible state of extinction.

13

Protective Management

W. G. Van Name once wrote that "the bald eagle, our national emblem and one of the largest, most unique [sic] and beautiful birds of North America . . . is now fast becoming a rare bird . . . much rarer than most people or even most ornithologists are aware. . . . No economic necessity whatever exists for the extermination of the bald eagle. . . . A federal law for the protection of the eagle in all parts of the United States is therefore greatly needed." (35) Van Name's concern for eagles is not unique, except that his words were published in 1921. It was a time of blatant disregard for all wild things. The territory of Alaska was paying out bounties on thousands of eagles killed every year, and this slaughter would not end until three decades after Van Name's outraged words appeared in print and after more than 128,000 eagles had been turned in for bounties. Pointedly, he finished his remarks with this: "That the extermination of a species so well known and inoffensive, with which so much patriotic sentiment is associated, and of such conspicuous beauty and interest from a scientific point of view, can go on unhindered will certainly not help to maintain public confidence in the organizations . . . to which the protection of our native fauna is entrusted."

Attitudes and opinions change slowly, if at all. Once responsible for condoning the eagle bounty, state and federal governments are now responsible for protecting eagles. With the current level of concern for eagles, it is difficult to understand the attitudes of our predecessors. Who would ever believe that funds would be appropriated to support eagle bounty hunters in the 1950s, but reward those helping to convict eagle killers in the 1970s. If a lesson is to be learned, it is this: Wildlife management decisions should be based on sound scientific knowledge, not on the desires of special interest groups, public outcry, or inane governmental directives.

Protective mangement for the bald eagle is the current program in practice. It is an interesting and exciting field. By studying and understanding the life history of the bald eagle, wildlife managers have amassed a small array of techniques that are now being used to protect and enhance many populations. (21) Additional methods undoubtedly will be developed and others discarded, but with the persistent diligence of many dedicated biologists, the bald eagle seems now to be in good hands.

LAWS

By the passage of several laws, the Congress of the United States has mandated that protective measures be used to prevent the bald eagle from becoming extinct. Protection is afforded by three federal laws: (1) the Endangered Species Act, (2) the Bald and Golden Eagle Protection Act, and (3) the Migratory Bird Treaty Act. Also, most states have laws designed to protect eagles. In Canada, protection is provided by provincial law.

The Endangered Species Act mandates that an endangered species be given special protection, and that research and management be increased to restore the species to levels necessary to remove them from the endangered species list. In 1978, the bald eagle was reclassified to an endangered status in forty-three states and to a threatened status in five states: Oregon, Washington, Michigan, Minnesota, and Wisconsin. (32) The threatened classification indicates that the species could become endangered in the near future. Bald eagles are not threatened or endangered in Alaska and do not occur in Hawaii.

Section 7 of the Endangered Species Act mandates that actions taken or condoned by federal agencies will not jeopardize the "continued existence" of an endangered species. Many state laws have similar provisions. An assessment of the possible effects of land-use changes is required under this section. In addition, the act mandates the appointment of recovery teams to develop research and management plans, provides funding, and allows for a fine of $20,000 and/or one year of imprisonment for violators.

Another law that protects bald eagles is the Bald and Golden Eagle Protection Act. It specifically defines illegal acts against bald eagles, outlines criminal penalties for violators, and rewards those who aid in the conviction of these violators. This act states that "no person shall take . . . any bald eagle . . . alive or dead, or any part, nest or egg thereof." It further states that "take" also includes "to pursue, shoot, shoot at, poison, wound, kill, capture, trap, collect, molest, or disturb." Special exemptions to these provisions include scientific research, public exhibitions, and religious uses by Indian tribes. Violators of this law face a $5,000 fine and/or one year of imprisonment; penalties for second and subsequent violations include a $10,000 fine and/or two years in jail. In addition, one-half of any such fine, but not exceeding $2,500, may be paid to the person giving information that leads to a conviction.

As is obvious from the language of this law, any type of action that disturbs bald eagles in any way is illegal. By the "letter of the law," even a bird-watcher or photographer who frightens an eagle from its perch has violated the act. But, as with many laws, convictions are based on the "spirit of the law," not on specific wording. This act has been used in numerous instances to convict irresponsible persons of violations against eagles. A rare few have received jail sentences, and these are usually suspended; fines are commonly handed down as a penalty. Violators are rarely given the maximum penalty.

Because the bald eagle is a migratory species, it also is protected by the Migratory Bird Treaty Act. Violation of this act calls for a $2,000 fine and/or two years in jail.

NEST PROTECTION

Safeguarding eagle nests is vital to the continued existence of the species. Management of nesting habitat has striven not only to maintain the current nesting population but also to protect or develop additional habitat to encourage more eagles to breed. This is the long-term goal of recovery efforts: to manage for an expanding population.

Protective Zoning   Three methods have been or are now being used to protect eagle nests: (1) circular zoning, (2) territory zoning, and (3) regional zoning. (30)

Circular zoning was the first approach used to protect nests and was initially employed by the U.S. Forest Service in Minnesota. (16) The concept is quite simple. Two buffer zones, called the primary and secondary zones, are drawn around the nest tree in concentric circles (Fig. 13.1). The primary zone extends 100 meters from the nest, and all human activities of any kind are prohibited there. The secondary zone is 100 to 200 meters from the nest. In this zone, activities are restricted only when the eagles are present in the territory and/or engaged in breeding activities. (16)

Circular zoning was a simple scheme to address a not-so-simple problem. Protection was not always sufficient because birds vary in their sensitivity to human activities. Circular zoning protected some nests adequately, but not others; consequently, this method has fallen into disfavor.

A new system, now in common use, is called *territory zoning*. It is a modified version of circular zoning, but more of the habitat features that eagles require are included in a protective zone. Hence, this system is more suited to the needs of individual breeding pairs and eliminates the drawing of zones of arbitrary widths. A primary zone of 100 meters surrounding the nest still is used; all human activities are prohibited there year round. The secondary zone, however, is irregular in shape, depending on the locations of alternate nests, roost and perch trees, feeding sites, and the degree to which forest cover screens these features from human activities (Fig 13.1). The shape of this secondary zone is determined by studying the habits of the nesting pair and mapping the various components of their territory. Once known, a boundary is drawn around the outermost territorial features, leaving a margin to protect those closest to the boundary. This margin is wide if the area is open and views are unrestricted, or if the eagles are sensitive to humans. It is narrow if screening cover is present or if the eagles are known to be tolerant of activity. Secondary zones can range up to 900 meters from the boundary of the primary zone. Because feeding areas may be some distance from the nest, a special feeding zone separate from the breeding territory may be needed. (30)

Human activity is restricted in the secondary zone only when eagles are present or during the breeding cycle. In some areas of the eagles' range, territories are continuously occupied, justifying year-round restrictions. In most other sites, however, occupancy occurs only during part of the year, and specific dates depend on several factors, especially latitude (see Chapter 5). The timing of restrictions for secondary zones is best made on a case-by-case basis.

The last nest-custody technique is called *regional zoning* (Fig. 13.1). This method was first put to use in the early 1980s; it has not yet gained favor with many land managers. It is, however, the most comprehensive scheme used thus far and has a long-range goal of providing for the recovery and expansion of the eagle population rather than just safeguarding individual territories.

This zoning plan requires the cooperation of wildlife and forest managers in order to care for a number of occupied or potential nest sites in a large geographic area. First implemented in Oregon, the plan protects each nesting pair using territory zones, but goes one step further by conserving adjacent lands to ensure that habitat is available for future populations. Managers use a combination of forest manipulative methods designed to enhance nesting, perching, and roosting habitats; conservation easements or land exchanges are made; and limits are placed on timber harvesting unless such forestry practices enhance eagle habitat. Foresters may manipulate the region to develop a multistoried, uneven-aged stand, thin and selectively harvest trees to promote growth of the remaining trees and to create a stand desired by eagles, and maintain old-growth trees that eagles frequently use. Preservation of old-growth forest may be the single most important objective in protecting nesting areas. (30)

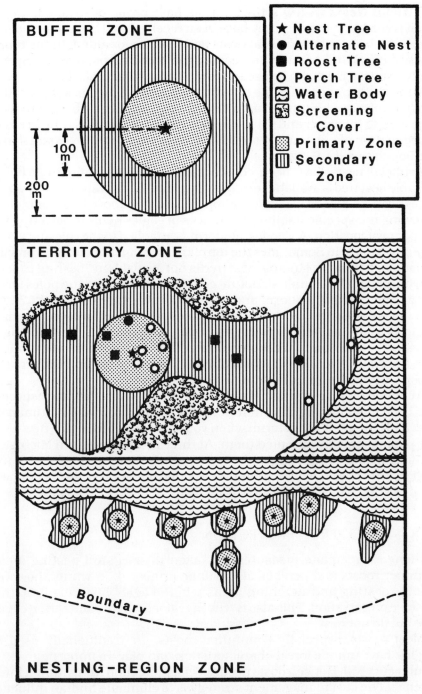

Fig. 13.1 Three management plans for protecting bald eagle nests. (30)

Artificial Nests A few artificial nests have been constructed, and in most recorded instances, they have been received well by breeding pairs. Thus, the building of artificial nests has promise for aiding in the reproductive effort and possibly increasing the breeding population. Specifically, artificial nests can be used (1) to replace natural nests that have been destroyed, (2) to encourage the breeding pair to move their nesting location away from excessive human activity or away from areas where activity is expected to increase, and (3) to encourage use of new breeding areas or reoccupation of old, unused territories, thus promoting an expansion of the population. (3, 9, 22)

Artificial nests have been constructed in several manners. When a suitable nest tree is available, one that is particularly tall and close to water, a nest can be placed close to the top between or above large branches. Knowing the specific habitat preferences of eagles helps in selecting the proper nest location. A wooden platform is attached to the tree and a nest is built on top of it. Sometimes the top of the tree must be cut off to provide a place for a nest. If a suitable nest tree is not available, a "nesting tripod" can be made. This simple structure consists of three gigantic poles forming a tripod, with a platform and nest constructed on top (Fig. 13.2). An ingenious method for providing artificial nest structures for ospreys, which could also be suitable for bald eagles in some situations, is the dropping of a nest structure from a helicopter. Like a giant dart, the nest pole plunges into the ground; it has a platform already fashioned on top, ready for the prospective pair to start building a nest. (9, 22,)

Although only a few artificial nests have been constructed, their success has been encouraging. The first nest ever made replaced a natural nest that had fallen in a windstorm; when young were placed in this new nest, the parents quickly accepted them. At three artificial nests in Michigan, six nesting attempts were made, two of which were successful, and five eaglets were raised in these nests over a period of several years. Eagles have used nesting tripods in Arizona. (3, 9, 22)

ROOST AND PERCH PROTECTION

As long as adequate measures are taken to safeguard nesting areas, summer roosts and perches also will be protected. In winter, however, many roosting and perching areas where eagles historically gather deserve preservation. This also is true in regions where summering eagles live but do not nest.

Most roosts, especially communal roosts, are traditionally used by eagles, have unique forest characteristics, and play an important role in winter survival. Hence, roosts need special protection from human interference. The best management strategy is to eliminate human influence within the roost and to restrict human activity along the outer perimeter of the roost. Widths of zones depend on the amount of screening cover that

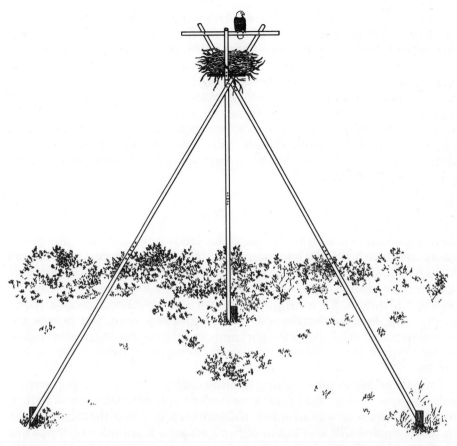

Fig. 13.2. Man-made bald eagle nest structure known as a nest tripod. (9)

is present. Where activity of humans is screened from view, 75 to 100 meters may be sufficient, but in open country, 250 to 300 meters will be needed to isolate eagles from humans. In the Klamath Basin in Oregon, one of the largest roosts in the country is protected by a 1,000-meter buffer zone. (29, 33)

A ban on logging in communal roost areas is essential unless selective harvesting will maintain or enhance the desired characteristics. Logging adjacent to roosts could result in roost trees being blown over in strong winds and could alter the favorable microclimate of the roost. Restrictions on activities that have no permanent effect need apply only during winter, from November to March or whenever eagles use the area. To provide roosts in the future, old-growth habitat should be maintained or developed. (30)

Because perching areas are usually close to water, protecting or enhancing waterfront habitat, particularly trees close to rivers and lakes, is the best means of safeguarding perch sites. Leaving or planting strips of tall trees approximately 50 meters wide along waterways is a well-known management objective; if these strips are 75 to 100 meters wide, they may also screen and ameliorate the effects of human activity. If no screening cover is present, buffer zones of 250 to 300 meters are needed. Preferred forest characteristics in these perching strips include a variety of trees of different heights, a dense understory for screening human activities, and a number of oversize trees, such as old snags, that have stout, easily accessible perches. In areas where few or no perch trees exist, trees can be planted or artificial perch structures can be erected. "Perch tripods," similar to nesting tripods, have been constructed, but natural perches are preferred. (30, 27, 29)

FOOD AND FEEDING HABITAT PROTECTION

Although food is a vital resource to the bald eagle, very few protective measures have been taken to maintain or enhance prey sources. Perhaps biologists and the public have difficulty in dealing with a management scheme that seems only remotely associated with eagle protection. In the Pacific Northwest, for example, salmon runs have been devastated by overfishing, habitat destruction, and mismanagement, but people are concerned about the effects to sport and commercial fishing, not to eagles. Unfortunately, the same attitudes exist throughout much of the eagles' range.

Food is the key to maintaining healthy eagles; without it, a population will not grow. A scant food source can lower survival in winter and reduce reproductive success in summer. If all other elements of their habitat are in place, eagles will still fail to occupy an area if abundant prey is not available. (18, 28, 30)

Methods by which food sources can be maintained or enhanced are as varied as the eagles' diet. No single technique is applicable in all situations, but food enhancement programs should take into account five features of the food supply. The *quantity* of food must, of course, be sufficient to satisfy the energy requirements of all eagles and the needs of an expanding population. The *quality* of food, specifically including the energy and nutrient content, is closely related to the quantity available; with higher quality, less prey is needed. Food may be abundant and nutritious, but if prey are not *accessible*, they have no value to an eagle. Thus, a reasonably good foraging success rate must exist or, alternatively, live prey sources must be vulnerable to capture. Other factors affecting accessibility include human presence, flooding, freezing, the existence of other predators, and a host of other conditions. Food must show a high level of *continuity* in its distribution, both in time and space, to have the maximum benefit. Although eagles can fast for long periods, disruptions in prey abundance may cause excessive nestling mortality, increase susceptibility to disease, or reduce the general health of the bird. Finally, food must be free of *contamination* that could be deleterious to eagles. This includes man-made chemicals and pollutants as well as natural disease organisms and pathogenic agents. (2)

Although artificial feeding of eagles has been conducted, the benefits and consequences of such actions are unknown. Artificial feeding of the white-tailed sea eagle, the bald eagle's closest cousin, has probably increased the survival of young birds. In Maine, a large-scale feeding program in the early 1980s has attracted hundreds of bald eagles and is thought to bolster the survival of juveniles and subadults; the effects to the breeding success of the adults is less certain. Many eagles are artificially fed in Washington as well. Biologists argue, however, that artificial feeding simply does not address the underlying problem of a lack of natural food. They also point out that this method can reduce the eagles' fear of humans and make them dependent on an unnatural food source, thus reducing their efficacy as predators. As more food sources dwindle, artificial feeding will likely increase, thereby increasing the number of eagles maintained in this state of welfare. Artificial feeding seems justified especially during critical periods when food is difficult to obtain and energy needs are high, but measures to restore depleted food stocks, the necessary long-term solution, should have higher priority. (18, 11, 27)

Feeding habitat requires protection to allow eagles to feed unmolested. This is a particularly critical concept because sensitivity to humans is acute when eagles forage and feed on the ground. Expansive, open areas for foraging are needed, and buffer zones around these areas must be at least 450 meters wide. Because foraging is most common in the morning, activities that occur early in the day are more likely to disturb feeding eagles. Food may be plentiful in an area, but as long as humans are present, the supply will be used little, if at all. (2, 29, 14)

SANCTUARIES

The protection of land from human encroachment is of paramount importance to ensure that eagles will have livable habitat in future years. Wilderness areas are relentlessly being developed; a scattering of small, isolated lands where habitat might still support eagles will soon be all that is left. If eagle populations are to be maintained, a sacrifice on the part of the populace is needed: large parcels of undeveloped land must be set aside and left alone.

If development forces the eviction of an eagle population, it is unlikely that the birds will move to a new location, as many people believe. Most wild animals, even those that can travel quickly, do not simply pick up and go elsewhere; their loss of habitat is manifested in poorer reproduction, increased mortality, and an attendant decline in population levels. It is not easy to document such effects, but with the increase in development along shorelines, there are few areas left for displaced eagles to occupy.

Sanctuaries have been established to protect both nesting and wintering habitat (see Chapter 4). Most eagle habitat is, however, located on federal lands where protective sanctions already exist. Not surprisingly, eagles often are residents of national parks, forests, wildlife refuges, and other federal holdings, not only because these still provide suitable habitat, but also because they are often the only areas left that can support eagles. Eagles are less common on private lands.

The methods by which land can be set aside are many. Outright purchases of lands have been made by conservation organizations such as the National Audubon Society, the National Wildlife Federation, and the Nature Conservancy. Donations from the public provide these agencies with their funding. In Minnesota, a save-the-eagle promotion resulted in funds donated to buy nesting territories. Each donor received a deed to a parcel of the land, usually several square feet, depending on the amount of money donated, and the acquired land was held in trust by the government to be administered for preservation. (17) Sometimes the federal government steps in and creates a special wildlife refuge for eagles, such as the Bear Valley National Wildlife Refuge in southern Oregon. (33) Other federal acquisitions, made possible by the Land and Water Conservation Fund Act, help preserve specific sites for nesting and roosting. Land exchanges between federal, state, and local governments also can be made, thus shifting the responsibility of eagle management to the most appropriate authorities. Sanctuaries also can be established at the state level. In an unprecedented move, the governor of Alaska signed a bill establishing the Chilkat Bald Eagle Preserve with the approval of numerous interest groups that were involved. (24) Even the private land holder has an opportunity to protect the national symbol. If a private holding is deemed important to the critical needs of a population, a conservation easement could be enacted on the parcel. In this, the owner agrees to specific measures to preserve habitat and, in return, the taxes on the land that is set aside are reduced. (34)

CAPTIVE BREEDING

Another technique to replenish dwindling bald eagle populations is to produce young by breeding captive pairs. This method has not been widely used, however, because it is expensive and most populations are now reproducing at acceptable rates. There is little justification for trapping wild birds, keeping them in captivity, and encouraging them to breed. Rather, those eagles that are on long-term exhibition or those that have permanent injuries are often placed in breeding programs so that some benefit is derived from holding them. Only the Patuxent Laboratory in Maryland, operated by the U.S. Fish and Wildlife Service, has an extensive captive breeding program, but many smaller facilities and zoos experiment with this technique. Eaglets that are produced in this way have been returned to the wild by hacking or by fostering (see section on Reintroduction later in this chapter).

With the possible exception of the Patuxent Laboratory, captive breeding programs for bald eagles have had many problems. It seems that conditions must be perfect if the breeding effort is to be successful. Apparently, the lack of one or several attributes found in the natural environment inhibits breeding in captivity. Problems arise at any point in the breeding cycle, from pair bonding, mating, nest building, egg laying, incubation, through to the rearing of young. This comes as no surprise because breeding attempts by wild birds often are unproductive. (7, 8)

Nevertheless, many captive pairs have produced young, and eaglets have been released to the wild from these efforts. In a summary of captive breeding before the 1970s, twenty-three clutches contained forty-nine eggs. Twenty young hatched from eleven of these clutches and only one chick died before fledging. These data do not, however, include the many failed efforts by many programs. (8, 10, 12, 15)

Captive pairs usually are provided with a large aviary with adequate isolation from human activity, an elevated and covered structure for the nest, materials for nest building, and a constant source of food. Although breeding success has occurred in an enclosure as small as $2 \times 2 \times 2$ meters, large, spacious aviaries are better. (10) One can provide a variety of conditions, but much of the rest is left to the mated pair. Recently, however, new techniques involving artificial insemination, artificial incubation, and hand-rearing of the young are replacing many of the functions once assumed by the breeding pair. Techniques for storing and later using the genetic material of endangered species, including bald eagles, may be available in the future. It seems unlikely, however, that artificial breeding will become an important management tool unless the eagle population declines to very low levels in the future.

REHABILITATION

The ultimate goal of rehabilitation—providing health care to injured or ill eagles—is to release the birds back into the wild, or at least keep them alive for exhibition, captive breeding, or scientific research. Hospitalization of bald eagles is more common than many people think and is becoming an increasingly important management technique for this endangered species.

In 1981, some 225 individuals or organizations held permits authorizing rehabilitation of raptors. One of the largest rehabilitation facilities, the Department of Veterinary Biology at the University of Minnesota, handled 200 cases involving bald eagles between 1972 and 1981, and patient care is expected to increase. At this laboratory, holding rooms, accommodating

300 to 400 raptors annually, are located among examination and treatment rooms, a surgical suite, and freezers used to hold carcasses of eagles that did not respond to treatment. Professional care here includes all phases of examination, diagnosis, surgery, treatment, convalescent care, physical reconditioning and therapy, and release.

Traumatic injuries—including shooting, trapping, and collisions—account for most cases at the University of Minnesota. Broken bones are a common malady, and amputations of a wing or leg often are necessary. One out of every three birds admitted has been shot, and one out of four has been captured in a leg-hold trap. Eagles struck by vehicles, caught in traps, or poisoned with lead contamination have the lowest recovery rates. On the brighter side, eagles admitted as orphans have a favorable prognosis and release rate. Because young eagles are inexperienced and have difficulty surviving in the wild, they account for twice as many admissions as do adults. Almost half of all patients eventually recover and are released.

Some biologists argue that health care for eagles is costly, that funds would be best spent in other endeavors, and that rehabilitated and released birds have poor survival rates. The cost of the program at the University of Minnesota, assuming a 50 percent success rate, ranges from about $2,000 to $5,000 per bird. Other manipulative management programs, such as hacking, have similar costs. A case for or against rehabilitation can be taken, but as long as the bald eagle is persecuted by humans, some health care seems to be warranted. (5, 25, 26)

REINTRODUCTION

Reintroduction is the process of reestablishing eagles in an area where the population has been extirpated or significantly reduced. There are four general approaches to reintroduce eagles: (1) egg translocation, (2) replacement clutching, (3) fostering and cross-fostering, and (4) hacking.

In areas where pesticides or other pollutants have caused eggshell thinning and poor hatching success, *egg translocations* from a healthy population to ailing nests can be conducted. Eggs have been translocated to Maine from nests in Minnesota and Wisconsin. This technique simply transfers members from one population to another. Only about 26 percent of substituted eggs hatch and result in successfully fledged birds. Because of this low success rate and the possibility of causing nest abandonment by both the donors and the recipients, this procedure is not commonly employed. (1, 4)

Egg translocations can result in the donor pair producing another clutch of eggs after the first is taken, but another technique known as *replacement clutching* is based on this principle. It has been successful in Florida, and the initial results are encouraging. Unlike translocations, the first clutch is removed and artificially incubated, the young are reared by hand,

and they are then fostered or hacked into the wild. Thus far, nearly all pairs that had eggs stolen from them laid a second clutch, though their second effort was delayed by a month. If successful, this technique can double the rate of production and provides eaglets for restoring populations in depleted areas. (19)

Fostering of nestlings is a method in which eaglets are taken from a healthy nest or from captive stocks and are transplanted in a nest where the eggs have failed to hatch or where the nestlings have died, but where the adults are still present. (4, 23) This procedure reintroduces eagles but also helps keep the adults from abandoning their territory. Ostensibly, the adults' instinctive behavior is not programmed for recognizing the young of other eagles, and they readily accept and raise them. Fledging of these fostered young—a measure of efficiency of this technique—averages 84 percent; this is close to nestling survival rates for natural young. (1, 4) Presently, experiments are being conducted to determine if other birds of prey, such as ospreys, might also accept and raise bald eaglets. This *cross-fostering* between two different species still needs more testing, especially to determine if the eaglets develop a false bond with the foster parent species.

Release of fledglings by *hacking* is the most common and successful method of reintroducing bald eagles. (4) Hacking is an old falconry technique in which nestlings are hand-reared in an artificial nest, allowed to fledge from the nest, and captured after they have mastered the art of flight. There is, of course, no need to recapture hacked eagles; it is expected that they will establish themselves in the general vicinity of the hack site. After the initial success of hacking programs for the endangered peregrine falcon in the 1970s, hacking of bald eagles was begun and is becoming an accepted and increasingly common management tool (Fig. 13.3)

The process of hacking is quite simple. Nestling bald eagles are obtained from captive stocks or from nests in areas where reproduction is high. They are then placed in hacking towers (Fig. 13.4)—a collection of cages atop a platform constructed on a shore. These nestlings are closely monitored, fed each day, and protected from harsh weather and predators. Caretakers feed the young from behind a visual barrier or with "eagle puppets" to prevent the eaglets from forming a false bond with humans (imprinting)—a development that could deter the eaglet from establishing a normal pair bond later on. When the eaglets are eleven to thirteen weeks old, the cages are opened, and they are allowed to fly away. Many birds stay near the hacking site after fledging because food is provided for a number of weeks after the eagles are released.

One of the most extensive hacking programs has been conducted in the state of New York where the entire bald eagle population has been annihilated. With the goal of reestablishing forty breeding pairs in the state by 1990, hacking was started in 1976 and done annually in the spring. As of 1981, forty-four eaglets had been hacked, and approximately 50 percent of

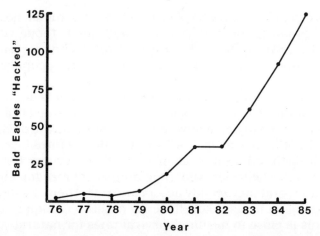

Fig. 13.3 Number of bald eagles hacked into the wild throughout North America. (1, 4, 20)

these were known to be surviving. Two of the birds released formed a pair bond four years after hacking and later successfully raised young of their own. This was the first productive nest in this state in many years. Another hacking program in California is helping to reestablish eagles in the Catalina Islands. As of 1983, hacking programs also existed in Ohio, Tennessee, Georgia, Missouri, Massachusetts, Pennsylvania, New Jersey, North Carolina, and Ontario. (20, 1, 4)

The costs of hacking are high. Acquiring, transporting, and raising one eaglet to hacking age can cost from $4,000 to $5,000, but this expense can be cut to about $2,000 if a large group of eagles is hacked together. (20) Costs increase rapidly as the mortality rate increases, so special efforts are used to keep the birds alive. Despite the expense, hacking seems destined to be one of the most important means by which bald eagles are reintroduced into areas where they were formerly abundant.

BIOCIDE RESTRICTION

Wildlife toxicologists and hazardous waste managers will be faced with many challenging problems in the future. Great strides have been made in restricting the use of biocides, but new toxic chemicals and pollutants are introduced into the industrial marketplace each year. (6) The contamination of the natural environment with these biocides—chemicals that indiscriminately kill animals and plants—is a particular concern because eagles often are most susceptible to their effects.

The banning of DDT in 1972 and subsequent improvement in the reproductive success of eagles is dramatic proof that restricting the use of biocides can help eagles. Other chemicals are now being closely monitored to determine if they affect eagles. The increase in acid rain could cause die-offs of many fish populations that serve as a prey base for eagles. Dieldrin poisoning continues to kill eagles year after year. Persistent organochlorines, heavy metals such as lead and mercury, and PCBs are also implicated in eagle deaths. Toxic chemicals are still being dumped indiscriminately in many areas; cleanup programs will take years to reverse the flow of chemicals into water tables, oceans, and natural ecosystems. Only by the prudent use and disposal of these substances will eagle populations finally be freed of their effects.

ELECTROCUTION PREVENTION

Electrocution of eagles perching on power poles is still a cause of death. When new power lines are constructed and older poles are being modified, special precautions are now being taken to eliminate this problem.

There are several ways in which power poles can be constructed so that the possibilities of electrocution are minimized. First, poles can be built without crossarms near the top thereby making them less attractive as perches. Second, where crossarms exist, some type of physical barrier can

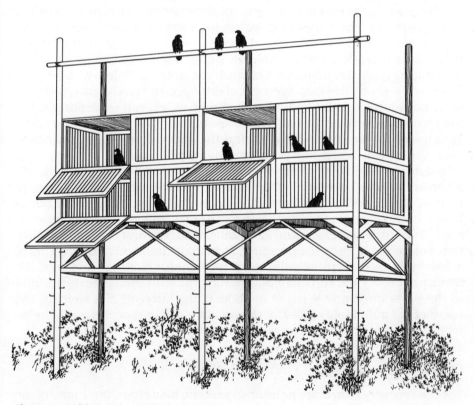

Fig. 13.4. Bald eagle hacking tower.

be installed to prevent the eagle from touching the two contacts necessary to pass an electric current. Third, artificial perches can be built above the pole to discourage or prevent perching on the crossarm where electrocutions usually occur. This method not only solves the problem but also provides perches in areas where perch trees may be scarce. (31)

Power lines can be a flight hazard because the lines are difficult to see. In areas where eagles are particularly common, rerouting of power lines is the best solution, but this can be quite expensive. (31)

RESEARCH

Research provides the basis for all management and recovery efforts. Without sound scientific background, management plans will not serve the needs of the eagle. Guesswork is not acceptable; with the limited number of bald eagles left in North America, it is often feasible to conduct studies on all populations, and recommendations for protective management can be made from on-site data bases.

Research and management are intimately intertwined, yet boundaries exist between the two. Research on any endangered species yields, or at least implies, some sort of management consideration; the more we learn about a species, the better able we are to protect it. Research biologists gather information on endangered species, but the wildlife managers put these ideas to work to solve problems. But a major problem exists in implementing recommendations. Scientific literature is replete with suggestions for the protective management of this species, but the application of this information lags far behind accepted knowledge. As an example, the five recovery teams for the bald eagle now have prepared their recommendations for protecting and enhancing the survival of eagles, but these suggestions will take many years to implement.

To date, research activities have had few adverse effects on bald eagles, whereas benefits have been many. In limited instances, a few eagles may be disturbed or even sacrificed. The overall benefits to the entire population, however, more than make up for the discomforts or misfortunes of a few. A compromise exists and all wildlife biologists and managers realize this. For example, does the trapping, color-marking, and radio-tagging of a few birds to determine migratory movements, habitat use, and life history aspects yield sufficient information to counterbalance the trauma to the birds involved? What is at stake is the survival of a species; the sacrifices of individual eagles for the well-being of the species is justifiable when such research helps prevent extinction.

PUBLIC CONCERN AND INVOLVEMENT

Special recovery efforts are helping to save the bald eagle, but many of the other sea eagles, though faced with greater dangers of extinction, receive less interest and concern. It is fortuitous that the bald eagle lives in countries where concern for wildlife is the highest in the world. But even in North America, many people are indifferent to or show outright contempt for wildlife; only a few will assume or support a stewardship role for the natural environment.

The bald eagle is a choice candidate for protection. It is a regal bird, one that is awe-inspiring, and the national symbol and national bird of the United States. But should endangered species management be prioritized based on such values? Many endangered species receive less consideration than the bald eagle even though they may be closer to extinction. In one survey, 90 percent of all people polled supported protective management of the bald eagle, but only 50 percent supported similar measures for an endangered snake. (13) It seems that species of value to humans, either economically or aesthetically, are those likely to receive the most public concern. If animals can act cute and appealing to the populace, they can be assured of a life of sheltered care. This self-interested manner of prioritizing the protection of endangered species has, of course, no ecological basis.

Emotionalism and sensationalism may help publicize the plight of endangered animals and raise public concern, but they have no place in the realm of sound protective management. Certain conservation groups play on the emotions of the public and sensationalize their efforts to protect endangered species. The press often is guilty of dramatizing events concerning eagles. This concern is well meant, but results of scientific research are the only means by which we will have an objective assessment of the truth. Scientists are obligated to manage eagles based on facts, not on human sentiment.

Appreciation of wildlife is a personal and individual matter. Ancient man lived in close harmony with nature and respected, even worshiped, animals. If he disturbed the natural order, he felt his very existence would be jeopardized. Once man assumed a more dominant and self-centerd role, he became the cause of most extinctions of animals. Only after man reaches a certain level of economic security and exploitative contentment do the needs of wildlife become recognized. Today, a renaissance of respect for wildlife is taking place. It is a slow transition, but perhaps some day in the course of human evolution we will again attain the level of appreciation for the natural world that we once had.

Appendixes

Appendix
1

Reference Tables A, B, and C

Table A. Major food sources of nesting bald eagles.

	Location	Fish:Bird:Mammal:Other (percentages)	Primary food sources	Chapter 8 references
1.	New Brunswick	90:9:1:0	Yellow perch, brown bullheads, gaspereaux, and pickerel (64%), 9 fish, 5 bird, 2 mammal species	77
2.	Nova Scotia	66:24:10:0	Cod (47%), great blue herons (9%), snowshoe hares (5%)	7
3.	Interior Maine	76:17:7:0	Brown bullheads, chain pickerels, white suckers (64%), 12 fish, 16 bird, 5 mammal species	74
4.	Coastal Maine	17:76:7:0	Black ducks and herring gulls (26%), 12 fish, 34 bird, 10 mammal species	74
5.	Coastal Maryland and Virginia	52:33:5:10	Catfishes (19%), 6 fish, 13 bird, and 1 mammal species	33
6.	North Central Florida	70:26:3:1	Brown bullheads and blue and white catfishes (59%), American coots (19%), a total of 10 fish, 12 bird, and 9 mammal species	45
7.	North Central Minnesota	90:8:1:1	Bullheads (35%), suckers (29%), and northern pike (14%)	13
8.	Louisiana	42:42:15:1	Catfish and coots (42%), waterfowl (16%), muskrats, nutria	12
9.	Arizona	76:10:14:0	Catfish (28%), carp (16%), suckers (12%)	32
10.	Grand Teton and Yellowstone National Parks	65:24:11:0	Suckers, trout, waterfowl most abundant in a varied diet	1

Table A. (cont.)

	Location	Fish:Bird:Mammal:Other (percentages)	Primary food sources	Chapter 8 references
11.	Yellowstone National Park	25:57:18:0	Various waterfowl species, cutthroat trout, 3 fish, 9 bird, 4 mammal species	72
12.	Northern Idaho	100:0:0:0	Yellow perch (72%), an all-fish diet	75
13.	Klamath Lake, Oregon	25:66:9:0	Grebes, ducks, chubs, suckers most common, 13 bird, 8 fish, and 5 mammal species	18
14.	Cascade Mountains, Oregon	36:55:8:1	Whitefish, trout, grebes, and coots (48% of diet containing at least 25 species)	18
15.	San Juan Islands, Washington	40:3:56:1	Primarily European hares and rock fishes, depending on time of year	54
16.	Amchitka Island, Alaska	14:49:36:1	Rock greenling, northern fulmar, sea otter most common of 11 fish, 30 bird, and 2 mammal species; also garbage	60
17.	Aleutian Islands, Alaska	9:81:7:3	Extreme diversity, northern fulmars (18%), 8 fish, 27 bird, 6 mammal, 4 invertebrate species	48
18.	Tanana River, Alaska	44:44:12:0	Northern pike, ducks, and snowshoe hares (59%)	55
19.	Southeastern Alaska, 1955	66:19:1:14	Salmon, trout, pollack, and cod (34%), a large diversity of prey and carrion	33
20.	Southeastern Alaska, 1975	91:1:3:5	Salmon, trout, and herring, majority of prey items	51

Table B. Tree species or other structures used for nests by bald eagles at 20 locations in North America.

Location	Number of nests	Tree species or structure type	Chapter 10 references
1. Ottawa National Forest, Michigan	79	White pine (52%); hardwoods (44%), predominantly yellow birch; red pine (2%); other trees (2%)	35
2. Maine	99	White pine (73%), red pine (1%), pitch pine (1%); white spruce (6%), red spruce (2%), and black spruce (2%); red oak (7%), sugar maple (4%), American beech (2%), trembling aspen (1%), paper birch (1%)	56
3. Nova Scotia	46	White pine (35%), poplars (35%), spruce (9%), maple (6%), snag (6%), eastern hemlock (4%), birch (4%)	16
4. Chesapeake Bay, Maryland	70	Loblolly pine (64%), Virginia pine (6%), oak (13%), 5 other deciduous species (17%)	2
5. Florida	286	Slash, loblolly, and longleaf pine (61%), red, white, and black mangrove (23%), cypress (14%), other species (2%)	38
6. Gulf Coast, Florida	140	Longleaf pine (96%), cypress (3%), black mangrove (1%)	6
7. Superior National Forest, Minnesota	102	White pine (80%), red pine (13%), aspen (4%), other unknown species (3%)	35
8. Chippewa National Forest, Minnesota	292	White pine (53%), red pine (27%), aspen (16%), other species (4%)	34
9. Yellowstone National Park, Wyoming	24	Lodgepole pine (71%), whitebark pine (12%), Engelmann spruce (12%), Douglas fir (4%)	54
10. Arizona	14	Cliff nests (57%), cliff and tree nests (21%), tree nests only (21%), cottonwood and willow in territories	19
11. Northern California	87	Ponderosa pine (71%), sugar pine (16%), and six other species of pine, fir, and cedar	31

Table B. (cont.)

	Location	Number of nests	Tree species or structure type	Chapter 10 references
12.	Eastern Oregon	124	Ponderosa pine (81%), Douglas fir (13%), sugar pine (4%), other species (3%)	3, 4
13.	Western Oregon	31	Douglas fir (74%), Sitka spruce (23%), western hemlock (3%)	3, 4
14.	Western Washington	218	Douglas fir (70%), Sitka spruce (17%), western hemlock (4%), black cotton-wood (3%), western red cedar (1%), others (5%)	18
15.	Southeast Alaska	136	Sitka spruce (73%), western hemlock (13%), snag (7%), cedar (1%), unknown species (6%)	9
16.	Amchitka Island, Alaska	252	Sea stacks or pinnacles (66%), ridges and hillsides (34%)	46
17.	Kodiak National Wildlife Refuge, Alaska	326	Cottonwood trees (81%), rocky cliffs (13%), alder cliffs (6%)	57
18.	Southeast Alaska	2,140	Sitka spruce (78%), western hemlock (20%), cedar (2%)	42
19.	Baja California	3	Two mangroves, one large cactus	24
20.	Saskatchewan and Manitoba	290	Trembling aspen (54%), spruce (30%), jack pine (15%), cliffs (1%)	14

Table C. Reproductive statistics for bald eagles throughout North America during the 1970s and early 1980s.

Location*	Years	Number of nests	Percent territories			Percent nests			Number of young per nest			Chapter 11 references
			Occupied	Active	Successful	Occupied & active	Active & successful	Occupied & successful	Occupied	Active	Successful	
1. Bernard Lake, Saskatchewan	1970–1981	268	91.0	78.0	63.4	85.7	81.3	69.7	1.11	1.29	1.59	18
2. Northwest Ontario	1970–1981	1,370						48.0	0.80		1.67	23
3. Labrador	1970–1973	24						45.4	0.54		1.20	68
4. Maine	1972–1978	521	53.7	50.3	17.5	93.6	34.7	32.5	0.44	0.47	1.35	65
5. Maryland and Virginia	1978–1981	343						53.8	0.81			13
6. Florida	1972–1975	491						57.4	0.82			44
7. Michigan	1973–1981	778						56.3	0.89		1.59	38, 48
8. Wisconsin	1973–1981	1,279						67.4	1.13		1.68	38
9. Minnesota	1973–1981	1,338						69.7	1.17		1.67	38
10. Arizona	1975–1980	53	84.9	79.2	41.5	93.3	52.4	48.9	0.80	0.86	1.64	25
11. Yellowstone National Park, Wyoming	1972–1979	107	69.2	50.5	19.6	73.0	38.9	28.4	0.41	0.56	1.43	2, 64
12. Oregon	1978–1982	1,058	67.0					61.0	0.92	1.04		34

Location	Years											
13. Washington	1975–1980	279	77.8	64.5	44.8	82.9	69.4	57.6	0.82	0.98	1.42	25
14. San Juan Islands, Washington	1975–1980	324	84.9	81.2	52.5	95.6	64.6	61.8	0.84	0.87	1.35	25, 43
15. Alaska Peninsula	1970	43						61.7	0.97		1.61	29
16. Chippewa National Forest, Minnesota	1970–1980	1,820	69.8	46.0		65.8				1.10	1.68	39
17. Amchitka Island, Alaska	1972	71		60.6						0.86	1.42	57
18. Southeast Alaska	1972–1981	864								1.41		31
19. Interior Alaska	1978–1980	42					64.3			1.07	1.67	53
20. Kenai Peninsula, Alaska	1979–1980	45					75.0			1.20	1.60	3
North America totals	1970–1982		70.6	67.6	43.0	89.3	61.6	58.2	0.92	1.05	1.61	

*Location numbers correspond to those in Figure 11.9.

Appendix
2

Metric Conversions

Units of Length

To convert from: Multiply by:

Kilometers	to	*Miles*	0.621
Meters	to	*Yards*	1.094
Meters	to	*Feet*	3.281
Centimeters	to	*Inches*	0.394
Millimeters	to	*Inches*	0.039

Units of Area

To convert from: Multiply by:

Square Kilometers	to	*Square Miles*	0.386
Hectares	to	*Acres*	2.471

Units of Mass

To convert from: Multiply by:

Kilograms	to	*Pounds*	2.205
Grams	to	*Ounces*	0.035

Units of Temperature

To convert from: Multiply by: And add:

Centigrade	to	*Fahrenheit*	1.8	32

Units of Energy

Kilocalorie is the same as *Calorie* (in popular usage).

Appendix
3

*Scientific Names of Animals and Plants Referred to
in this Book*

BIRDS

Loon	*Gavia* spp.
Northern fulmer	*Fulmarus glacialis*
Brown pelican	*Pelecanus occidentalis*
Cormorant	*Phalacrocorax* spp.
Canada goose	*Branta canadensis*
Mallard	*Anas platyrhynchos*
Black duck	*Anas rubripes*
Pintail	*Anas acuta*
Widgeon	*Mareca americana*
Merganser	*Mergus* spp.
Turkey vulture	*Cathartes aura*
Black vulture	*Coragyps atratus*
Indian Brahminy kite	*Haliastur indus*
Lesser fishing eagle	*Ichthyophaga nana*
Grey-headed fishing eagle	*Ichthyophaga ichthyaetus*
Vulturine fish eagle	*Gypohierax angolensis*
African fish eagle	*Haliaeetus vocifer*
Madagascar fish eagle	*Haliaeetus vociferoides*
White-bellied sea eagle	*Haliaeetus leucogaster*
Sanford's sea eagle	*Haliaeetus sanfordi*
White-tailed sea eagle	*Haliaeetus albicilla*
White-headed sea eagle	*Haliaeetus leucocephalus*
Pallas' sea eagle	*Haliaeetus leucoryphus*
Steller's sea eagle	*Haliaeetus pelagicus*
Serpent eagle	*Spilornis* spp.
Northern harrier	*Circus cyaneus*
Black hawk	*Buteogallus anthracinus*
Broad-winged hawk	*Buteo platypterus*
Red-tailed hawk	*Buteo jamaicensis*
Golden eagle	*Aquila chrysaetos*
Osprey	*Pandion haliaetus*
Peregrine falcon	*Falco peregrinus*

BIRDS (cont.)

Chukar	*Alectoris graeca*
Great blue heron	*Ardea herodias*
American coot	*Fulica americana*
Herring gull	*Larus argentatus*
Cassin's auklet	*Ptychoramphus aleutica*
Crow	*Corvus* spp.
Magpie	*Pica* spp.

MAMMALS

Opossum	*Didelphis marsupialis*
White-tailed jackrabbit	*Lepus townsendi*
Black-tailed jackrabbit	*Lepus californicus*
Snowshoe hare	*Lepus americanus*
European rabbit	*Oryctolagus cuniculus*
Prairie dog	*Cynomys* spp.
Muskrat	*Ondatra zibethica*
Brown rat	*Rattus norvegicus*
Porcupine	*Erethizon dorsatum*
Nutria	*Myocastor coypus*
Beaked whale	*Mesoplodon* spp.
Sperm whale	*Physeter catodon*
Coyote	*Canis latrans*
Black bear	*Ursus americana*
Raccoon	*Procyon lotor*
River otter	*Lutra canadensis*
Sea otter	*Enhydra lutris*
Bobcat	*Lynx rufus*
Sea lion	*Eumetopias jubata*
Deer	*Odocoileus* spp.
Elk	*Cervus canadensis*
Bison	*Bison bison*

FISHES

Herring	*Alosa* spp. and *Clupea* spp.
Alewife or Gaspereaux	*Alosa pseudoharengus*
Gizzard shad	*Dorosoma cepedianum*
Cutthroat trout	*Salmo clarki*
Chum salmon	*Oncorhynchus keta*
Kokanee or Sockeye salmon	*Onocorhynchus nerka*
Char	*Salvelinus* spp.
Whitefish	*Prosopium williamsoni*
Oolichan	*Thaleichthys pacificus*
Northern pike	*Esox lucius*

FISHES (cont.)

Chain pickerel	*Esox niger*
Carp	*Cyprinus carpio*
Chub	*Gila* spp.
Northern squawfish	*Ptychocheilus oregonensis*
White sucker	*Catostomus commersoni*
Largescale sucker	*Catostomus macrocheilus*
Brown bullhead	*Ictalurus nebulosus*
Blue catfish	*Ictalurus furcatus*
White catfish	*Ictalurus catus*
Rock fish	*Sebastodes* spp.
Yellow perch	*Perca flavescens*
Rock greenling	*Nexagrammos lagocephalus*
Cod	*Gadus* spp.
Pollack	*Theragra chalcogramma*

TREES

Pine	*Pinus* spp.
White pine	*Pinus strobus*
Red pine	*Pinus resinosa*
Pitch pine	*Pinus rigida*
Loblolly pine	*Pinus taeda*
Virginia pine	*Pinus virginiana*
Slash pine	*Pinus elliottii*
Longleaf pine	*Pinus palustris*
Lodgepole pine	*Pinus contorta*
Whitebark pine	*Pinus albicaulis*
Ponderosa pine	*Pinus ponderosa*
Sugar pine	*Pinus monticola*
Jack pine	*Pinus banksiana*
Larch	*Larix* spp.
Western larch	*Larix occidentalis*
Spruce	*Picea* spp.
White spruce	*Picea glauca*
Red spruce	*Picea rubens*
Black spruce	*Picea mariana*
Engelmann spruce	*Picea engelmannii*
Sitka spruce	*Picea sitchensis*
Eastern hemlock	*Tsuga canadensis*
Western hemlock	*Tsuga heterophylla*
Douglas fir	*Pseudotsuga menziesii*
Fir	*Abies* spp.
Western red cedar	*Thuja plicata*
Cypress	*Cupressus* spp.
Willow	*Salix* spp.

TREES (cont.)

Black willow	*Salix nigra*
Cottonwood and Poplar	*Populus* spp.
Black cottonwood	*Populus trichocarpa*
Trembling aspen	*Populus tremuloides*
Hickory	*Carya* spp.
Pecan	*Carya illinoensis*
Birch	*Betula* spp.
Paper birch	*Betula papyrifera*
Yellow birch	*Betula alleghaniensis*
Alder	*Alnus* spp.
Red alder	*Alnus rubra*
American beech	*Fagus grandifolia*
Oak	*Quercus* spp.
Red oak	*Quercus rubra*
Elm	*Ulmus* spp.
Sycamore	*Platanus* spp.
Maple	*Acer* spp.
Sugar maple	*Acer saccharum*
Bigleaf maple	*Acer macrophyllum*
Red mangrove	*Rhizophora mangle*
White mangrove	*Laguncularia racemosa*
Persimmon	*Diospyros virginiana*
Ash	*Fraxinus* spp.
Black mangrove	*Avicennia nitida*

REPTILES

Diamondback terrapin	*Malaclemys terrapin*
Musk turtle	*Sternotherus odoratus*
Black swamp snake	*Seminatrix pygaea*

INVERTEBRATES

Snail	Gastropoda
Abalone	*Haliotis* spp.
Blue mussel	*Mytilus edulis*
Clam	Heterodonta
Squid	*Loligo pealei*
Octopus	Octopoda
Shrimp	Decapoda
Crab	*Cancer* spp.
Starfish	Asteroidea

Literature Cited

Chapter 1.
1. Herrick, F. H. 1934. *The American Eagle: A Study in Natural and Civil History.* New York: Appleton-Century.

Chapter 2.
1. Amadon, D. 1983. The bald eagle and its relatives. In *Biology and Management of Bald Eagles and Ospreys,* ed. D. M. Bird. Ste. Anne de Bellevue, Quebec: Harpell Press, pp. 1–4.
2. Brown, L. 1976. *Eagles of the World.* New York: Universe Books.
3. ———. 1980. *The African Fish Eagle.* Cape Town: Purnell.
4. Brown, L. H., and D. Amadon. 1968. *Eagles, Hawks and Falcons of the World.* Vol. 1. New York: McGraw-Hill.
5. Feduccia, A. 1980. *The Age of Birds.* Cambridge, Mass.: Harvard University Press.
6. Grossman, M. L., and J. Hamlet. 1964. *Birds of Prey of the World.* New York: Clarkson N. Potter.
7. Laycock, G. 1973. *Autumn of the Eagle.* New York: Scribners.
8. Lincer, J. L., W. S. Clark, and M. N. LeFranc, Jr. 1979. *Working Bibliography of the Bald Eagle.* Washington, D.C.: National Wildlife Federation.
9. Miller, L. 1957. Bird remains from an Oregon Indian midden. *Condor* 59:59–63.
10. Murphy, J. R. 1979. The sea eagles of the world: Current status and concerns. In *Proceedings of the 1979 Bald Eagle Days,* ed. T. Ingram. Apple River, Ill.: Eagle Valley Environmentalists, pp. 152–58.

Chapter 3.
1. Amadon, D. 1983. The bald eagle and its relatives. In *Biology and Management of Bald Eagles and Ospreys,* ed. D. M. Bird, Ste. Anne de Bellevue, Quebec: Harpell Press, pp. 1–4.
2. Baird, S. F., T. M. Brewer, and R. Ridgeway. 1974. *History of North American Birds.* Vol. 3. New York: Arno Press.
3. Bent, A. C. 1937. *Life Histories of North American Birds of Prey.* Part 1. Washington, D.C.: U.S. National Museum Bulletin 167, pp. 321–49.
4. Bortolotti, G. R. 1984. Sexual size dimorphism and age-related size variation in bald eagles. *Journal of Wildlife Management* 48:72–81.
5. Brewster, W. 1925. The birds of the Lake Umbagog region of Maine. *Bulletin of the Museum of Comparative Zoology* 66:211–402.
6. Brodkorb, P. 1955. Number of feathers and weights of various systems in the bald eagle. *Wilson Bulletin* 67:142.
7. Brown, L. 1976. *Eagles of the World.* New York: Universe Books.
8. Chrest, H. R. 1964. Nesting of the bald eagle in the Karluk Lake drainage on Kodiak Island, Alaska. Master's thesis, Colorado State University, Fort Collins.
9. Clark, W. S. 1983. The field identification of North American eagles. *American Birds* 37:822–26.
10. Friedmann, H. 1950. *The Birds of North and Middle America.* Part 11. Washington, D.C.: U.S. National Museum Bulletin 50.

11. Garcelon, D. K., M. S. Martell, P. T. Redig, and L. C. Buoen. 1985. Morphometric, karyotypic, and laparoscopic techniques for determining sex in bald eagles. *Journal of Wildlife Management* 49: 595–99.

12. Gerrard, J. M., D. W. A. Whitfield, P. Gerrard, P. N. Gerrard, and W. J. Maher. 1978. Migratory movements and plumage of subadult Saskatchewan bald eagles. *Canadian Field-Naturalist* 92:375–82.

13. Gerrard, P. N., S. N. Wiemeyer, and J. M. Gerrard. 1979. Some observations on the behavior of captive bald eagles before and during incubation. *Raptor Research* 13:57–64.

14. Gilbert, S., P. Tomassoni, and P. A. Kramer. 1981. History of captive management and breeding of bald eagles. *International Zoo Yearbook* 21:101–09.

15. Grubb, T. G., and D. M. Rubink. 1978. First bald eagle eggs collected for analysis in Arizona. Tempe, Ariz.: Rocky Mountain Forest and Range Experiment Station, U.S. Forest Service Research Note RM-352.

16. Hancock, D. 1973. Captive propagation of bald eagles. *International Zoo Yearbook* 13:244–49.

17. Harmata, A. R. 1984. Bald eagles of the San Luis Valley, Colorado: Their winter ecology and spring migration. Ph.D. diss., Montana State University, Bozeman.

18. Hensel, R. J., and W. A. Troyer. 1964. Nesting studies of the bald eagle in Alaska. *Condor* 66:282–86.

19. Herrick, F. R. 1934. *The American Eagle: A Study in Natural and Civil History.* New York: Appleton-Century.

20. Hunt, W. G., B. S. Johnson, J. B. Bulger, and C. Thelander. 1980. Impacts of a proposed Copper Creek Dam on bald eagles. Unpublished report. San Francisco: Biosystems Analysis, Inc.

21. Imler, R. H., and E. R. Kalmbach. 1955. The bald eagle and its economic status. Washington, D.C.: U.S. Department of Interior, Fish and Wildlife Circular No. 30.

22. Jollie, M. S. 1947. Plumage changes in golden eagles. *Auk* 64:549–76.

23. Laycock, G. 1973. *Autumn of the Eagle.* New York: Scribner's.

24. McClelland, B. R., L. S. Young, D. S. Shea, P. T. McClelland, H. L. Allen, and E. B. Spettigue. 1981. The bald eagle concentration in Glacier National Park, Montana: Origin, growth, and variation in numbers. *Living Bird* 21:133–55.

25. Mengel, R. M. 1953. On the name of the northern bald eagle and the identity of Audubon's gigantic "Bird of Washington." *Wilson Bulletin* 65:145–51.

26. Murie, O. J. 1975. *A Field Guide to Animal Tracks.* Boston: Houghton Mifflin.

27. Newton, I. 1979. *Population Ecology of Raptors.* Vermillion, S. D.: Buteo Books.

28. Oberholser, H. C. 1906. *The North American Eagles and Their Economic Relations.* Washington, D.C.: U.S. Department of Agriculture, Biological Survey Bulletin No. 27.

29. Orians, G. H. 1980. Why are bald eagles bald? In *Proceedings of the Washington Bald Eagle Symposium,* ed. R. L. Knight, G. T. Allen, M. V. Stalmaster, and C. W. Servheen. Seattle: The Nature Conservancy, pp. 3–11.

30. Retfalvi, L. I. 1965. Breeding behavior and feeding habits of the bald eagle (*Haliaeetus leucocephalus* L.) on San Juan Island, Washington. Master's thesis, University of British Columbia, Vancouver.

31. Robards, F. C. 1966. Capture, handling and banding of bald eagles. Juneau, Alaska: U.S. Fish and Wildlife Service Research Report.

32. Sell, R. J., and D. W. Anderson. 1979. Regression analysis of latitudinal trends

in bald eagle egg size—taxonomic implications. Raptor Research Annual Meeting, Davis, California (Abstract).

33. Servheen, C. W. 1975. Ecology of the wintering bald eagles on the Skagit River, Washington. Master's thesis, University of Washington, Seattle.

34. ———. 1976. Deck-feather molt in bald and golden eagles in relation to feather mounting of radio transmitters. *Raptor Research* 10:58–60.

35. Shlaer, R. 1972. An eagle's eye: Quality of the retinal image. *Science* 176: 1920–22.

36. Snyder, N. F. R., and J. W. Wiley. 1976. Sexual size dimorphism in hawks and owls of North America. *Ornithological Monograph* 20:1–96.

37. Southern, W. E. 1964. Additional observations on winter bald eagle populations: Including remarks on biotelemetry techniques and immature plumages. *Wilson Bulletin* 76:121–37.

38. ———. 1967. Further comments on subadult bald eagle plumages. *Jack-Pine Warbler* 45:70–80.

39. Stott, K., Jr. 1948. Notes on the longevity of captive birds. *Auk* 65:402–05.

40. Verner, J., and R. N. Lehman. 1979. Sonographic identification of individual bald eagles and peregrine falcons in California—A feasibility study. Raptor Research Annual Meeting, Davis, California (Abstract).

Chapter 4.

1. Andrew, J. M., and J. A. Mosher. 1982. Bald eagle nest site selection and nesting habitat in Maryland. *Journal of Wildlife Management* 46:383–90.

2. Braun, C. E., F. Hamerstrom, T. Ray, and C. M. White. 1975. Conservation committee report on status of eagles. *Wilson Bulletin* 87:140–43.

3. Broley, C. L. 1947. Migration and nesting of Florida bald eagles. *Wilson Bulletin* 59:3–20.

4. Broley, M. J. 1952. *Eagle Man.* New York: Pellegrini & Cudahy.

5. Donohoe, M. 1981. A council of eagles. *Oceans* 14:3–5.

6. Dunstan, T. C. 1978. Our bald eagle: Freedom's symbol survives. *National Geographic* 153:186–99.

7. Dunstan, T. C., J. E. Mathisen, and J. F. Harper. 1975. The biology of bald eagles in Minnesota. *Loon* 47:5–10.

8. Gerrard, J. M. 1983. A review of the current status of bald eagles in North America. In *Biology and Management of Bald Eagles and Ospreys,* ed. D. M. Bird. Ste. Anne de Bellevue, Quebec: Harpell Press, pp. 5–21.

9. Gerrard, J. M., D. W. A. Whitfield, P. Gerrard, P. N. Gerrard, and W. J. Maher. 1978. Migratory movements and plumage of subadult Saskatchewan bald eagles. *Canadian Field-Naturalist* 92:375–82.

10. Graham, F., Jr. 1976. Will the bald eagle survive to 2076? *Audubon* 78:99–101.

11. Green, N. 1985. The bald eagle. In *Audubon Wildlife Report—1985,* ed. A. M. Enos and R. L. Di Silvestro. New York: National Audubon Society, pp. 508–31.

12. Grier, J. W. 1974. Reproduction, organochlorines, and mercury in northwestern Ontario bald eagles. *Canadian Field-Naturalist* 88:469–75.

13. Griffin, C. R. 1978. The ecology of bald eagles wintering at Swan Lake National Wildlife Refuge, with emphasis on eagle-waterfowl relationships. Master's thesis, University of Missouri, Columbia.

14. Griffin, C. R., J. M. Southern, and L. D. Frenzel. 1980. Origins and migratory

movements of bald eagles wintering in Missouri. *Journal of Field Ornithology* 51:161–67.

15. Hancock, D. 1965. West Coast eagle survey. *Canadian Audubon* 27:37–41.

16. Hansen, A. J., 1984. Behavioral ecology of bald eagles along the Pacific Northwest Coast: A landscape perspective. Ph.D. diss., University of Tennessee, Knoxville.

17. Harmata, A. R. 1984. Bald eagles of the San Luis Valley, Colorado: Their winter ecology and spring migration. Ph.D. diss., Montana State University, Bozeman.

18. Harper, J. F., and T. C. Dunstan. 1976. Dispersal and migration of fledgling bald eagles. In *Proceedings of the 1976 Bald Eagle Days*, ed. T. Ingram. Apple River, Ill.: Eagle Valley Environmentalists, pp. 94–100.

19. Hodges, J. I., Jr., J. G. King, and R. Davies. 1984. Bald eagle breeding population survey of coastal British Columbia. *Journal of Wildlife Management* 48:993–98.

20. Hodges, J. I., J. G. King, and F. C. Robards. 1979. Resurvey of the bald eagle breeding population in southeast Alaska. *Journal of Wildlife Management* 43:219–21.

21. Howard, R. P., and L. J. Van Daele. 1980. An overview of the status of bald eagles in Idaho. In *Proceedings of the Washington Bald Eagle Symposium*, ed. R. L. Knight, G. T. Allen, M. V. Stalmaster, and C. W. Servheen, Seattle: The Nature Conservancy, pp. 23–33.

22. Hunt, W. G., and B. S. Johnson. 1981. Impacts of a proposed Copper Creek Dam on bald eagles: Second winter study. Unpublished report. San Francisco: Biosystems Analysis, Inc.

23. Keister, G. P., Jr. 1981. Characteristics of winter roosts and populations of bald eagles in the Klamath Basin. Master's thesis, Oregon State University, Corvallis.

24. King, J. G., F. C. Robards, and C. J. Lensink. 1972. Census of the bald eagle breeding population in southeast Alaska. *Journal of Wildlife Management* 36:1292–95.

25. Korhel, A. H., and T. W. Clark. 1981. Bald eagle winter survey in the Snake River Canyon, Wyoming. *Great Basin Naturalist* 41:461–64.

26. Krause, F. 1981. Winter gathering on the Skagit. *Nature Conservancy News* 31:16–21.

27. Leighton, F. A., J. M. Gerrard, P. Gerrard, D. W. A. Whitfield, and W. J. Maher. 1979. An aerial census of bald eagles in Saskatchewan. *Journal of Wildlife Management* 43:61–69.

28. Lint, J. B. 1975. A report of the bald eagles of Wolf Lodge Bay. U.S. Department of Interior, Bureau of Land Management, Coeur d'Alene, Idaho.

29. Lish, J. W., and J. C. Lewis. 1975. Status and ecology of bald eagles wintering in Oklahoma. In *Proceedings of the 29th Annual Conference of the Southeastern Association of Game and Fish Commissioners*, pp. 415–23.

30. McClelland, B. R. 1973. Autumn concentrations of bald eagles in Glacier National Park. *Condor* 75:121–23.

31. McClelland, B. R., L. S. Young, D. S. Shea, P. T. McClelland, H. L. Allen, and E. B. Spettigue. 1981. The bald eagle concentration in Glacier National Park, Montana: Origin, growth, and variation in numbers. *Living Bird* 21:133–55.

32. National Wildlife Federation. 1983. Results of the mid-winter bald eagle survey: 1979, 1980, 1981, 1982, and 1983. Washington, D.C.: National Wildlife Federation News Release.

33. Nye, P. E. 1977. Ecological relationships of bald eagles on a wintering area in New York State. Master's thesis, College of Saint Rose, Albany, New York.
34. Platt, J. B. 1976. Bald eagles wintering in a Utah desert. *American Birds* 30:783–88.
35. Postupalsky, S. 1976. Banded northern bald eagles in Florida and southern states. *Auk* 93:835–36.
36. Retfalvi, L. 1965. Breeding behavior and feeding habits of the bald eagle *(Haliaeetus leucocephalus)* on San Juan Island, Washington. Master's thesis, University of British Columbia, Vancouver.
37. Servheen, C. W. 1975. Ecology of the wintering bald eagles on the Skagit River, Washington. Master's thesis, University of Washington, Seattle.
38. Servheen, C. W., and W. English. 1979. Movements of rehabilitated bald eagles and proposed seasonal movement patterns of bald eagles in the Pacific Northwest. *Raptor Research* 13:79–88.
39. Shea, D. S. 1978. Bald eagle concentrations in Glacier National Park. *Western Birds* 9:35–37.
40. Southern, W. E. 1964. Additional observations on winter bald eagle populations: Including remarks on biotelemetry techniques and immature plumages. *Wilson Bulletin* 76:121–37.
41. Spencer, D. A., ed. 1976. Wintering of the migrant bald eagle in the lower 48 states. Washington, D.C.: National Agricultural Chemicals Association.
42. Sprunt, A., IV. 1969. Population trends of the bald eagle in North America. In *Peregrine Falcon Populations: Their Biology and Decline*, ed. J. J. Hickey. Madison: University of Wisconsin Press, pp. 347–51.
43. Stalmaster, M. V., J. R. Newman, and A. J. Hansen. 1979. Population dynamics of wintering bald eagles on the Nooksack River, Washington. *Northwest Science* 53:126–31.
44. Steenhof, K. 1976. The ecology of wintering bald eagles in southeastern South Dakota. Master's thesis, University of Missouri, Columbia.
45. Swenson, J. E. 1975. Ecology of the bald eagle and osprey in Yellowstone National Park. Master's thesis, Montana State University, Bozeman.
46. Todd, C. S. 1979. The ecology of the bald eagle in Maine. Master's thesis, University of Maine, Orono.
47. Welty, C. 1962. *The Life of Birds*. Philadelphia: Saunders.
48. Wetmore, S. P., and D. I. Gillespie. 1976. Osprey and bald eagle populations in Labrador and northeastern Quebec, 1969–1973. *Canadian Field-Naturalist* 90:330–37.
49. Whitfield, D. W. A., J. M. Gerrard, W. J. Maher, and D. W. Davis. 1974. Bald eagle nesting habitat, density, and reproduction in central Saskatchewan and Manitoba. *Canadian Field-Naturalist* 88:399–407.
50. Young, L. S. 1983. Movements of bald eagles associated with autumn concentrations in Glacier National Park. Master's thesis, University of Montana, Missoula.

Chapter 5.

1. Alt, K. L. 1980. Ecology of the breeding bald eagle and osprey in the Grand Teton–Yellowstone National Parks Complex. Master's thesis, Montana State University, Bozeman.
2. Anderson, R. J., and A. M. Bruce. 1980. A comparison of selected bald and

golden eagle nests in western Washington. In *Proceedings of the Washington Bald Eagle Symposium*, ed. R. L. Knight, G. T. Allen, M. V. Stalmaster, and C. W. Servheen. Seattle: The Nature Conservancy, pp 117–20.

3. Bailey, A. M. 1919. The bald eagle in Louisiana. *Wilson Bulletin* 31:52–55.

4. Bent, A. C. 1937. Life histories of North American birds of prey. Part I. Washington, D.C.: National Museum Bulletin 167, pp. 321–49.

5. Bortolotti, G. R. 1984. Evolution of growth rate and nestling sex ratio in bald eagles *(Haliaeetus leucocephalus)*. Ph.D. diss., University of Toronto.

6. ———. 1984. Physical development of nestling bald eagles with emphasis on the timing of growth events. *Wilson Bulletin* 96:524–42.

7. Broley, C. L. 1947. Migration and nesting of Florida bald eagles. *Wilson Bulletin* 59:3–20.

8. Broley, M. J. 1952. *Eagle Man.* New York: Pellegrini & Cudahy.

9. Brown, L. 1977. *Eagles of the World.* New York: Universe Books.

10. Chrest, H. R. 1964. Nesting of the bald eagle in the Karluk Lake drainage on Kodiak Island, Alaska. Master's thesis, Colorado State University, Fort Collins.

11. Corr, P. O. 1974. Bald eagle *(Haliaeetus leucocephalus alaskanus)* nesting related to forestry in southeastern Alaska. Master's thesis, University of Alaska, College.

12. Fraser, J. D. 1981. The breeding biology and status of the bald eagle on the Chippewa National Forest. Ph.D. diss., University of Minnesota, St. Paul.

13. Fraser, J. D., L. D. Frenzel, J. E. Mathisen, and M. E. Shough. 1983. Three adult bald eagles at an active nest. *Raptor Research* 17:29–30.

14. Gerrard, J. M., P. N. Gerrard, G. R. Bortolotti, and D. W. A. Whitfield. 1983. A 14-year study of bald eagle reproduction on Besnard Lake, Saskatchewan. In *Biology and Management of Bald Eagles and Ospreys*, ed. D. M. Bird. Ste. Anne de Bellevue, Quebec: Harpell Press, pp. 47–57.

15. Gerrard, J. M., P. N. Gerrard, and D. W. A. Whitfield. 1980. Behavior in a non-breeding bald eagle. *Canadian Field-Naturalist* 94:391–97.

16. Gerrard, P. N., S. N. Wiemeyer, and J. M. Gerrard. 1979. Some observations of the behavior of captive bald eagles before and during incubation. *Raptor Research* 13:57–64.

17. Gilbert, S., P. Tomassoni, and P. A. Kramer. 1981. History of captive management and breeding of bald eagles. *International Zoo Yearbook* 21:101–09.

18. Gittens, E. F. 1968. A study on the status of the bald eagle in Nova Scotia. Master's thesis, Acadia University, Wolfville, Nova Scotia.

19. Grier, J. W. 1969. Bald eagle behavior and productivity responses to climbing to nests. *Journal of Wildlife Management* 33:961–66.

20. Grubb, T. G. 1976. A survey and analysis of bald eagle nesting in western Washington. Master's thesis, University of Washington, Seattle.

21. ———. 1976. Nesting bald eagles attack researcher. *Auk* 93:842–43.

22. Hancock, D. 1965. West Coast eagle survey. *Canadian Audubon* 27:37–41.

23. ———. 1973. Captive propagation of bald eagles *(Haliaeetus leucocephalus)*— A review. *International Zoo Yearbook* 13:244–49.

24. Harmata, A. R. 1984. Bald eagles of the San Luis Valley, Colorado: Their winter ecology and spring migration. Ph.D. diss., Montana State University, Bozeman.

25. Hehnke, M. F. 1973. Nesting ecology and feeding behavior of bald eagles on the Alaska peninsula. Master's thesis, California State University, Humboldt.

26. Hensel, R. J., and W. A. Troyer. 1964. Nesting studies of the bald eagle in Alaska. *Condor* 66:282–86.
27. Herrick, F. H. 1924. Nests and nesting habits of the American eagle. *Auk* 41:213–31.
28. ———. 1932. Daily life of the American eagle: Early phase. *Auk* 49:307–23.
29. ———. 1934. *The American Eagle: A Study in Natural and Civil History.* New York: Appleton-Century.
30. Hodges, J. I., Jr. 1981. Chilkat River Valley bald eagle nest surveys—1966, 1979 and 1980. Unpublished report. U.S. Fish and Wildlife Service, Juneau, Alaska.
31. ———. 1982. Bald eagle nesting studies in Seymour Canal, southeast Alaska. *Condor* 84:125–27.
32. Hodges, J. I., Jr., and F. C. Robards. 1982. Observations of 3,850 bald eagle nests in southeast Alaska. In *Proceedings of a Symposium and Workshop, Raptor Management and Biology in Alaska and Western Canada,* ed. W. N. Ladd and P. F. Schempf. U.S. Fish and Wildlife Service, Alaska Regional Office, Anchorage, pp. 37–46.
33. Howell, J. C. 1967. Comparison of nesting sites of bald eagles in central Florida from 1930 to 1965. *Auk* 84:602–03.
34. Isaacs, F. B., R. G. Anthony, and R. J. Anderson. 1983. Distribution and productivity of nesting bald eagles in Oregon, 1978–1982. *Murrelet* 64:33–38.
35. Lehman, R. N. 1978. An analysis of habitat parameters and site selection criteria for nesting bald eagles in California. Part 1. Unpublished report. U.S. Forest Service, San Francisco.
36. Maestrelli, J. R., and S. N. Wiemeyer. 1975. Breeding bald eagles in captivity. *Wilson Bulletin* 87:45–53.
37. Mahaffy, M. S. 1981. Territorial behavior of the bald eagle on the Chippewa National Forest. Master's thesis, University of Minnesota, St. Paul.
38. Mathisen, J. E. 1980. Bald eagle–osprey status report, 1980. U.S. Forest Service, Chippewa National Forest, Cass Lake, Minnesota.
39. Mathisen, J., and J. Stewart. 1970. A band for an eagle. *Loon* 42:84–87.
40. Mattsson, J. P. 1974. Interaction of a breeding pair of bald eagles with subadults at Sucker Lake, Michigan. Master's thesis, St. Cloud State College, Minnesota.
41. McEwan, L. C., and D. H. Hirth. 1979. Southern bald eagle productivity and nest site selection. *Journal of Wildlife Management* 43:585–94.
42. Murphy, J. R. 1962. Aggressive behavior of a bald eagle. *Auk* 79:712–13.
43. Newton, I. 1979. *Population Ecology of Raptors.* Vermillion, S.D.: Buteo Books.
44. Nice, M. M. 1953. The earliest mention of territory. *Condor* 55:316–17.
45. Ogden, J. C. 1975. Effects of bald eagle territoriality on nesting ospreys. *Wilson Bulletin* 87:496–505.
46. Ohmart, R. D., and R. J. Sell. 1980. The bald eagle of the Southwest with special emphasis on the breeding population of Arizona. Unpublished report. Arizona State University, Tempe.
47. Retfalvi, L. I. 1965. Breeding behavior and feeding habits of the bald eagle (*Haliaeetus leucocephalus* L.) on San Juan Island, Washington. Master's thesis, University of British Columbia, Vancouver.
48. Ritchie, R. J. 1982. Investigations of bald eagles, Tanana River, Alaska, 1977–80. In *Proceedings of a Symposium and Workshop, Raptor Manage-*

ment and Biology in Alaska and Western Canada, ed. W. N. Ladd and P. F. Schempf. U.S. Fish and Wildlife Service, Alaska Regional Office, Anchorage, pp. 55–67.

49. Robards, F. C., and J. I. Hodges. 1977. Observations from 2,760 bald eagle nests in southeast Alaska. U.S. Fish and Wildlife Service, Juneau.

50. Robards, F. C., and J. G. King. 1966. Nesting and productivity of bald eagles, southeast Alaska—1966. U.S. Fish and Wildlife Service, Juneau.

51. Sell, R. J., and D. W. Anderson. 1979. Regression analysis of latitudinal trends in bald eagle egg size—taxonomic implications. Raptor Research Annual Meeting, Davis, Calif. (Abstract.)

52. Sherrod, S. K., C. M. White, and F. S. L. Williamson. 1976. Biology of the bald eagle on Amchitka Island, Alaska. *Living Bird* 15:143–82.

53. Smith, F. R. 1936. The food and nesting habits of the bald eagle. *Auk* 53:301–05.

54. Sprunt, A., IV., W. B. Robertson, Jr., S. Postupalsky, R. J. Hensel, C. E. Knoder, and F. J. Ligas. 1973. Comparative productivity of six bald eagle populations. *Transactions of the 28th North American Wildlife and Natural Resources Conference* 38:96–106.

55. Todd, C. S. 1979. The ecology of the bald eagle in Maine. Master's thesis, University of Maine, Orono.

56. Welty, J. C. 1962. *The Life of Birds.* Philadelphia: Saunders.

57. Whitfield, D. W. A., J. M. Gerrard, W. J. Maher, and D. W. Davis. 1974. Bald eagle nesting habitat, density, and reproduction in central Saskatchewan and Manitoba. *Canadian Field-Naturalist* 88:399–407.

58. Wiemeyer, S. N. 1981. Captive propagation of bald eagles at Patuxent Wildlife Research Center and introductions into the wild, 1976–80. *Raptor Research* 15:68–82.

59. Young, L. S. 1983. Movements of bald eagles associated with autumn concentrations in Glacier National Park. Master's thesis, University of Montana, Missoula.

Chapter 6.

1. Altman, R. L. 1983. Post-release flight and foraging behavior of a bald eagle hacked in western Kentucky. *Raptor Research* 17:37–42.

2. Bent, A. C. 1937. Life histories of North American birds of prey. Part 1. Washington, D.C.: U.S. National Museum Bulletin 167, pp. 321–49.

3. Bortolotti, G. R. 1984. Evolution of growth rate and nestling sex ratio in bald eagles *(Haliaeetus leucocephalus).* Ph.D. diss., University of Toronto.

4. ———. 1984. Criteria for determining age and sex of nestling bald eagles. *Journal of Field Ornithology* 55:467–81.

5. ———. 1984. Physical development of nestling bald eagles with emphasis on the timing of growth events. *Wilson Bulletin* 96:524–42.

6. Brown, L. 1977. *Eagles of the World.* New York: Universe Books.

7. Chrest, H. R. 1964. Nesting of the bald eagle in the Karluk Lake drainage on Kodiak Island, Alaska. Master's thesis, Colorado State University, Fort Collins.

8. Evans, D. L. 1982. Status reports on twelve raptors. U.S. Fish and Wildlife Service, Special Scientific Report—Wildlife No. 238. Washington, D.C., pp. 1–13.

9. Fraser, J. D. 1981. The breeding biology and status of the bald eagle on the Chippewa National Forest. Ph.D. diss., University of Minnesota, St. Paul.

10. Gerrard, P., J. M. Gerrard, D. W. A. Whitfield, and W. J. Maher. 1974. Post-fledging movements of juvenile bald eagles. *Blue Jay* 32:218–26.

11. Gilbert, S., P. Tomassoni, and P. A. Kramer. 1981. History of captive management and breeding of bald eagles. *International Zoo Yearbook* 21:101–09.

12. Grier, J. W. 1969. Bald eagle behavior and productivity responses to climbing to nests. *Journal of Wildlife Management* 33:961–66.

13. Harper, J. F. 1974. Activities of fledgling bald eagles in north central Minnesota. Master's thesis, Western Illinois University, Macomb.

14. Hensel, R. J., and W. A. Troyer. 1964. Nesting studies of the bald eagle in Alaska. *Condor* 66:282–86.

15. Herrick, F. H. 1932. Daily life of the American eagle: Early phase. *Auk* 49:307–23.

16. ———. 1933. Daily life of the American eagle: Early phase (concluded). *Auk* 50:35–53.

17. ———. 1934. *The American Eagle: A Study in Natural and Civil History*. New York: Appleton-Century.

18. Kussman, J. V. 1977. Post-fledging behavior of the northern bald eagle *(Haliaeetus leucocephalus alascanus)* on the Chippewa National Forest, Minnesota. Ph.D. diss., University of Minnesota, St. Paul.

19. Maestrelli, J. R., and S. N. Wiemeyer. 1975. Breeding bald eagles in captivity. *Wilson Bulletin* 87:45–53.

20. Mattsson, J. P. 1974. Interaction of a breeding pair of bald eagles with sub-adults at Sucker Lake, Michigan. Master's thesis, St. Cloud State College, Minnesota.

21. Milburn, E. H. 1979. An evaluation of the hacking technique for establishing bald eagles *(Haliaeetus leucocephalus)*. Master's thesis, Cornell University, Ithaca, New York.

22. Pramstaller, M. E. 1977. Nocturnal, preroosting, and postroosting behavior of breeding adult and young of the year bald eagles *(Haliaeetus leucocephalus alascanus)* on the Chippewa National Forest, Minnesota. Master's thesis, University of Minnesota, St. Paul.

23. Retfalvi, L. I. 1965. Breeding behavior and feeding habits of the bald eagle *(Haliaeetus leucocephalus* L.) on San Juan Island, Washington. Master's thesis, University of British Columbia, Vancouver.

24. Sherrod, S. K., C. M. White, and F. S. L. Williamson. 1976. Biology of the bald eagle on Amchitka Island, Alaska. *Living Bird* 15:143–82.

25. Weekes, F. M. 1975. Behavior of a young bald eagle at a southern Ontario nest. *Canadian Field-Naturalist* 89:35–40.

Chapter 7.

1. Allen, H. L., and L. S. Young. 1982. *An Annotated Bibliography of Avian Communal Roosting*. Olympia: Washington Department of Game.

2. Boeker, E. L., A. J. Hansen, and J. I. Hodges. 1982. Third annual progress report: Chilkat River cooperative bald eagle study. New York: National Audubon Society.

3. Edwards, C. C. 1969. Winter behavior and population dynamics of American eagles in Utah. Ph.D. diss., Brigham Young University, Provo.

4. Fischer, D. L. 1982. The seasonal abundance, habitat use and foraging behavior

of wintering bald eagles, *Haliaeetus leucocephalus*, in west-central Illinois. Master's thesis, Western Illinois University, Macomb.

5. Griffin, C. R. 1981. Interactive behavior among bald eagles wintering in north-central Missouri. *Wilson Bulletin* 93:259–64.

6. Griffin, C. R., T. S. Baskett, and R. D. Sparrowe. 1982. Ecology of bald eagles wintering near a waterfowl concentration. Washington, D.C.: U.S. Department of Interior, Fish and Wildlife Service Special Wildlife Report, Wildlife No. 247.

7. Grubb, T. G., and C. E. Kennedy. 1982. Bald eagle winter habitat on southwestern national forests. U.S. Department of Agriculture, Forest Service Research Paper RM-237, Fort Collins, Colorado.

8. Hancock, D. 1964. Bald eagles wintering in the southern Gulf Islands, British Columbia. *Wilson Bulletin* 76:111–20.

9. Hansen, A. J., M. V. Stalmaster, and J. R. Newman. 1980. Habitat characteristics, function, and destruction of bald eagle communal roosts in western Washington. In *Proceedings of the Washington Bald Eagle Symposium*, ed. R. L. Knight, G. T. Allen, M. V. Stalmaster, and C. W. Servheen. Seattle: The Nature Conservancy, pp. 221–29.

10. Harmata, A. R. 1984. Bald eagles of the San Luis Valley, Colorado: Their winter ecology and spring migration. Ph.D. diss., Montana State University, Bozeman.

11. Harper, R. G. 1983. An ecological investigation of wintering bald eagles at Lock and Dam 24, Mississippi River. Master's thesis, Western Illinois University, Macomb.

12. Joseph, R. A. 1977. Behavior and age class structure of wintering northern bald eagles *(Haliaeetus leucocephalus alascanus)* in western Utah. Master's thesis, Brigham Young University, Provo.

13. Keister, G. P., Jr. 1981. Characteristics of winter roosts and populations of bald eagles in the Klamath Basin. Master's thesis, Oregon State University, Corvallis.

14. Knight, R. L., J. B. Athern, J. J. Brueggeman, and A. W. Erickson. 1979. Observations on wintering bald and golden eagles on the Columbia River, Washington. *Murrelet* 60:99–105.

15. Knight, S. K. 1981. Aspects of food finding and avoidance behavior of wintering bald eagles. Master's thesis, Western Washington University, Bellingham.

16. Knight, S. K., and R. L. Knight. 1983. Aspects of food finding by wintering bald eagles. *Auk* 100:477–84.

17. Lish, J. W. 1973. Status and ecology of bald eagles and nesting of golden eagles in Oklahoma. Master's thesis, Oklahoma State University, Stillwater.

18. McClelland, B. R., L. S. Young, D. S. Shea, P. T. McClelland, H. L. Allen, and E. B. Spettigue. 1981. The bald eagle concentration in Glacier National Park, Montana: Origin, growth, and variation in numbers. *Living Bird* 21:133–55.

19. Millsap, B. A. 1984. Midwinter bald eagle survey. *Eyas* 7:2–4.

20. National Wildlife Federation. 1983. Results of the midwinter bald eagle survey: 1979, 1980, 1981, 1982, and 1983. Washington, D.C.: National Wildlife Federation News Release.

21. Platt, J. B. 1976. Bald eagles wintering in a Utah desert. *American Birds* 30:783–88.

22. Russock, H. I. 1979. Observations on the behavior of wintering bald eagles. *Raptor Research* 13:112–15.

23. Servheen, C. W. 1975. Ecology of the wintering bald eagles on the Skagit River, Washington. Master's thesis, University of Washington, Seattle.

24. Shea, D. S. 1973. A management-oriented study of bald eagle concentrations in Glacier National Park. Master's thesis, University of Montana, Missoula.

25. ———. 1978. Bald eagle concentrations in Glacier National Park. *Western Birds* 9:35–37.

26. Southern, W. E. 1963. Winter populations, behavior, and seasonal dispersal of bald eagles in northwestern Illinois. *Wilson Bulletin* 75:42–55.

27. ———. 1964. Additional observations on winter bald eagle populations: Including remarks on biotelemetry techniques and immature plumages. *Wilson Bulletin* 76:121–37.

28. Spencer, D. A., ed. 1976. *Wintering of the Migrant Bald Eagle in the Lower 48 States.* Washington, D.C.: National Agricultural Chemicals Association.

29. Sprunt, A., IV., and F. J. Ligas. 1966. Audubon bald eagle studies, 1960–1966. *Proceedings of the 62nd National Audubon Society Meeting,* Sacramento, Calif. pp. 25–30.

30. Stalmaster, M. V. 1976. Winter ecology and effects of human activity on bald eagles in the Nooksack River Valley, Washington. Master's thesis, Western Washington University, Bellingham.

31. ———. 1981. Ecological energetics and foraging behavior of wintering bald eagles. Ph.D. diss., Utah State University, Logan.

32. ———. 1983. An energetics simulation model for managing wintering bald eagles. *Journal of Wildlife Management* 47:349–59.

33. Stalmaster, M. V., and J. A. Gessaman. 1984. Ecological energetics and foraging behavior of overwintering bald eagles. *Ecological Monographs* 54:407–28.

34. Steenhof, K. 1976. The ecology of wintering bald eagles in southeastern South Dakota. Master's thesis, University of Missouri, Columbia.

35. ———. 1978. Management of wintering bald eagles. Washington, D.C.: U.S. Department of Interior, Fish and Wildlife Service Publication FWS/OBS-78/79.

36. ———. 1983. Activity patterns of bald eagles wintering in South Dakota. *Raptor Research* 17:57–62.

37. Ward, P., and A. Zahavi. 1973. The importance of certain assemblages of birds as "information centres" for food-finding. *Ibis* 115:517–34.

38. Young, L. S. 1983. Movements of bald eagles associated with autumn concentrations in Glacier National Park. Master's thesis, University of Montana, Missoula.

Chapter 8.

1. Alt, K. L. 1980. Ecology of the breeding bald eagle and osprey in the Grand Teton–Yellowstone National Parks Complex. Master's thesis, Montana State University, Bozeman.

2. Baldwin, W. P. 1940. Bald eagle robbing marsh hawk. *Auk* 57:413.

3. Bent, A. C. 1937. Life histories of North American birds of prey. Part 1. Washington, D.C.: National Museum Bulletin 167, pp. 321–49.

4. Broley, C. L. 1947. Migration and nesting of Florida bald eagles. *Wilson Bulletin* 59:3–20.

5. Brooks, A. 1922. Notes on the abundance and habits of the bald eagle in British Columbia. *Auk* 39:556–59.

6. Campbell, R. W. 1969. Bald eagle swimming in ocean with prey. *Auk* 86:561.

7. Cash, K. J., P. J. Austin-Smith, D. Banks, D. Harris, and P. C. Smith. 1985. Food

remains from bald eagle nest sites on Cape Breton Island, Nova Scotia. *Journal of Wildlife Management* 49:223–25.

8. Clark, W. S. 1982. Incidences of turtles in the diet of nesting bald eagles. *Journal of Field Ornithology* 53:49–51.

9. DeGrange, A. R., and J. W. Nelson. 1982. Bald eagle predation on nocturnal seabirds. *Journal of Field Ornithology* 53:407–09.

10. Dixon, J. 1909. A life history of the northern bald eagle. *Condor* 11:187–93.

11. Donohoe, M. 1981. A council of eagles. *Oceans* 14:3–5.

12. Dugoni, J. A. 1980. Habitat utilization, food habits, and productivity of nesting southern bald eagles in Louisiana. Master's thesis, Louisiana State University, Loyola.

13. Dunstan, T. C., and J. F. Harper. 1975. Food habits of bald eagles in north-central Minnesota. *Journal of Wildlife Management* 39:140–43.

14. Edwards, C. C. 1969. Winter behavior and population dynamics of American eagles in Utah. Ph.D diss., Brigham Young University, Provo.

15. Erskine, A. J. 1968. Encounters between bald eagles and other birds in winter. *Auk* 85:681–83.

16. Fielder, P. C. 1982. Food habits of bald eagles along the mid–Columbia River, Washington. *Murrelet* 63:46–50.

17. Fischer, D. L. 1982. The seasonal abundance, habitat use and foraging behavior of wintering bald eagles, *Haliaeetus leucocephalus,* in west-central Illinois. Master's thesis, Western Illinois University, Macomb.

18. Frenzel, R. W. 1985. Environmental contaminants and ecology of bald eagles in south central Oregon. Ph.D. diss., Oregon State University, Corvallis.

19. Griffin, C. R. 1981. Interactive behavior among bald eagles wintering in north-central Missouri. *Wilson Bulletin* 93:259–64.

20. Griffin, C. R., T. S. Baskett, and R. D. Sparrowe. 1982. Ecology of bald eagles wintering near a waterfowl concentration. Washington, D.C.: U.S. Department of Interior, Fish and Wildlife Service Special Wildlife Report, Wildlife No. 247.

21. Grubb, T. G., and M. A. Coffey. 1982. Evidence of bald eagles feeding on freshwater mussels. *Auk* 94:84–85.

22. Grubb, T. G., and R. J. Hensel. 1978. Food habits of nesting bald eagles on Kodiak Island, Alaska. *Murrelet* 59:70–72.

23. Halter, D. F. 1974. Bald eagle preys upon Arctic loon. *Auk* 91:825–27.

24. Hancock, D. 1964. Bald eagles wintering in the southern Gulf Islands, British Columbia. *Wilson Bulletin* 76:111–20.

25. Hansen, A. J. 1984. Behavioral ecology of bald eagles along the Pacific Northwest coast: A landscape perspective. Ph.D. diss., University of Tennessee, Knoxville.

26. Harmata, A. R. 1984. Bald eagles of the San Luis Valley, Colorado: Their winter ecology and spring migration. Ph.D. diss., Montana State University, Bozeman.

27. Harper, R. G. 1983. An ecological investigation of wintering bald eagles at Lock and Dam 24, Mississippi River. Master's thesis, Western Illinois University, Macomb.

28. Hawbecker, A. C. 1958. Abalones eaten by bald eagles. *Condor* 60:407–08.

29. Hayward, J. L., Jr., W. H. Gillett, C. J. Amlaner, Jr., and J. F. Stout. 1977. Predation on gulls by bald eagles in Washington. *Auk* 94:375.

30. Hehnke, M. F. 1973. Nesting ecology and feeding behavior of bald eagles on the Alaska peninsula. Master's thesis, California State University, Humboldt.

31. Herrick, F. R. 1934. *The American Eagle: A Study in Natural and Civil History.* New York: Appleton-Century.

32. Hildebrandt, T. D. 1981. The ecology of breeding southern bald eagles *(Haliaeetus leucocephalus leucocephalus)* in Arizona, 1977 and 1978. Master's thesis, Arizona State University, Tempe.

33. Imler, R. H., and E. R. Kalmbach. 1955. The bald eagle and its economic status. Washington, D.C.: U.S. Department of Interior, Fish and Wildlife Service Circular No. 30.

34. Jackson, F. L. 1981. King of the heap. *National Wildlife* 19:36–39.

35. Jonen, J. R. 1973. The winter ecology of the bald eagle in west-central Illinois. Master's thesis, Western Illinois University, Macomb.

36. Keister, G. P., Jr. 1981. Characteristics of winter roosts and populations of bald eagles in the Klamath Basin. Master's thesis, Oregon State University, Corvallis.

37. Kenyon, K. W. 1961. Birds of Amchitka Island, Alaska. *Auk* 78:304–26.

38. Knight, S. K. 1981. Aspects of food finding and avoidance behavior of wintering bald eagles. Master's thesis, Western Washington University, Bellingham.

39. Knight, S. K., and R. L. Knight. 1983. Aspects of food finding by wintering bald eagles. *Auk* 100:477–84.

40. Laycock, G. 1973. *Autumn of the Eagle.* New York: Scribner's.

41. Levenson, H. 1976. Behavior and energetics of ospreys nesting in northern California. Master's thesis, California State University, Humboldt.

42. Lish, J. W., and J. C. Lewis. 1975. Status and ecology of bald eagles wintering in Oklahoma. In *Proceedings of the 29th Annual Conference of the Southeastern Association of Game and Fish Commissioners,* pp. 415–23.

43. McClelland, B. R. 1973. Autumn concentrations of bald eagles in Glacier National Park. *Condor* 75:121–23.

44. McClelland, B. R., L. S. Young, D. S. Shea, P. T. McClelland, H. L. Allen, and E. B. Spettigue. 1981. The bald eagle concentration in Glacier National Park, Montana: Origin, growth, and variation in numbers. *Living Bird* 21:133–55.

45. McEwan, L. C., and D. H. Hirth. 1980. Food habits of the bald eagle in north-central Florida. *Condor* 82:229–31.

46. Merrell, T. R., Jr. 1970. A swimming bald eagle. *Wilson Bulletin* 82:220.

47. Munro, J. A. 1938. The northern bald eagle in British Columbia. *Wilson Bulletin* 50:28–35.

48. Murie, O. J. 1940. Food habits of the northern bald eagle in the Aleutian Islands, Alaska. *Condor* 42:198–202.

49. Nye, P. E. 1977. Ecological relationships of bald eagles on a wintering area in New York State. Master's thesis, College of Saint Rose, Albany.

50. Oberholser, H. C. 1906. The North American eagles and their economic relations. Washington, D.C.: U.S. Department of Agriculture, Biological Survey Bulletin No. 27.

51. Ofelt, C. H. 1975. Food habits of nesting bald eagles in southeast Alaska. *Condor* 77:337–38.

52. Platt, J. B. 1976. Bald eagles wintering in a Utah desert. *American Birds* 30:783–88.

53. Prevost, Y. 1979. Osprey–bald eagle interactions at a common foraging site. *Auk* 96:413–14.

54. Retfalvi, L. 1970. Food of nesting bald eagles on San Juan Island, Washington. *Condor* 72:358–61.

55. Ritchie, R. J. 1982. Investigations of bald eagles, Tanana River, Alaska, 1977–80. In *Proceedings of a Symposium and Workshop: Raptor Management and Biology in Alaska and Western Canada*, ed. W. N. Ladd and P. F. Schempf. U.S. Fish and Wildlife Service, Alaska Regional Office, Anchorage, pp. 55–67.

56. Russock, H. I. 1979. Observations on the behavior of wintering bald eagles. *Raptor Research* 13:112–15.

57. Servheen, C. W., and W. English. 1979. Movements of rehabilitated bald eagles and proposed seasonal movement patterns of bald eagles in the Pacific Northwest. *Raptor Research* 13:79–88.

58. Shea, D. S. 1973. A management-oriented study of bald eagle concentrations in Glacier National Park. Master's thesis, University of Montana, Missoula.

59. Sherrod, S. K., J. A. Estes, and C. M. White. 1975. Depredation of sea otter pups by bald eagles at Amchitka Island, Alaska. *Journal of Mammalogy* 56:701–03.

60. Sherrod, S. K., C. M. White, and F. S. L. Williamson. 1976. Biology of the bald eagle on Amchitka Island, Alaska. *Living Bird* 15:143–82.

61. Smith, F. R. 1936. The food and nesting habits of the bald eagle. *Auk* 53:301–05.

62. Southern, W. E. 1963. Winter populations, behavior, and seasonal dispersal of bald eagles in northwestern Illinois. *Wilson Bulletin* 75:42–55.

63. ———. 1964. Additional observations on winter bald eagle populations: Including remarks on biotelemetry techniques and immature plumages. *Wilson Bulletin* 76:121–37.

64. ———. 1966. Utilization of shad as winter food by birds. *Auk* 83:309–11.

65. Spencer, D. A., ed. 1976. *Wintering of the Migrant Bald Eagle in the Lower 48 States*. Washington, D.C.: National Agricultural Chemicals Association.

66. Stalmaster, M. V. 1976. Winter ecology and effects of human activity on bald eagles in the Nooksack River Valley, Washington. Master's thesis, Western Washington University, Bellingham.

67. ———. 1981. Ecological energetics and foraging behavior of wintering bald eagles. Ph.D. diss., Utah State University, Logan.

68. Stalmaster, M. V., and J. A. Gessaman. 1984. Ecological energetics and foraging behavior of overwintering bald eagles. *Ecological Monographs* 54:407–28.

69. Stalmaster, M. V., J. R. Newman, and A. J. Hansen. 1979. Population dynamics of wintering bald eagles on the Nooksack River, Washington. *Northwest Science* 53:126–31.

70. Steenhof, K. 1976. The ecology of wintering bald eagles in southeastern South Dakota. Master's thesis, University of Missouri, Columbia.

71. Stewart, P. A. 1970. Weight changes and feeding behavior of a captive-reared bald eagle. *Bird-Banding* 41:103–10.

72. Swenson, J. E. 1975. Ecology of the bald eagle and osprey in Yellowstone National Park. Master's thesis, Montana State University, Bozeman.

73. Tate, J. L., Jr., and S. Postupalsky. 1965. Food remains at a bald eagle nest. *Jack-Pine Warbler* 43:146–47.

74. Todd, C. S., L. S. Young, R. B. Owen, Jr., and F. J. Gramlich. 1982. Food habits of bald eagles in Maine. *Journal of Wildlife Management* 46:636–45.

75. Van Daele, L. J., and H. A. Van Daele. 1980. Observations of breeding bald eagles in Idaho. *Murrelet* 61:108–10.

76. Wheeler, R. J., and L. E. Raice. 1967. Note on the predatory behavior of the bald eagle. *Murrelet* 48:20–21.

77. Wright, B. S. 1953. The relation of bald eagles to breeding ducks in New Brunswick. *Journal of Wildlife Management* 17:55–62.
78. Young, L. S. 1983. Movements of bald eagles associated with autumn concentrations in Glacier National Park. Master's thesis, University of Montana, Missoula.

Chapter 9.

1. Brown, L. H., and D. Amadon. 1968. *Eagles, Hawks and Falcons of the World.* Vol. 1. New York: McGraw-Hill.
2. Chura, N. J., and P. A. Stewart. 1967. Care, food consumption, and behavior of bald eagles used in DDT tests. *Wilson Bulletin* 79:441–48.
3. Collopy, M. W. 1980. Food consumption and growth energetics of nestling golden eagles. Ph.D. diss., University of Michigan, Ann Arbor.
4. Duke, G. E., O. A. Evanson, and A. Jegers. 1976. Meal to pellet intervals in 14 species of captive raptors. *Comparative Biochemistry and Physiology* 53A:1–6.
5. Hayes, S. R., and J. A. Gessaman. 1980. The combined effects of air temperature, wind and radiation on the resting metabolism of avian raptors. *Journal of Thermal Biology* 5:119–25.
6. Jonen, J. R. 1973. The winter ecology of the bald eagle in west-central Illinois. Master's thesis, Western Illinois University, Macomb.
7. Oberholser, H. C. 1906. The North American eagles and their economic relations. Washington, D.C.: U.S. Department of Agriculture Biological Survey, Bulletin No. 27.
8. Stalmaster, M. V. 1981. Ecological energetics and foraging behavior of wintering bald eagles. Ph.D. diss., Utah State University, Logan.
9. ———. 1981. *An Energetics Simulation Model for Managing Wintering Bald Eagles in Washington.* Olympia: Washington Department of Game.
10. ———. 1983. An energetics simulation model for managing wintering bald eagles. *Journal of Wildlife Management* 47:349–59.
11. Stalmaster, M. V., and J. A. Gessaman. 1982. Food consumption and energy requirements of captive bald eagles. *Journal of Wildlife Management* 46:646–54.
12. ———. 1984. Ecological energetics and foraging behavior of overwintering bald eagles. *Ecological Monographs* 54:407–28.
13. Stewart, P. A. 1970. Weight changes and feeding behavior of a captive-reared bald eagle. *Bird-Banding* 41:103–10.

Chapter 10.

1. Alt, K. L. 1980. Ecology of the breeding bald eagle and osprey in the Grand Teton–Yellowstone National Parks Complex. Master's thesis, Montana State University, Bozeman.
2. Andrew, J. M., and J. A. Mosher. 1982. Bald eagle nest site selection and nesting habitat in Maryland. *Journal of Wildlife Management* 46:382–90.
3. Anthony, R. G., and F. B. Isaacs. 1981. Characteristics of bald eagle nest sites in Oregon. Unpublished paper. Oregon State University, Corvallis.
4. Anthony, R. G., R. L. Knight, G. T. Allen, B. R. McClelland, and J. I. Hodges.

1982. Habitat use by nesting and roosting bald eagles in the Pacific Northwest. *Transactions of the 47th North American Wildlife and Natural Resources Conference* 48:332–42.

5. Boeker, E. L., A. J. Hansen, and J. I. Hodges. 1982. Third annual progress report: Chilkat River Cooperative Bald Eagle Study. New York: National Audubon Society.

6. Broley, C. L. 1947. Migration and nesting of Florida bald eagles. *Wilson Bulletin* 59:3–20.

7. Bromley, R. G., and D. L. Trauger. 1974. Ground nesting of bald eagles near Yellowknife, Northwest Territories. *Canadian Field-Naturalist* 88:73–75.

8. Chrest, H. R. 1964. Nesting of the bald eagle in the Karluk Lake drainage on Kodiak Island, Alaska. Master's thesis, Colorado State University, Fort Collins.

9. Corr, P. O. 1974. Bald eagle *(Haliaeetus leucocephalus alascanus)* nesting related to forestry in southeastern Alaska. Master's thesis, University of Alaska, College.

10. Crenshaw, J. G., and B. R. McClelland. 1983. Western larch bald eagle roosts in Glacier National Park, Montana. Paper presented at Workshop on Habitat Management for Nesting and Roosting Bald Eagles in the Western United States. Oregon State University, Corvallis.

11. Fielder, P. C., and R. G. Starkey. 1980. Wintering bald eagle use along the upper Columbia River, Washington. In *Proceedings of the Washington Bald Eagle Symposium,* ed. R. L. Knight, G. T. Allen, M. V. Stalmaster, and C. W. Servheen. Seattle: The Nature Conservancy, pp. 177–93.

12. Forbis, L. A., B. Johnston, A. M. Camarena, and D. McKinney. 1977. Bald eagle habitat management guidelines. U.S. Department of Agriculture, Forest Service, Region 5, San Francisco.

13. Fraser, J. D. 1981. The breeding biology and status of the bald eagle on the Chippewa National Forest. Ph.D. diss., University of Minnesota, St. Paul.

14. Gerrard, J. M., P. Gerrard, W. J. Maher, and D. W. A. Whitfield. 1975. Factors influencing nest site selection of bald eagles in northern Saskatchewan and Manitoba. *Blue Jay* 33:169–76.

15. Gerrard, J. M., P. N. Gerrard, and D. W. A. Whitfield. 1980. Behavior in a non-breeding bald eagle. *Canadian Field-Naturalist* 94:391–97.

16. Gittens, E. F. 1968. A study on the status of the bald eagle in Nova Scotia. Master's thesis, Acadia University, Wolfville, Nova Scotia.

17. Griffin, C. R. 1978. The ecology of bald eagles wintering at Swan Lake National Wildlife Refuge, with emphasis on eagle-waterfowl relationships. Master's thesis, University of Missouri, Columbia.

18. Grubb, T. G. 1976. A survey and analysis of bald eagle nesting in western Washington. Master's thesis, University of Washington, Seattle.

19. Grubb, T. G., and W. L. Eakle. 1983. Characteristics of bald eagle nesting habitat in the Sonoran desert type of Arizona. Paper presented at the Workshop on Habitat Management for Nesting and Roosting Bald Eagles in the Western United States. Oregon State University, Corvallis.

20. Grubb, T. G., and C. E. Kennedy. 1982. Bald eagle winter habitat on southwestern national forests. U.S. Department of Agriculture, Forest Service Research Paper RM-237, Fort Collins, Colorado.

21. Hansen, A. J., and J. W. Bartelme. 1980. Winter ecology and management of bald eagles on the Skykomish River, Washington. In *Proceedings of the Wash-*

ington Bald Eagle Symposium, ed. R. L. Knight, G. T. Allen, M. V. Stalmaster, and C. W. Servheen. Seattle: The Nature Conservancy, pp. 133–44.

22. Hansen, A. J., M. V. Stalmaster, and J. R. Newman. 1980. Habitat characteristics, function, and destruction of bald eagle communal roosts in western Washington. In *Proceedings of the Washington Bald Eagle Symposium*, ed. R. L. Knight, G. T. Allen, M. V. Stalmaster, and C. W. Servheen. Seattle: The Nature Conservancy, pp. 221–29.

23. Harper, R. G. 1983. An ecological investigation of wintering bald eagles at Lock and Dam 24, Mississippi River. Master's thesis, Western Illinois University, Macomb.

24. Henny, C. J., D. W. Anderson, and C. E. Knoder. 1978. Bald eagles nesting in Baja California. *Auk* 95:424.

25. Hodges, J. I., and F. C. Robards. 1982. Observations of 3,850 bald eagle nests in southeast Alaska. In *Proceedings of a Symposium and Workshop: Raptor Management and Biology in Alaska and Western Canada*, ed. W. N. Ladd and P. F. Schempf. U.S. Department of Interior, Fish and Wildlife Service, Alaska Regional Office, Anchorage, pp. 37–46.

26. Hunt, W. G., B. S. Johnson, J. B. Bulger, and C. Thelander. 1980. Impacts of a proposed Copper Creek Dam on bald eagles. Unpublished report. San Francisco: Biosystems Analysis, Inc.

27. Juenemann, B. G. 1973. Habitat evaluations of selected bald eagle nest sites on the Chippewa National Forest. Master's thesis, University of Minnesota, St. Paul.

28. Keister, G. P., Jr. 1981. Characteristics of winter roosts and populations of bald eagles in the Klamath Basin. Master's thesis, Oregon State University, Corvallis.

29. Keister, G. P., Jr., and R. G. Anthony. 1983. Characteristics of bald eagle communal roosts in the Klamath Basin, Oregon and California. *Journal of Wildlfe Management* 47:1072–79.

30. Korhel, A. H., and T. W. Clark. 1978. Bald eagle winter survey in the Snake River Canyon, Wyoming. *Great Basin Naturalist* 41:461–64.

31. Lehman, R. N. 1979. A survey of selected habitat features of 95 bald eagle nest sites in California. California Department of Fish and Game Report, Sacramento.

32. Lish, J. W. 1973. Status and ecology of bald eagles and nesting of golden eagles in Oklahoma. Master's thesis, Oklahoma State University, Stillwater.

33. Lish, J. W., and J. C. Lewis. 1975. Status and ecology of bald eagles wintering in Oklahoma. *Proceedings of the 29th Annual Conference of the Southeastern Association of Game and Fish Commissioners* 29:415–23.

34. Mathisen, J. E. 1983. Nest site selection by bald eagles on the Chippewa National Forest. In *Biology and Management of Bald Eagles and Ospreys*, ed. D. M. Bird. Ste. Anne de Bellevue, Quebec: Harpell Press, pp. 95–100.

35. Mattsson, J. P., and A. H. Grewe. 1976. Bald eagle nesting in the Superior National Forest. U.S. Department of Agriculture, North Central Forest Experiment Station, Forest Service Research Note NC-198.

36. McEwan, L. C. 1977. Nest site selection and productivity of the bald eagle. Master's thesis, University of Florida, Gainesville.

37. McEwan, L. C., and D. H. Hirth. 1979. Southern bald eagle productivity and nest site selection. *Journal of Wildlife Management* 43:585–94.

38. Nesbitt, S. A., R. R. Roth, and W. B. Robertson, Jr. 1975. The status of the bald

eagle in Florida 1972–1975. *Proceedings of the 29th Annual Conference of the Southeastern Association of Game and Fish Commissioners* 29:424–28.

39. Nye, P. E. 1977. Ecological relationships of bald eagles on a wintering area in New York State. Master's thesis, College of Saint Rose, Albany.

40. Platt, J. B. 1976. Bald eagles wintering in a Utah desert. *American Birds* 30: 783–88.

41. Pramstaller, M. E. 1977. Nocturnal, preroosting, and postroosting behavior of breeding adult and young of the year bald eagles *(Haliaeetus leucocephalus alascanus)* on the Chippewa National Forest, Minnesota. Master's thesis, University of Minnesota, St. Paul.

42. Robards, F. C., and J. I. Hodges. 1977. Observations from 2,760 bald eagle nests in southeast Alaska. Progress Report 1969–1976. U.S. Department of Interior, Fish and Wildlife Service, Juneau.

43. Servheen, C. W. 1975. Ecology of the wintering bald eagles on the Skagit River, Washington. Master's thesis, University of Washington, Seattle.

44. Shea, D. S. 1973. A management-oriented study of bald eagle concentrations in Glacier National Park. Master's thesis, University of Montana, Missoula.

45. ———. 1978. Bald eagle concentrations in Glacier National Park. *Western Birds* 9:35–37.

46. Sherrod, S. K., C. M. White, and F. S. L. Williamson. 1976. Biology of the bald eagle on Amchitka Island, Alaska. *Living Bird* 15:143–82.

47. Stalmaster, M. V. 1983. An energetics simulation model for managing wintering bald eagles. *Journal of Wildlife Management* 47:349–59.

48. Stalmaster, M. V., and J. A. Gessaman. 1984. Ecological energetics and foraging behavior of overwintering bald eagles. *Ecological Monographs* 54:407–28.

49. Stalmaster, M. V., R. L. Knight, B. L. Holder, and R. J. Anderson. 1985. Bald eagles. In *Management of Wildlife and Fish Habitats in Forests of Western Oregon and Washington*, Publication No. R6-F&WL-192-1985. Washington, D.C.: U.S. Department of Agriculture, Forest Service, pp. 269–90.

50. Stalmaster, M. V., and J. R. Newman. 1979. Perch-site preferences of wintering bald eagles in northwest Washington. *Journal of Wildlife Management* 43: 221–24.

51. Steenhof, K. 1976. The ecology of wintering bald eagles in southeastern South Dakota. Master's thesis, University of Missouri, Columbia.

52. ———. 1978. Management of wintering bald eagles. Washington, D.C.: U.S. Department of Interior, Fish and Wildlife Service Publication FWS/OBS-78/79.

53. Steenhof, K., S. S. Berlinger, and L. H. Fredrickson. 1980. Habitat use by wintering bald eagles in South Dakota. *Journal of Wildlife Management* 44:798–805.

54. Swenson, J. E. 1975. Ecology of the bald eagle and osprey in Yellowstone National Park. Master's thesis, Montana State University, Bozeman.

55. Swisher, J. F. 1964. A roosting area of the bald eagle in northern Utah. *Wilson Bulletin* 76:186–87.

56. Todd, C. S. 1979. The ecology of the bald eagle in Maine. Master's thesis, University of Maine, Orono.

57. Troyer, W. A., and R. J. Hensel. 1965. Nesting and productivity of bald eagles on the Kodiak National Wildlife Refuge, Alaska. *Auk* 82:636–38.

58. Whitfield, D. W. A., J. M. Gerrard, W. J. Maher, and D. W. Davis. 1974. Bald eagle nesting habitat, density, and reproduction in central Saskatchewan and Manitoba. *Canadian Field-Naturalist* 88:399–407.

59. Wood, B. 1980. Winter ecology of bald eagles at Grand Coulee Dam,

Washington. In *Proceedings of the Washington Bald Eagle Symposium*, ed. R. L. Knight, G. T. Allen, M. V. Stalmaster, and C. W. Servheen. Seattle: The Nature Conservancy, pp. 195–204.

Chapter 11.
1. Abbott, J. M. 1978. Chesapeake Bay bald eagle breeding survey—1978. Unpublished report.
2. Alt, K. L. 1980. Ecology of the breeding bald eagle and osprey in the Grand Teton–Yellowstone National Parks Complex. Master's thesis, Montana State University, Bozeman.
3. Bangs, E. E., T. N. Bailey, and V. D. Berns. 1982. Ecology of nesting bald eagles on the Kenai National Wildlife Refuge, Alaska. In *Proceedings of a Symposium and Workshop: Raptor Management and Biology in Alaska and Western Canada*, ed. W. N. Ladd and P. F. Schempf. U.S. Fish and Wildlife Service, Alaska Regional Office, Anchorage, pp. 47–54.
4. Belisle, A. A., W. L. Reichel, L. N. Locke, T. G. Lamont, B. M. Mulhern, R. M. Prouty, R. B. DeWolf, and E. Cromartie. 1972. Residues of organochlorine pesticides, polychlorinated biphenyls, and mercury and autopsy data for bald eagles, 1969 and 1970. *Pesticides Monitoring Journal* 6:133–38.
5. Braun, C. E., F. Hamerstrom, T. Ray, and C. M. White. 1975. Conservation committee report on status of eagles. *Wilson Bulletin* 87:140–43.
6. Broley, C. L. 1947. Migration and nesting of Florida bald eagles. *Wilson Bulletin* 59:3–20.
7. ———. 1950. The plight of the Florida bald eagle. *Audubon* 52:42–49.
8. ———. 1958. The plight of the American bald eagle. *Audubon* 60:162–71.
9. Broley, M. J. 1952. *Eagle Man*. New York: Pellegrini & Cudahy.
10. Brown, L. H., and D. Amadon. 1968. *Eagles, Hawks and Falcons of the World*. New York: McGraw-Hill.
11. Chrest, H. R. 1964. Nesting of the bald eagle in the Karluk Lake drainage on Kodiak Island, Alaska. Master's thesis, Colorado State University, Fort Collins.
12. Chura, N. J., and P. A. Stewart. 1967. Care, food consumption, and behavior of bald eagles used in DDT tests. *Wilson Bulletin* 79:441–48.
13. Cline, K. W. 1983. Chesapeake Bay bald eagle banding project. National Wildlife Federation, Raptor Information Center Report, Washington, D.C.
14. Coon, N. C., L. N. Locke, E. Cromartie, and W. L. Reichel. 1970. Causes of bald eagle mortality, 1960–1965. *Journal of Wildlife Diseases* 6:72–76.
15. Cromartie, E., W. L. Reichel, L. N. Locke, A. A. Belisle, T. E. Kaiser, T. G. Lamont, B. M. Mulhern, R. M. Prouty, and D. M. Swineford. 1975. Residues of organochlorine pesticides and polychlorinated biphenyls and autopsy data for bald eagles, 1971–72. *Pesticides Monitoring Journal* 9:11–14.
16. Fraser, J. D. 1981. The breeding biology and status of the bald eagle on the Chippewa National Forest. Ph.D. diss., University of Minnesota, St. Paul.
17. Fyfe, R. W., and R. R. Olendorff. 1976. Minimizing the dangers of nesting studies to raptors and other sensitive species. Canadian Wildlife Service Occasional Paper No. 23.
18. Gerrard, J. M., P. N. Gerrard, G. R. Bortolotti, and D. W. A. Whitfield. 1983. A 14-year study of bald eagle reproduction on Besnard Lake, Saskatchewan. In *Biology and Management of Bald Eagles and Ospreys*, ed. D. M. Bird. Ste. Anne de Bellevue, Quebec: Harpell Press, pp. 47–57.

19. Gerrard, J. M., D. W. A. Whitfield, P. Gerrard, P. N. Gerrard, and W. J. Maher. 1978. Migratory movements and plumage of subadult Saskatchewan bald eagles. *Canadian Field-Naturalist* 92:375–82.

20. Grier, J. W. 1969. Bald eagle behavior and productivity responses to climbing to nests. *Journal of Wildlife Management* 33:961–66.

21. ———. 1974. Reproduction, organochlorines, and mercury in northwestern Ontario bald eagles. *Canadian Field-Naturalist* 88:469–75.

22. ———. 1980. Modeling approaches to bald eagle population dynamics. *Wildlife Society Bulletin* 8:316–22.

23. ———. 1982. Ban of DDT and subsequent recovery of reproduction in bald eagles. *Science* 218:1232–35.

24. Grubb, T. G. 1976. A survey and analysis of bald eagle nesting in western Washington. Master's thesis, University of Washington, Seattle.

25. Grubb, T. G., R. L. Knight, D. M. Rubink, and C. H. Nash. 1983. A five-year comparison of bald eagle productivity in Washington and Arizona. In *Biology and Management of Bald Eagles and Ospreys*, ed. D. H. Bird. Ste. Anne de Bellevue, Quebec: Harpell Press, pp. 35–45.

26. Hancock, D. 1973. Captive propagation of bald eagles, *Haliaeetus leucocephalus*—a review. *International Zoo Yearbook* 13:244–49.

27. Hansen, A. J. 1984. Behavioral ecology of bald eagles along the Pacific Northwest coast: A landscape perspective. Ph.D. diss., University of Tennessee, Knoxville.

28. Haywood, D. D., and R. D. Ohmart. 1983. Preliminary report on habitat utilization by two pairs of breeding bald eagles in Arizona. In *Biology and Management of Bald Eagles and Ospreys*, ed. D. M. Bird. Ste. Anne de Bellevue, Quebec: Harpell Press, pp. 87–94.

29. Hehnke, M. F. 1973. Nesting ecology and feeding behavior of bald eagles on the Alaska Peninsula. Master's thesis, California State University, Humboldt.

30. Hensel, R. J., and W. A. Troyer. 1964. Nesting studies of the bald eagle in Alaska. *Condor* 66:282–86.

31. Hodges, J. I., Jr. 1982. Bald eagle nesting studies in Seymour Canal, southeast Alaska. *Condor* 84:125–27.

32. Howell, J. C. 1941. Bald eagle killed by lightning while incubating its eggs. *Wilson Bulletin* 53:42–43.

33. ———. 1973. The 1971 status of 24 bald eagle nest sites in east central Florida. *Auk* 90:678–80.

34. Isaacs, F. B., R. G. Anthony, and R. J. Anderson. 1983. Distribution and productivity of nesting bald eagles in Oregon, 1978–1982. *Murrelet* 64:33–38.

35. Kaiser, T. E., W. L. Reichel, L. N. Locke, E. Cromartie, A. J. Krynitsky, T. G. Lamont, B. M. Mulhern, R. M. Prouty, C. J. Stafford, and D. M. Swineford. 1980. Organochlorine pesticide, PCB, and PBB residues and necropsy data for bald eagles from 29 states—1975–77. *Pesticides Monitoring Journal* 13:145–49.

36. Krantz, W. C., B. M. Mulhern, G. E. Bagley, A. Sprunt IV, F. J. Ligas, and W. B. Robertson, Jr. 1970. Organochlorine and heavy metal residues in bald eagle eggs. *Pesticides Monitoring Journal* 3:136–40.

37. Laycock, G. 1973. *Autumn of the Eagle*. New York: Scribner's.

38. Madsen, C. R., T. J. Sheldrake, and J. T. Leach, eds. 1982. Bald eagle production in the Great Lakes States 1973–1981. U.S. Fish and Wildlife Service, Region 3, Twin Cities, Minnesota.

39. Mathisen, J. E. 1980. Bald eagle–osprey status report, 1980. U.S. Forest Service, Chippewa National Forest, Cass Lake, Minnesota.

40. McEwan, L. C., and D. H. Hirth. 1979. Southern bald eagle productivity and nest site selection. *Journal of Wildlife Management* 43:585–94.

41. McKelvey, R. W., and D. W. Smith. 1979. A black bear in a bald eagle nest. *Murrelet* 60:106.

42. Mulhern, B. M., W. L. Reichel, L. N. Locke, T. G. Lamont, A. Belisle, E. Cromartie, G. E. Bagley, and R. M. Prouty. 1970. Organochlorine residues and autopsy data from bald eagles 1966–68. *Pesticides Monitoring Journal* 4:141–44.

43. Nash, C., M. Pruett-Jones, and G. T. Allen. 1980. The San Juan Islands bald eagle nesting survey. In *Proceedings of the Washington Bald Eagle Symposium,* ed. R. L. Knight, G. T. Allen, M. V. Stalmaster, and C. W. Servheen. Seattle: The Nature Conservancy, pp. 105–15.

44. Nesbitt, S. A., and M. Collopy. 1985. State Report: Florida–Raptor Research and Management in Florida. *Eyas* 8:26–28.

45. Nye, P., and B. Loucks. 1984. The status of raptors in New York. *Eyas* 7:14–17.

46. Postupalsky, S. 1974. Raptor reproductive success: Some problems with methods, criteria, and terminology. *Raptor Research Report* 2:21–31.

47. ———. 1978. The bald eagles return. *Natural History* 87:62–63.

48. ———. 1983. 1983 bald eagle and osprey nesting surveys in Michigan. Lansing: Michigan Department of Natural Resources, Wildlife Division Report No. 2964.

49. Prouty, R. M., W. L. Reichel, L. N. Locke, A. A. Belisle, E. Cromartie, T. E. Kaiser, T. G. Lamont, B. M. Mulhern, and D. M. Swineford. 1977. Residues of organochlorine pesticides and polychlorinated biphenyls and autopsy data for bald eagles, 1973–74. *Pesticides Monitoring Journal* 11:134–37.

50. Redig, P. T., G. E. Duke, and P. Swanson. 1983. The rehabilitation and release of bald and golden eagles: A review of 245 cases. In *Biology and Management of Bald Eagles and Ospreys,* ed. D. M. Bird. Ste. Anne de Bellevue, Quebec: Harpell Press, pp. 137–47.

51. Reichel, W. L., E. Cromartie, T. G. Lamont, B. M. Mulhern, and R. M. Prouty. 1969. Pesticide residues in eagles. *Pesticides Monitoring Journal* 3:142–44.

52. Retfalvi, L. I. 1965. Breeding behavior and feeding habits of the bald eagle (*Haliaeetus leucocephalus* L.) on San Juan Island, Washington. Master's thesis, University of British Columbia, Vancouver.

53. Ritchie, R. J. 1982. Investigations of bald eagles, Tanana River, Alaska, 1977–80. In *Proceedings of a Symposium and Workshop: Raptor Management and Biology in Alaska and Western Canada,* ed. W. N. Ladd and P. F. Schempf, U.S. Fish and Wildlife Service, Alaska Regional Office, Anchorage, pp. 55–67.

54. Robards, F. C., and J. C. King. 1966. Nesting and productivity of bald eagles, southeast Alaska—1966. U.S. Bureau of Sport Fisheries and Wildlife, Juneau.

55. Seattle *Post-Intelligencer.* 1983. Watt hunts down eagle killers. 16 June.

56. Servheen, C., and W. English. 1976. Bald eagle rehabilitation techniques in western Washington. *Raptor Research* 10:84–87.

57. Sherrod, S. K., C. M. White, and F. S. L. Williamson. 1976. Biology of the bald eagle on Amchitka Island, Alaska. *Living Bird* 15:143–82.

58. Sprunt, A., IV. 1963. Bald eagles aren't producing enough young. *Audubon* 65:32–35.

59. ———. 1965. Population trends of the bald eagle in North America. In *Peregrine*

Falcon Populations: Their Biology and Decline, ed. J. J. Hickey. Madison: University of Wisconsin Press, pp. 347–51.

60. Sprunt, A., IV. and F. J. Ligas. 1966. Audubon bald eagle studies—1960–1966. *Proceedings of the 62nd National Audubon Society Meeting*, Sacramento, pp. 25–30.

61. Sprunt, A., IV, W. B. Robertson, Jr., S. Postupalsky, R. J. Hensel, C. E. Knoder, and F. J. Ligas. 1973. Comparative productivity of six bald eagle populations. *Transactions of the 38th North American Wildlife and Natural Resources Conference*, Washington, D.C., 38:96–106.

62. Stickel, L. F., N. J. Chura, P. A. Stewart, C. M. Menzie, R. M. Prouty, and W. L. Reichel. 1966. Bald eagle pesticide relations. Transactions of the 31st North American Wildlife and Natural Resources Conference, Washington, D.C., 31:190–200.

63. Stone, W. B., and P. E. Nye. 1981. Trichomoniasis in bald eagles. *Wilson Bulletin* 93:109.

64. Swenson, J. E. 1975. Ecology of the bald eagle and osprey in Yellowstone National Park. Master's thesis, Montana State University, Bozeman.

65. Todd, C. S. 1979. The ecology of the bald eagle in Maine. Master's thesis, University of Maine, Orono.

66. Troyer, W. A., and R. J. Hensel. 1965. Nesting and productivity of bald eagles on the Kodiak National Wildlife Refuge, Alaska. *Auk* 82:636–38.

67. Weekes, F. 1974. A survey of bald eagle nesting attempts in southern Ontario, 1969–1973. *Canadian Field-Naturalist* 88:415–19.

68. Wetmore, S. P., and D. I. Gillespie. 1976. Osprey and bald eagle populations in Labrador and northeastern Quebec, 1969–1973. *Canadian Field-Naturalist* 90:330–37.

69. Wiemeyer, S. N., B. M. Mulhern, F. J. Ligas, R. J. Hensel, J. E. Mathisen, F. C. Robards, and S. Postupalsky. 1972. Residues of organochlorine pesticides, polychlorinated biphenyls, and mercury in bald eagle eggs and changes in shell thickness, 1969 and 1970. *Pesticides Monitoring Journal* 6:50–55.

70. Young, H. 1968. A consideration of insecticide effects on hypothetical avian populations. *Ecology* 49:991–94.

Chapter 12.

1. Anonymous. 1983. 200–300 bald eagles reported killed. *Eyas* 6:3.

2. Anthony, R. G., and F. B. Isaacs. 1981. Characteristics of bald eagle nest sites in Oregon. Unpublished paper. Oregon State University, Corvallis.

3. Bailey, G. 1981. Idaho man gets 5 years in eagle case. Seattle *Post-Intelligencer.* 14 November.

4. Bangs, E. E., T. N. Bailey, and V. D. Berns. 1982. Ecology of nesting bald eagles on the Kenai National Wildlife Refuge, Alaska. In *Proceedings of a Symposium and Workshop: Raptor Management and Biology in Alaska and Western Canada*, ed. W. N. Ladd and P. F. Schempf. U.S. Department of Interior, Fish and Wildlife Service, Alaska Regional Office, Anchorage, pp. 47–54.

5. Braun, C. E., F. Hamerstrom, T. Ray, and C. M. White. 1975. Conservation committee report on status of eagles. *Wilson Bulletin* 87:140–43.

6. Chura, N. J., and P. A. Stewart. 1967. Care, food consumption, and behavior of bald eagles used in DDT tests. *Wilson Bulletin* 79:441–48.

7. Corr, P. O. 1974. Bald eagle *(Haliaeetus leucocephalus alascanus)* nesting

related to forestry in southeastern Alaska. Master's thesis, University of Alaska, College.

8. Dale, F. H. 1936. Eagle "control" in northern California. *Condor* 38:208–10.

9. Ewers, J. C. 1958. *The Blackfeet: Raiders on the Northwestern Plains.* Norman: University of Oklahoma Press.

10. Feierabend, J. S., and O. Myers. 1984. A national summary of lead poisoning in bald eagles and waterfowl. Unpublished paper. National Wildlife Federation, Washington, D. C.

11. Fraser, J. D. 1981. The breeding biology and status of the bald eagle on the Chippewa National Forest. Ph.D. diss., University of Minnesota, St. Paul.

12. Fraser, J. D., L. D. Frenzel, and J. E. Mathisen. 1985. The impact of human activities on breeding bald eagles in north central Minnesota. *Journal of Wildlife Management* 49:585–92.

13. Fyfe, R. W., and R. R. Olendorff. 1976. Minimizing the dangers of nesting studies to raptors and other sensitive species. Canadian Wildlife Service Occasional Paper No. 23.

14. Green, N. H. 1985. The bald eagle. In *Audubon Wildlife Report—1985,* ed. A. M. Enos and R. L. Di Silvestro. New York: National Audubon Society, pp. 508–31.

15. Grier, J. W. 1969. Bald eagle behavior and productivity responses to climbing to nests. *Journal of Wildlife Management* 33:961–66.

16. ———. 1980. Modeling approaches to bald eagle population dynamics. *Wildlife Society Bulletin* 8:316–22.

17. Grier, J. W., F. J. Gramlich, J. Mattsson, J. E. Mathisen, J. V. Kussman, J. B. Elder, and N. F. Green. 1983. The bald eagle in the northern United States. In *Bird Conservation,* Vol. 1, ed. S. A. Temple. Madison: University of Wisconsin Press, pp. 41–66.

18. Grubb, T. G. 1976. A survey and analysis of bald eagle nesting in western Washington. Master's thesis, University of Washington, Seattle.

19. Hansen, A. J., E. L. Boeker, J. I. Hodges, and D. R. Cline. 1984. *Bald Eagles of the Chilkat Valley, Alaska: Ecology, Behavior, and Management.* Washington, D.C.: National Audubon Society.

20. Harmata, A. R. 1984. Bald eagles of the San Luis Valley, Colorado: Their winter ecology and spring migration. Ph.D. diss., Montana State University, Bozeman.

21. Hickey, J. J., and D. W. Anderson. 1968. Chlorinated hydrocarbons and eggshell changes in raptorial and fish-eating birds. *Science* 162:271–73.

22. Hodge, F. W., ed. 1959. *Handbook of American Indians North of Mexico.* Part 1. New York: Pageant Books.

23. Hoffman, D. J., O. H. Pattee, S. N. Wiemeyer, and B. Mulhern. 1981. Effects of lead shot ingestion on alpha-aminolevulinic acid dehydratase activity, hemoglobin concentration, and serum chemistry in bald eagles. *Journal of Wildlife Diseases* 17:423–31.

24. Hunt, W. B. 1954. The Complete Book of Indian Crafts and Lore. New York: Golden Press, Western Publishing.

25. Jacobson, E., J. W. Carpenter, and M. Novilla. 1977. Suspected lead toxicosis in a bald eagle. *Journal of the American Veterinary Medicine Association* 171:952–54.

26. Juenemann, B. G. 1973. Habitat evaluations of selected bald eagle nest sites on the Chippewa National Forest. Master's thesis, University of Minnesota, St. Paul.

27. Kendall, R. J. 1981. Are we poisoning our wildlife? *Washington Wildlife* 31: 13–17.

28. King, J. G., F. C. Robards, and C. J. Lensink. 1972. Census of the bald eagle breeding population in southeast Alaska. *Journal of Wildlife Management* 36:1292–95.

29. Knight, R. L., and S. K. Knight. 1984. Responses of wintering bald eagles to boating activity. *Journal of Wildlife Management* 48:999–1004.

30. Laycock, G. 1973. *Autumn of the Eagle.* New York: Scribner's.

31. Lockie, J. D., and D.A. Ratcliffe. 1964. Insecticides and Scottish golden eagles. *British Birds* 57:88–102.

32. Mathisen, J. E. 1968. Effects of human disturbance on nesting of bald eagles. *Journal of Wildlife Management* 32:1–6.

33. McClelland, B. R., L. S. Young, D. S. Shea, P. T. McClelland, H. L. Allen, and E.B. Spettigue. 1981. The bald eagle concentration in Glacier National Park, Montana: Origin, growth, and variation in numbers. *Living Bird* 21:133–55.

34. Miller, L. 1957. Bird remains from an Oregon Indian midden. *Condor* 59:59–63.

35. Mulhern, B. M., W. L. Reichel, L. N. Locke, T. G. Lamont, A. Belisle, E. Cromartie, G. E. Bagley, and R. M. Prouty. 1970. Organochlorine residues and autopsy data from bald eagles, 1966–1968. *Pesticide Monitoring Journal* 4:141–44.

36. Obee, B. 1983. Bald eagle. *Wildlife Review* 10:22–24.

37. O'Ryan, J. 1981. 22 indicted for killing eagles and other birds. Seattle *Post-Intelligencer.* 25 July.

38. Pattee, O. H., and S. K. Hennes. 1983. Bald eagles and waterfowl: The lead shot connection. *Transactions of the 48th North American Wildlife and Natural Resources Conference,* Washington, D.C. 48:230–37.

39. Pattee, O. H., S. N. Wiemeyer, B. M. Mulhern, L. Sileo, and J. W. Carpenter. 1981. Experimental lead-shot poisoning in bald eagles. *Journal of Wildlife Management* 45:806–10.

40. Prouty, R. M., W. L. Reichel, L. N. Locke, A. A. Belisle, E. C. Cromartie, T. E. Kaiser, T. G. Lamont, B. M. Mulhern, and D. M. Swineford. 1977. Residues of organochlorine pesticides and polychlorinated biphenyls and autopsy data for bald eagles, 1973–74. *Pesticide Monitoring Journal* 11:134–37.

41. Redig, P. T., G. E. Duke, and P. Swanson. 1983. The rehabilitation and release of bald and golden eagles: A review of 245 cases. In *Biology and Management of Bald Eagles and Ospreys,* ed. D. M. Bird. Ste. Anne de Bellevue, Quebec: Harpell Press, pp. 137–47.

42. Robards, F. C., and J. G. King. 1966. Nesting and productivity of bald eagles, southeast Alaska—1966. U.S. Bureau of Sport Fisheries and Wildlife, Juneau.

43. Russell, D. 1980. Occurrence and human disturbance sensitivity of wintering bald eagles on the Sauk and Suiattle rivers, Washington. In *Proceedings of the Washington Bald Eagle Symposium,* ed. R. L. Knight, G. T. Allen, M. V. Stalmaster, and C. W. Servheen. Seattle: The Nature Conservancy, pp. 165–74.

44. Sayre, R., ed. 1973. Several hundred eagles in Nevada were caught accidentally. . . *Audubon* 75:124.

45. Schueler, D. G. 1978. Incident at eagle ranch. *Audubon* 80:41–72.

46. Shapiro, A. E., F. Montabano III, and D. Mager. 1982. Implications of construction of a flood control project upon bald eagle nesting activity. *Wilson Bulletin* 94:55–63.

47. Sherrod, S. K., C. M. White, and F. S. L. Williamson. 1976. Biology of the bald eagle on Amchitka Island, Alaska. *Living Bird* 15:143–82.

48. Skagen, S. K. 1980. Behavioral responses of wintering bald eagles to human activity. In *Proceedings of the Washington Bald Eagle Symposium*, ed. R. L. Knight, G. T. Allen, M. V. Stalmaster, and C. W. Servheen. Seattle: The Nature Conservancy, pp. 231–41.

49. Smith, H. I. 1924. Eagle snaring among the Bellacoola Indians. *Canadian Field-Naturalist* 38:167–68.

50. Snow, C. 1973. Habitat management series for endangered species. Report No. 5: Southern bald eagle and northern bald eagle. Washington, D.C.: U.S. Department of Interior, Bureau of Land Management Technical Note T-N-171.

51. Stalmaster, M. V. 1980. Management strategies for wintering bald eagles in the Pacific Northwest. In *Proceedings of the Washington Bald Eagle Symposium*, ed. R. L. Knight, G. T. Allen, M. V. Stalmaster, and C. W. Servheen. Seattle: The Nature Conservancy, pp. 49–67.

52. ———. 1983. An energetics simulation model for managing wintering bald eagles. *Journal of Wildlife Management* 47:349–59.

53. Stalmaster, M. V., and J. A. Gessaman. 1982. Food consumption and energy requirements of captive bald eagles. *Journal of Wildlife Management* 46:646–54.

54. ———. 1984. Ecological energetics and foraging behavior of overwintering bald eagles. *Ecological Monographs* 54:407–28.

55. Stalmaster, M. V., and J. R. Newman. 1978. Behavioral responses of wintering bald eagles to human activity. *Journal of Wildlife Management* 42:506–13.

56. Steenhof, K. 1978. Management of wintering bald eagles. Washington, D.C.: U.S. Department of Interior, Fish and Wildlife Service Publication FWS/OBS-78/79.

57. Thelander, C. G. 1973. Bald eagle reproduction in California, 1972–1973. California Department of Fish and Game, Administrative Report No. 73-5, Sacramento.

58. Verbeek, N.A.M. 1982. Egg predation by northwestern crows: Its association with human and bald eagle activity. *Auk* 99:347–52.

59. White, J. M. 1979. *Everyday Life of the North American Indian*. New York: Holmes & Meier.

60. Young, L. S. 1980. A quantitative evaluation of human disturbance impacts on breeding ecology of bald eagles in the San Juan Islands, Washington. Washington Department of Game Report, Olympia.

Chapter 13.

1. Anonymous. 1984. Summary of bald eagle translocations. *Eyas* 7:5–6.

2. Dombeck, M., J. Hammill, and W. Bullen. 1984. Fisheries management and fish dependent birds. *Fisheries* 9:2–4.

3. Dunstan, T. C., and M. Borth. 1970. Successful reconstruction of active bald eagle nest. *Wilson Bulletin* 82:326–27.

4. Engel, J. M., and F. B. Isaacs. 1982. Bald eagle translocation techniques. U.S. Department of Interior, Fish and Wildlife Service, North Central Region Report, Twin Cities, Minnesota.

5. English, W., J. W. Foster, and C. Servheen. 1980. Bald eagle rehabilitation in

western Washington, an update. In *Proceedings of the Washington Bald Eagle Symposium*, ed. R. L. Knight, G. T. Allen, M. V. Stalmaster, and C. W. Servheen. Seattle: The Nature Conservancy, pp. 69–73.

6. Fleming, W. J., and D. R. Clark, Jr. 1983. Organochlorine pesticides and PCBs: A continuing problem for the 1980s. *Transactions of the 48th North American Wildlife and Natural Resources Conference*, 49:186–99.

7. Gerrard, P. N., S. N. Wiemeyer, and J. M. Gerrard. 1979. Some observations on the behavior of captive bald eagles before and during incubation. *Raptor Research* 13:57–64.

8. Gilbert, S., P. Tomassoni, and P. A. Kramer. 1981. History of captive management and breeding of bald eagles. *International Zoo Yearbook* 21:101–09.

9. Grubb, T. G. 1980. An artificial bald eagle nest structure. U.S. Department of Agriculture, Forest Service, Research Note RM-383.

10. Hancock, D. 1973. Captive propagation of bald eagles. *International Zoo Yearbook* 13:244–49.

11. Helander, B. 1978. Feeding white-tailed sea eagles in Sweden. In *Endangered Birds: Management Techniques for Preserving Threatened Species*, ed. S. A. Temple. Madison: University of Wisconsin Press, 149–59.

12. Johnson, M. J., and R. Gayden. 1975. Breeding the bald eagle *Haliaeetus leucocephalus* at the National Zoological Park, Washington. *International Zoo Yearbook* 15:98–100.

13. Kellert, S. R. 1984. Conceptual framework for exploring attitudes toward western energy development impacts on wildlife and related findings. In *Proceedings of the Issues and Technology in the Management of Impacted Western Wildlife Symposium*, ed. R. D. Comer, J. M. Merino, J. W. Monarch, C. Pustmueller, M. Stalmaster, R. Stoecker, J. Todd, and W. Wright. Thorne Ecological Institute Technical Publication Number 14, Boulder, Colorado, pp. 169–78.

14. Knight, R. L., and S. K. Knight. 1984. Responses of wintering bald eagles to boating activity. *Journal of Wildlife Management* 48:999–1004.

15. Maestrelli, J. R., and S. N. Wiemeyer. 1975. Breeding bald eagles in captivity. *Wilson Bulletin* 87:45–53.

16. Mathisen, J. E. 1968. Effects of human disturbance on nesting of bald eagles. *Journal of Wildlife Management* 32:1–6.

17. Mathisen, J. E., D. J. Sorenson, L. D. Frenzel, and T. C. Dunstan. 1977. A management strategy for bald eagles. *Transactions of the 41st North American Wildlife and Natural Resources Conference* 42:86–92.

18. McCollough, M.A. 1986. The post-fledging ecology and population dynamics of bald eagles in Maine. Ph.D. diss., University of Maine, Orono.

19. Nesbitt, S. A., and M. Collopy. 1985. Raptor research and management in Florida: Bald eagles. *Eyas* 8:26–28.

20. Nye, P. E. 1983. A biological and economic review of the hacking process for the restoration of bald eagles. In *Biology and Management of Bald Eagles and Ospreys*, ed. D. M. Bird. Ste. Anne de Bellevue, Quebec: Harpell Press, pp. 127–35.

21. Olendorff, R. R., R. S. Motroni, and M. W. Call. 1980. Raptor management—The state of the art in 1980. Washington, D.C.: U.S. Department of Interior, Bureau of Land Management Technical Note Number 345.

22. Postupalsky, S. 1978. Artificial nesting platforms for ospreys and bald eagles.

In *Endangered Birds: Management Techniques for Preserving Threatened Species*, ed. S. A. Temple. Madison: University of Wisconsin Press, pp. 35–45.

23. Postupalsky, S., and J. B. Holt, Jr. 1975. Adoption of nestlings by breeding bald eagles. *Raptor Research* 9:18–20.

24. Rearden, J. 1984. The Chilkat miracle. *Audubon* 86:40–54.

25. Redig, P. T., G. E. Duke, and P. Swanson. 1983. The rehabilitation and release of bald and golden eagles: A review of 245 cases. In *Biology and Management of Bald Eagles and Ospreys*, ed. D. M. Bird. Ste. Anne de Bellevue, Quebec: Harpell Press, pp. 137–47.

26. Servheen, C., and W. English. 1976. Bald eagle rehabilitation techniques in western Washington. *Raptor Research* 10:84–87.

27. Stalmaster, M. V. 1980. Management strategies for wintering bald eagles in the Pacific Northwest. In *Proceedings of the Washington Bald Eagle Symposium*, ed. R. L. Knight, G. T. Allen, M. V. Stalmaster, and C. W. Servheen. Seattle: The Nature Conservancy, pp. 49–67.

28. Stalmaster, M. V., and J. A. Gessaman. 1984. Ecological energetics and foraging behavior of overwintering bald eagles. *Ecological Monographs* 54:407–28.

29. Stalmaster, M. V., and J. R. Newman. 1978. Behavioral responses of wintering bald eagles to human activity. *Journal of Wildlife Management* 42:506–13.

30. Stalmaster, M. V., R. L. Knight, B. L. Holder, and R. J. Anderson. 1985. Bald eagles. In *Management of Wildlife and Fish Habitats in Forests of Western Oregon and Washington*, ed. E. R. Brown. Washington, D.C.: U.S. Department of Agriculture, Forest Service, Publication No.: R6-F&WL-192-1985, pp. 269–90.

31. Steenhof, K. 1978. Management of wintering bald eagles. Washington, D.C.: U.S. Department of Interior, Fish and Wildlife Service Publication FWS/OBS-78/79.

32. U.S. Department of Interior. 1978. Determination of certain bald eagle populations as endangered or threatened. *Federal Register* 43:6230–6233.

33. ———. 1978. Acquisition of the Bear Valley National Wildlife Refuge, Klamath County, Oregon. Environmental Impact Assessment, U.S. Fish and Wildlife Service, Portland, Oregon.

34. ———. 1980. Conservation easements in Washington. Heritage Conservation and Recreation Service.

35. Van Name, W. G. 1921. Threatened extinction of the bald eagle. *Ecology* 2:76–78.

Index

A

Accipitridae family, 7
activity
   daily, 84–85, 124
   energy cost of, 113
   feeding, 85–86
   social, 85–91
   weather, influence of, 84–85
aerial surveys, 133
African fish eagle, 8, 10, 111
aging technique
   juveniles and subadults,
      17–21
   nestlings, 70
American Eagle, The (Herrick),
   45
Aristotle, 49
artificial feeding, 171
artificial nests
   reasons for construction, 168
   success, 168
   types, 168
attacks on humans, 61, 96
attributes (those admired), 1–2,
   179
Audubon, John James, 14, 97
autopsies of eagles, 145

B

Bald Eagle Protection Act,
   164–65
banding, 42, 144
bathing, 90–91
Bent, Arthur, 160
Bergmann's rule, 109–10
Bering, Vitus, 10
bill (and beak)
   size, 15–17, 70
   uses, 26

biomagnification, 156
birth, 65–66
body temperature, 110–11
bounty, eagle, 144, 153, 163–64
breeding chronology, 62–64
   influence of:
   elevation, 64
   latitude, 63
   relaying, 175
   weather, 63–64
Broley, Charles, 42, 134–35
brood size, 57, 139, 141–42
brooding, 59–62

C

captive breeding, 172–73
carrying capacity, 146
cartwheel display, 46–47, 91
casting, 116-17
censuses
   nest, 133–34
   winter, 80–81, 83
Chilkat River Bald Eagle
   Preserve, 36–38, 82, 172
clutch size, 56–57, 173
color-marking, 42, 144
Congress, United States, 2, 164
Continental Bald Eagle Project,
   135
copulation, 47–48
courtship, 46–47
crop, 26, 116

D

DDT (and DDE) poisoning, 114,
   135, 139, 142–43, 156,
   176–77